Robeson

Sincerely
Paul Robeson

Robeson

An American Ballad

Arnold H. Lubasch

THE SCARECROW PRESS, INC.
Lanham • Toronto • Plymouth, UK
2012

Published by Scarecrow Press, Inc.
A wholly owned subsidiary of The Rowman & Littlefield Publishing Group, Inc.
4501 Forbes Boulevard, Suite 200, Lanham, Maryland 20706
www.rowman.com

10 Thornbury Road, Plymouth PL6 7PP, United Kingdom

British Library Cataloguing in Publication Information Available

Library of Congress Cataloging-in-Publication Data

Lubasch, Arnold H., 1932–
    Robeson : an American ballad / Arnold H. Lubasch.
        p. cm.
    Includes bibliographical references and index.
    ISBN 978-0-8108-8522-6 (cloth : alk. paper) — ISBN 978-0-8108-8523-3 (ebook)
    1. Robeson, Paul, 1898–1976. 2. African Americans—Biography. 3. Singers—United
States—Biography. 4. Actors—United States—Biography. 5. Political activists—United
States—Biography. I. Title.
    E185.97.R63L83 2012
    782.0092—dc23 [B]   2012020971

∞™ The paper used in this publication meets the minimum requirements of
American National Standard for Information Sciences—Permanence of Paper
for Printed Library Materials, ANSI/NISO Z39.48-1992.

Printed in the United States of America

Contents

Preface

Our Paul

*S*imply stated, Paul Robeson was one of the most extraordinary men of the twentieth century.

He was a Phi Beta Kappa student, an all-American football player at Rutgers College, and the quintessential scholar-athlete who worked his way through Columbia Law School by playing professional football on weekends. He went on to become a groundbreaking black actor in plays and films, as well as the most celebrated concert singer of his time, overcoming racial prejudice all the way. He also became a political activist and a vigorous crusader for civil rights and world peace.

His fight for black people and his support of the Soviet Union—at a time when racism and communism aroused the most intense emotions—produced an overwhelming storm of political hostility that devastated his career, damaged his health, and banished his name from American history for many years. If Robeson's uncritical support of Soviet policies was mistaken, as it assuredly was, he paid an excessively high price for it.

* * *

From the Harlem Renaissance of the 1920s to the turbulent 1930s, World War II, the Cold War, and the years leading to the civil rights movement, Paul Robeson was a significant figure in New York, London, Moscow, and around the world.

His starring role in *Othello* won the highest acclaim in the theater. His singing of "Ballad for Americans" was a historic event. He raised Negro spirituals to an art form and was hailed as the voice of his people. He promoted African culture long before it became popular to do so, one of the many ways in which he was ahead of his time. And he transformed the musical lament of "Ol' Man River" into his signature song of defiance.

The remarkable range of his talents and activities brought Robeson into contact with a wide array of prominent people. Among his friends were Eugene O'Neill, Sergei Eisenstein, Albert Einstein, George Gershwin, Jerome Kern, George Bernard Shaw, W. E. B. Du Bois, Lorraine Hansberry, and Marian Anderson.

He confronted President Harry S. Truman and campaigned with Henry Wallace, was a guest of Soviet premier Nikita Khrushchev, befriended Jawaharlal Nehru of India before that man became a world leader, and mentored Harry Belafonte, Sidney Poitier, and Lena Horne.

Beyond his achievements, Robeson had a unique personal quality—a sense of enormous decency and dignity—that you felt immediately upon meeting him. The people of Harlem often called him "Our Paul." And many other people of all colors shared that feeling of affection for him, the feeling that he belonged to them too.

Astute critics likened him to the great redwood trees of California and described him as "the tallest tree in our forest."

* * *

Paul Robeson Jr. stressed in a television interview in 1971 that his father had survived unprecedented attacks against him. "And there's a certain majes-

Former New York City mayor David Dinkins in his office with Robeson's photograph in 2005. Photo courtesy Richard Perry, *New York Times*.

tic triumph in the fact that he has retired a sort of undefeated champion. He never took a word back, and he retired unbowed and undefeated."

Since Robeson's death in 1976, his son has worked consistently to preserve and promote his father's legacy. His efforts culminated in 1998 with widespread celebrations of the centennial anniversary of Robeson's birth, and he gave the bulk of his father's papers to the Moorland-Spingarn Research Center at Howard University in Washington, DC. He also wrote a perceptive two-volume biography, *The Undiscovered Paul Robeson*, containing personal insights into the complex relationship of his parents.

* * *

On a personal note, I have firsthand memories of Paul Robeson. I saw him perform many times, visited him backstage several times, and spoke with him briefly on those occasions. This experience encourages me to hope that I can add something to the remembrance of this remarkable man.

My research includes everything that I could track down about him in books, newspapers, magazines, and television documentaries, as well as thousands of original documents, diaries, speeches, and letters. Writing at this time gives me access to extensive information that has come to light in recent years, helping to illuminate his life. And the passage of time provides additional perspective in viewing the events and controversy that swirled around him.

Since one's political perspective can influence the view of communism and the McCarthy era, it might be appropriate for me to note that I am politically mainstream, with no ideological agenda, then or now. I still agree with the view of my late mother, a fiercely patriotic lady, who said more than once, "I wish our Paul didn't like Russia so much."

I worked as a reporter for the *New York Times* for more than thirty years before I retired from daily journalism. By inclination and experience, I am a reporter rather than an academic or an ideologue. It is my intent to tell the Robeson story as accurately, clearly, and fairly as I can, in the context of the times.

Paul Robeson is a man worth remembering, a notable part of our nation's history. And for the happy few who remember him well, he remains "Our Paul."

Arnold H. Lubasch

Acknowledgments

$\mathcal{M}$y personal thanks to the following people:

Paul Robeson Jr. and his wife, Marilyn, for their long friendship and informative conversations. And to Paul Jr.'s publisher for granting permission to use limited material from his father's books.

Pete Seeger for his firsthand account of the Peekskill concert and rioting, in a long telephone interview with me.

Robert Sherman for his recollections of his aunt, Clara Rockmore, and her friend Paul Robeson, in a telephone interview with me.

Dr. John Rosen for confirming a key quote about "Our Paul," although he declined to discuss his family's relationship with Robeson.

Ruby Dee for sharing her memories of Paul Robeson in a telephone interview with me.

Sterling Stuckey for discussing Robeson with me and recommending pertinent reading.

* * *

To the following research libraries:

Lincoln University of Pennsylvania—with thanks to Susan Pevar, special collections librarian, for original material about Robeson's father.

Princeton, NJ: Historical Society, Public Library, University Library.

Somerville High School—thanks to June Ambs for finding many articles in *The Valkyrie* about Robeson's years at the high school.

Rutgers University—Alexander Library, in New Brunswick, New Jersey, where I spent several days reading original documents, articles, and issues of *The Targum.*

New York Public Library and its Schomburg Center for Research in Black Culture, in Harlem, where I studied numerous documents, articles, and programs of Paul Robeson and Lawrence Brown.

Special thanks to the Moorland-Spingarn Research Center, where I spent a week studying its extensive collection of Paul and Eslanda Robeson papers, including original documents, diaries, and letters, with the assistance of Joellen ElBashir, curator of manuscripts, and her staff, at Howard University in Washington, DC.

Akademie der Künste, Music Archive, in Berlin, where I studied many of the documents and articles in its Paul Robeson Archive with the help of its staff.

Also, the Library of Congress in Washington, DC; Yale University—Beinecke Rare Book and Manuscript Library; University of Maryland—the Clara Rockmore Collection; University of Arizona library in Tucson—old newspaper files; and Hayden Library of Arizona State University in Tempe—complete transcripts of key congressional hearings with the kind assistance of librarians Shirley Whitehouse and Kathleen Jones.

* * *

As a veteran newspaperman, I made extensive use of newspaper stories in the archives of the press, particularly the following:

New York Times and *London Times*
Amsterdam News, Chicago Defender, and *Pittsburgh Courier*
Archives of ProQuest Historical Newspapers
And many, many more newspapers in the United States and overseas

* * *

I consulted more than one hundred books for source material and background information; many of them are cited in my chapter notes. The most interesting and helpful authors included the following:

Paul Robeson's own *Here I Stand*—as a primary source on his childhood.
Eslanda Goode Robeson—for her insights into her husband.
Paul Robeson Jr.—for insights into his parents' complex relationship and medical history.
Lloyd L. Brown—for his research into Robeson origins and Paul's early life.

Marie Seton—for her knowledge of Robeson in London and Moscow.
Martin Duberman—for his research and interviews with Uta Hagen and
  Helen Rosen, which he generously allowed me to use.

My thanks to Phyllis Collazo of the *New York Times* and Cathy Gonzales of
AP Images for their help in obtaining photographs.

* * *

Special personal thanks to the following:

David Markson, Susan Davis, Gerald Lechter, and especially Lawrence
  Van Gelder for reading my manuscript, offering valuable suggestions,
  and providing early encouragement.
Gail Markson for sterling assistance in solving my computer problems.
My wife, Helga Lubasch, for listening patiently to my Robeson stories
  for so many years and providing her loving support.

• 1 •

Destiny's Child

"I got a home in that rock, don't you see?"

—spiritual

$\mathcal{T}$he year was 1898, an exciting time in America. The traumatic Civil War had been fought barely a generation earlier, ending the brutal institution of slavery. The short-lived Reconstruction period following the war extended the rights of the freed slaves, but this soon gave way to repressive racial segregation.

Many in the population of 75 million Americans retained firsthand memories of slavery and the war. Almost two-thirds of the people lived in rural areas, many working on family farms, but a thriving new industrial age created jobs that attracted a growing number to big cities. The horse and buggy provided much of the transportation, now on the brink of great changes.

The young nation seemed bursting with energy. But life was hard for the country's Negroes mired in poverty. And many of them found themselves subjected to grievous violence in the form of race riots and deadly lynchings, particularly in the Old South and sections of the Middle West.

In the North, in the small town of Princeton, New Jersey, dominated by its elite university, there was a section for Negroes, many of whom held menial jobs tending the university's campus. With the aura of a somnolent Southern town, Princeton maintained a rigid segregation, which made the many Virginians who attended the university feel comfortably at home.

It was here, in Princeton, that a former slave, William Drew Robeson, served as pastor of a black church. He was born on July 27, 1845, son of Sabra and Benjamin, slaves on a plantation in North Carolina. At age seventeen, a year after the start of the Civil War, William escaped from the plantation, fled to the North, and worked as a farmhand before attending a school for freed Negroes.[1]

* * *

William entered Lincoln University, a new Pennsylvania school dedicated to "enlightening and elevating the freedom of the South," in 1867, two years after the Civil War ended. Here he obtained a classical education that stressed Latin and Greek. He graduated in 1873 and stayed at Lincoln to earn a degree in sacred theology three years later.[2] His transformation from slave to clergyman, not only literate but learned, was a testament to this man's intelligence, determination, and character.

While at Lincoln, he met Maria Louisa Bustill, a tall, slender, light-skinned schoolteacher from Philadelphia. She came from a prominent family of free Negroes with some Native American and English Quaker ancestors. Her father, Charles Bustill, a plastering contractor, had served as an abolitionist leader.[3]

William married Louisa, as she was called, on July 11, 1878, two years after completing his divinity studies at Lincoln. They settled in Princeton, where he was appointed pastor of the Witherspoon Street Presbyterian Church. His wife gave birth to seven children, two of whom died in infancy.

* * *

Paul Leroy Robeson, last of the couple's children, arrived on April 9, 1898, a chilly day with cloudy skies in Princeton, the day before Easter Sunday. Like all the Robeson children, Paul was born in the modest three-story parsonage at 72 Witherspoon Street, down the block from the small wood-framed church. His father was fifty-two years old, and his mother was forty-four.[4] Paul made his appearance, coincidentally, on the thirty-third anniversary of the date General Robert E. Lee surrendered to General Ulysses S. Grant at Appomattox Court House in Virginia, effectively ending the Civil War.

The family's other children included three boys—Bill, a bright, restless student, who became a doctor; Reeve, a rebellious youth, who faded from the family; and Benjamin, who emulated his father by becoming a minister. The lone girl, Marian, became a schoolteacher like her mother. At the time of Paul's birth, Bill was sixteen, Reeve twelve, Benjamin five, and Marian three.

Reverend Robeson, with a strong sense of dignity, delivered his sermons in a deep, sonorous voice. In the custom of the era, his last name came from the name of the plantation where he was born. His brothers, John and Ben, followed him to Princeton and formed an extended family. In his church, he installed a stained glass window inscribed, "In Loving Remembrance of Sabra Robeson."

Paul resembled his father's side of the family, with dark skin and broad African features. And he identified emotionally with his paternal relatives, who came out of slavery in the South.

* * *

The country Paul Robeson was born into appeared quite different from the one that Americans know today. Race relations were strongly influenced by a major Supreme Court decision rendered two years before Paul was born, *Plessy v. Ferguson*, which accepted "separate but equal" facilities as constitutional, effectively endorsing racial segregation as the law of the land. Segregation laws came to be called Jim Crow, the name of a stereotypical black character in minstrel shows.[5]

As the twentieth century neared, the growing Industrial Revolution propelled the young country into the ranks of the great powers. Thomas Edison had already developed a light bulb at his laboratory in New Jersey, producing electric lights to replace candles and kerosene lamps. And a Virginia-born scholar, Woodrow Wilson, taught politics and law at Princeton University, about forty miles south of Edison's new laboratory in West Orange, New Jersey.[6]

* * *

The beginning of the new century brought misfortune to the Robeson family in Princeton.

Originally, the town's white First Presbyterian Church had allowed Negroes to sit in the balcony. When the Presbyterians built a new church for themselves, they turned over a small church to the Negroes, who then formed the Witherspoon Street congregation. But the white hierarchy still held control of the black church.

Rev. Robeson spoke out for his people's rights during the two decades that he served as the Witherspoon Street pastor. In November 1898, he allowed "the colored people of Princeton" to hold a mass meeting in his church to discuss recent violence against Negroes in several states. Presbyterian leaders eventually decided to replace him with a more pliable pastor. His removal went into effect on February 1, 1901, but he was permitted to remain in the parsonage until May 1.[7]

Stripped of his position, Robeson moved his family from the comfortable parsonage to a smaller house around the corner on Green Street when Paul was just three years old. Robeson had earned barely $700 a year as pastor, and now even harder times prevailed, but he retained the respect of his black community. He bought a horse and wagon and earned his living by hauling away ashes from the coal stoves of many houses in town.

Parish house where Paul was born on April 9, 1898, on Witherspoon Street in Princeton, New Jersey. By Katherine Elgin for Arnold Lubasch.

One of Paul's earliest memories was of "the growing mound of dusty ashes dumped into our backyard at 13 Green Street."[8]

* * *

Cruel tragedy struck the Robeson family on the morning of January 19, 1904, with the sudden death of Louisa, by all accounts an intelligent, gentle woman who often helped write her husband's sermons and still used the terms "thee" and "thou" of her Quaker upbringing.

Louisa, who suffered from chronic asthma and failing eyesight, was cleaning her parlor, which contained a coal stove, when a burning ember fell on her long skirt and set it afire. The only one at home with her at the time was young Ben. Failing to beat out the fire, he ran to neighbors for help, which arrived too late. Louisa suffered severe burns and died several hours later.

Paul, only five years old when his mother died, said later that the shock of her death wiped out his memories of her. It was his father—whom he invariably called "Pop"—who exerted the great, enduring influence on his life. Father and son would grow increasingly close in the coming years.

"There must have been moments when I felt the sorrows of a motherless child," Paul Robeson recalled many years later, "but what I most remember from my youngest days was an abiding sense of comfort and security." He received loving care from his father, from his brothers and sister, and from the close-knit black community that surrounded them.

With nostalgia, he described the Negroes of his Princeton childhood as hard-working people, poor in worldly goods but rich in compassion. He said they shared "songs of love and longing, songs of trials and triumphs . . . and the healing comfort to be found in the illimitable sorrow of the spirituals."[9]

* * *

As an intelligent and sensitive youngster, Paul certainly saw the racism and poverty that afflicted the Negroes all around him. But he concealed any anger and resentment that he felt. Only on rare occasions, when greatly provoked, did his anger burst forth. He learned from his father that he should keep his emotions within himself, remaining silent, stoic, and strong.

Naturally, young Paul sang hymns and spirituals in the choir of his father's church on Sundays. He also sang some of the popular songs of the day with his brothers and friends when they entertained themselves at home, in an era long before radio, television, and electronic gadgets.

Bill, Ben, and Paul began singing some songs one evening, harmonizing on the popular ballad of the day "Down by the Old Mill Stream." Bill suddenly exclaimed, "Paul you can sing." Neither Paul nor Ben took their older brother seriously at this point. And they quickly went on to other things. Ben fondly recalled the incident many years later.[10]

* * *

Paul also became aware early in his life that the people of Princeton's black community saw something special about him—they said that he was destined to achieve great things.

He did not understand what made people feel this way about him. But he knew that they held great expectations for his future. And this placed an added responsibility on him, a duty to advance the cause of his people.

Beyond being taller and smarter than anyone his age in the all-black elementary school, he had a certain inner stillness. It was a deep sense of responsibility and purpose, an exceptional gravitas in one so young. He seemed to be that unusual child of destiny who would make his people proud.

* * *

Reverend Robeson, a Presbyterian since his days at Lincoln University, transferred his religious affiliation to the African Methodist Episcopal (AME) Zion Church, an independent black denomination founded in New York in 1796. It gave him an opportunity to start over with a new church in another town.

Paul was nine years old in 1907 when the Robesons moved from Princeton to the working-class town of Westfield, about thirty miles to the northwest. Here, Reverend Robeson built the Downer Street AME Zion Church with the help of Paul, Ben, and a small black congregation. Until the church and its parsonage could be completed, the reverend worked in a grocery and lived with Paul in cramped quarters above the store.

Living in Westfield for three years, Paul attended a predominantly white elementary school that included the town's few Negro children. It was a lonely time, although he moved easily between his black community and the white environment of his school. He was cut off from his friends back in Princeton, and his siblings were away most of the time, leaving him with his father.

His brother Bill, who taught him how to study and analyze subjects, went to medical school at the University of Pennsylvania. Bill worked as a railroad porter between periods of medical school, eventually earned his degree, and settled in Washington, DC. Their stern father ordered another brother, the rebellious, troublesome Reeve, to leave home because he set a bad example for young Paul. He drifted to Detroit and faded from the family.[11]

Paul's favorite brother, Ben, went away to a prep school and then to college in North Carolina, but during his frequent visits home, he continued to teach Paul to play football and baseball. Their sister, Marian, went to the Scotia Seminary, also in North Carolina, where helpful Robeson relatives still lived.

It was the elderly Reverend Robeson who dominated Paul's youth. He idolized his father, describing him later as "the greatest influence" in his life. He remembered his father as a man of ordinary height, with broad shoulders, whose bearing "reflected the rock-like strength and dignity of his character."[12]

Paul noted that his father was not demonstrative or quick to praise his children, adding that the Robesons refrained from expressing their deepest feelings. The powerful example set by his father helped make Paul a man of spiritual values and strong principles.

When he brought home a report card with all As except for one B, his father gently chided him about that one B. This family story was told by Paul's first biographer, his wife, Eslanda, who said he accepted his father's admonition to strive for perfection. With this unobtainable goal in mind, he always remained modest, even after his many achievements. She said, "He never became conceited because he was always working toward perfection."[13]

* * *

In 1910, Reverend Robeson accepted a transfer to become pastor of the larger St. Thomas AME Zion Church in the town of Somerville, about half-way between Westfield and Princeton. The reverend would stay in Somerville for the rest of his life. Paul attended the eighth grade at an all-black elementary school there and graduated at the top of his class.

While the Robesons moved to Somerville, W. E. B. Du Bois, the first Negro to earn a doctorate at Harvard University, helped start the National Association for the Advancement of Colored People, or NAACP, in 1910. He urged Negroes to strive for higher education and equality.

Paul entered Somerville High School on September 5, 1911, the start of the new school year. He was one of seventy-seven freshmen, all listed in the student newspaper, *The Valkyrie*. Most of the students were white. Paul was a bright boy, agile and big for his age, who excelled in studies as well as sports and adjusted quickly to high school. He played football, baseball, and basketball for the school and participated in the debate, drama, and glee clubs.[14]

His father instilled a love of learning in Paul and supervised his recitation of famous speeches, including the words of Homer and Virgil, in sessions at home, turning him into a skilled orator. Then, after nightly studies, father and son often played checkers together.[15]

That summer, following his freshman year in high school, Paul made his first venture beyond the small towns of New Jersey. His brother Ben had obtained a summer job as a waiter at Narragansett Pier in Rhode Island, where many black students worked in the resorts of the rich, and he took fourteen-year-old Paul with him to serve as a kitchen boy. Paul would return to Narragansett Pier to work as a busboy and as a waiter for several more summers.

* * *

In the fall of Paul's sophomore year at Somerville, *The Valkyrie* printed a photograph of the school's fifteen-man football team. It shows a slender Paul in the center row. He played fullback on the team, which won four of its seven games, but lost 33–0 and 45–0 to two larger schools with better-trained teams.

The next season ended on Thanksgiving Day with a 10–0 loss to Bound Brook. *The Valkyrie* reported that "Robeson, the star fullback, was tackled . . . thrown heavily to the ground" and suffered a broken collarbone.

During his senior year, which began in the fall of 1914, Paul not only continued his exploits on the playing field but served as athletic editor of the student newspaper. The December issue included an editor's note: "Since Robeson, who is athletic editor, has failed to give full honor to himself," it said, "we have taken the liberty of so doing. Robeson, at full-back, was the mainstay of the team in every game. His steady playing on the defense and never-failing rushes on the offense gained him the reputation of being one of the best players ever turned out by Somerville High School."

Small church where his father was minister, on the same block as the family's house. By Katherine Elgin for Arnold Lubasch.

In the assembly hall on Friday evening, February 26, 1915, the seniors presented a show of adolescent humor, which they called "The Shakespeare Water Cure." The characters included Hamlet and Ophelia, Romeo and Juliet, Shylock and Macbeth, all entwined in a broad farce set at a spa, with Paul as Othello. *The Valkyrie* reported, "The class realized $95 on this play and is much pleased with the result."

"On Friday, April 23, Paul Robeson, who was chosen as our delegate to the oratorical contest, delivered his speech entitled 'Toussaint L'Ouverture' in chapel. In this he displayed excellent articulation and force of speech which held his audience attentive to the last." He finished third, with honorable mention.

The June 1915 issue of *The Valkyrie* served as the yearbook for the senior class, complete with a formal photograph of each of the thirty students. It reported the average height of the seniors was five feet, five inches, and their average weight was 131 pounds. Listed as favorite studies were German, English, and history; favorite colleges for girls were Vassar and Mt. Holyoke; for boys, Princeton and Rutgers.

Class president was J. Douglas Brown, one of Paul's best friends, later dean of faculty at Princeton University, who remembered Paul as "a warm and loyal friend."

Next to Paul's senior photograph, the yearbook said, "Doing all with a deal of skill." It listed his activities as school orator, debate team, athletic editor of *The Valkyrie*, senior play, and glee club; he had varsity letters in football, basketball, baseball, and track.

* * *

During his years at Somerville High School, Paul had several white teachers who took an interest in him, including one who supervised the show with Paul prophetically portraying Othello. His only complaint from those high school years concerned the school's principal, whom he could never please.[16]

One classmate remembered that Paul had "a habit of oversleeping and was often late." Sleeping late would become a lifelong habit.

Despite the racial insults sometimes shouted by opposing fans at sports events, he enjoyed an exceptional childhood for a Negro of his era. Certainly, as an intelligent black youngster, he felt an inner tension while growing up amid blatant racism. But his academic and athletic success smoothed his path.

The parents of his classmates welcomed him as a clergyman's polite, popular son. Paul seemed to move easily between his own black neighborhood and the homes of his white classmates. But he was keenly aware of social restrictions, learning to contain his emotions and to compartmentalize his life.

Paul continued to prefer the word "Negro"—the most acceptable reference when he was growing up—even after terms like black and African American came into popular usage. The biography that his wife wrote was titled *Paul Robeson, Negro*, and the first sentence of his own book three decades later read, "I am a Negro."

* * *

The core of Paul's character—his rock-solid home—consisted of his family, his father's church, and the Negro community around it. These forces provided young Paul with an enduring strength of his own. He knew who he was and where he came from. He did not yet know where he was going, but he felt an obligation to do his best for his people, the Negroes of America.

As his senior year neared an end, he planned to go to Lincoln University, as his father had done, and possibly follow his father into the ministry. But then Paul heard about a competitive examination open to all high school seniors in New Jersey. The student who achieved the highest score would win a four-year scholarship to Rutgers College, a highly regarded white school in New Brunswick, only some twelve miles from his home in Somerville.

He decided to take the examination, a difficult two-day written test that covered all the academic subjects of his four years in high school. He studied hard for the examination held in the Somerville Courthouse. When the results were announced, his score was the highest ever recorded in the state.

Paul Robeson would go to Rutgers—and he rightly called it "a decisive point in my life."[17]

* * *

I Got a Home in That Rock

I got a home in that rock, don't you see?
I got a home in that rock, don't you see?
Between earth and sky,
Thought I heard my savior cry,
He got a home in that rock, don't you see?

Rich man died, he'd lived so well, don't you see?
Rich man died, he'd lived so well, don't you see?
Rich man died, he'd lived so well,
When he died he found a home in hell,
He had no home in that rock, don't you see?

God gave Noah the rainbow sign, don't you see?
God gave Noah the rainbow sign, don't you see?
God gave Noah the rainbow sign,
No more water but fire next time,
Better get a home in that rock, don't you see?

—arranged by Lawrence Brown

• 2 •

Robeson of Rutgers

There's a man going 'round taking names.

—spiritual

On an autumnal morning in September 1915, Paul Robeson walked onto the campus of Rutgers College, on the banks of the Raritan River in New Brunswick, New Jersey. Rutgers was only a dozen miles from his home in Somerville, but it must have felt as if he had entered a new world—a white world. The only black faces he could see were those of gardeners, janitors, and other menial workers because the teachers and the students included not a single Negro other than himself.

The seventeen-year-old Robeson, standing six feet, two inches tall and now weighing 190 pounds, moved along the quiet paths of Rutgers, a private men's college of some five hundred students. Just two black students had attended the college in the past, but they were long gone.[1]

Rutgers, founded in 1766, was one of the oldest colleges in the country. The first intercollegiate football game had been played here between Rutgers and its rival, Princeton, in 1869, a game that Rutgers won. The college would become a large, diverse state university many years later.

Despite his scholarship, Paul did not have a dormitory room when he arrived, since no white student could be expected to accept a black roommate. Instead, he found a room in the home of a Negro family named Cummings, who lived on Morrell Street, not far from the campus. On campus, most students and professors simply ignored him. Paul was polite and friendly to all; he had already learned to conceal any anger that he might feel.

* * *

11

Of course, he wanted to play football, so as soon as he settled into his classes, he went out to the playing field. He had won an academic scholarship, not one for football, and he had not been invited to the preseason practice. The team's highly regarded coach, George Foster Sanford, allowed him to try out for the team as a defensive end. But the players quickly made it clear that they did not want a black teammate.

"On the first day of scrimmage, they set about making sure that I wouldn't get on their team," Robeson recalled. "One boy slugged me in the face and smashed my nose, just smashed it. . . . And then when I was down, flat on my back, another boy got me with his knee, just came over and fell on me. He managed to dislocate my right shoulder."

"Well, that night I was a very, very sorry boy," he continued. He was ready to quit. But his brother Ben came to him and said he did not want to think "our family had a quitter in it."

So after spending ten days in bed, Paul returned for another scrimmage. He made a tackle and was on the ground, his right hand palm down on the ground, when a player came over and stamped on his hand with cleats, tearing the fingernails off. And "that's when I knew rage."

"The next play came around my end, the whole first-string backfield came at me." He swept out his long arms and knocked down the three block-ers—they just went down. Then, he grabbed the ball carrier, Frank Kelly, in his two hands and lifted him over his head. "I was going to smash him so hard to the ground that I'd break him right in two, and I could have done it."

But just then, the coach yelled, "Robey, you're on the varsity!" That calmed Robeson and saved Kelly.[2]

With the help of Coach Sanford, who became a strong supporter, Paul went on to win the acceptance of the Rutgers players. The coach gradually inserted him into games as a substitute at end or tackle, and he played in half of the team's eight games. The strong Rutgers team won seven of its games. Paul summed up his own performance as "promising."

* * *

In his classes, Paul earned an A or B in all his subjects, except for one C in English composition, a record that displeased his father, who told him to forget about going out for basketball and to concentrate on his studies. His grades improved sufficiently, so his father agreed he could play baseball in the spring.

His freshman year ended, and Paul went back to Narragansett for the summer, working again as a waiter at the Imperial Hotel. He became a friend of Frederick "Fritz" Pollard, a football star from nearby Brown University, who also worked for the hotel. Pollard spent hours coaching Robeson on the best ways to play his position and catch passes.

Fritz Pollard and Paul Robeson would be good friends for many years.

* * *

Robeson returned to Rutgers for his sophomore year in September 1916. The school had now admitted another black student, Robert Davenport of West Orange, who then became Paul's roommate. They moved into Winants Hall, a student dormitory on the campus.

On the football field, Paul played regularly, mostly at left tackle and left end, helping Rutgers to a winning season. But his Scarlet Knights lost to Brown University, 21–3, as Fritz Pollard raced past the defense for three touchdowns.

Paul's worst disappointment came at the homecoming game against Washington and Lee, a Southern college that asked Rutgers not to use its black player. The accommodating Rutgers administration told Coach Sanford to keep him off the field. The coach reluctantly complied, and the players took the field without Paul. They played the Southern team to a 13–13 tie. Paul kept silent, concealing the anger he certainly felt. He adhered to his father's admonition that he should always appear polite to make it easier for other blacks to follow him.

His father had emphasized to him that he was going to Rutgers not just for himself but as a representative of all the Negroes who lacked his opportunity. Paul recalled that just before he left for Rutgers, his father told him that, as a Negro, he must always "lean over backwards to be a clean player." And he did just that.[3]

He was also very durable, playing both offense and defense, all sixty minutes of the game, in an era when players just wore light leather helmets and little padding in their uniforms. The hard protective helmets with face guards and heavy shoulder pads so familiar today were unknown in those days.

* * *

Paul also played center and forward on the basketball team and catcher on the baseball team; he joined the track team as well, competing in discus throwing and shot put. He especially loved playing baseball and made sure he was in the center of the action as the catcher; and when not catching, he liked to play the key infield position of shortstop. He was a good fielder but a weak hitter.

He became the star of the varsity debating team and won oratorical contests every year. But his lovely young baritone voice was heard rarely, if ever, in the glee club, because a Negro could not travel with the club and take part in its social affairs. And no fraternity invited him to join despite his star status. Any distress these social slights caused him he concealed behind his consistently modest and genial manner.

In the spring of 1917, the latter part of his sophomore year, Paul met Geraldine Mamie Neale. She was a petite and lovely Negro in her senior year of high school when he first saw her at a YMCA event in her hometown of Freehold. Their initial meeting was brief, but Paul made sure that he would meet beautiful "Gerry" again.[4]

September 1917 found Paul Robeson returning to Rutgers for his junior year after another summer working in Narragansett. This was an era when most players were under six feet tall, so he was considered a giant—not only big, strong, and fast but also agile and extremely quick thinking on the football field.

In a nine-game season, the Scarlet Knights of Rutgers won seven, lost one, and tied one. Robeson's play stood out as the central force that held six of the opponents scoreless. The Rutgers student newspaper, *The Targum*, called it the best season in the college's history, with the team ranked among the best in the country.[5]

The Scarlet Knights, led by Robeson, won their first two games at home by one-sided scores, shutting out their opponents. Then, playing away, they lost a hard-fought battle to Syracuse, 14–10, but bounced back the next Saturday with a 33–7 victory over Lafayette in Easton, Pennsylvania.

For its fifth game, Rutgers traveled to the Bronx to play highly regarded Fordham. The *New York Tribune's* report of the game, written by Charles A. Taylor, opened with these words: "A dark cloud upset the hopes of the Fordham eleven yesterday afternoon. Its name was Robeson. . . . The score was 28–0 in favor of the dark cloud."

The next Saturday, a tough away game against West Virginia ended in a 7–7 tie. West Virginia had asked Rutgers not to play Robeson, but this time the team refused, standing up for its black star. Rutgers demolished its next two opponents by scores of 61–0 and 27–0.

The final—and biggest—game of the season took Rutgers to Ebbets Field in Brooklyn to play the powerful Newport Naval Reserves. With the nation still at war, the military team included several former all-Americans. But they were stymied 14–0 by the Rutgers defense.

* * *

The sportswriters who covered the Rutgers-Newport game that Saturday produced stories that praised Paul Robeson in dramatic style. Walter Camp wrote that "the giant Robeson" did not confine himself to left end but roamed "all over the field until the Newport team began to believe that there were, at least, eleven Robesons, and their entire horizon was obscured by him."[6]

Robeson in his football uniform at Rutgers in 1917 when he was an all-American. Courtesy Associated Press.

The *New York Sunday Tribune* of November 25 reported, "It was Robeson, a veritable Othello of battle who led the dashing little Rutgers eleven to a 14–0 victory over the widely heralded Newport Naval Reserves." Three days later, the *New York World* published a feature under this headline: "Robeson Takes a Place with Elect of Football—All Around Ability of Rutgers' End Puts Him with Greatest and Best of the Game."

"Paul Robeson, the big Negro end of the Rutgers eleven, is a football genius," began the article by George Daley. He praised his blocking on offense, tackling on defense, catching forward passes, playing defensive quarterback, and kicking off. "And the greatest perhaps of his accomplishments is accurate diagnosing. His ability to size up plays and quickly get to the point of danger is almost uncanny. He is so rarely at fault that he is at the centre of practically every play."

Robeson was a virtually unanimous selection for first-team all-American. Many sportswriters named him as the best college player in the country in 1917. He was the third black all-American in football history; the second was Fritz Pollard, a year earlier. The leading football authority, Walter Camp, called Robeson "the most powerful defensive end that ever trod the gridiron, a veritable superman."[7]

* * *

In winter, he played center on the varsity basketball team, valued for his size, versatility, and alert thinking on the court. In spring, he served as full-time catcher on the baseball team. And on the track team, he threw the discus and heaved the shot, thus winning varsity letters in all four major sports.

A teammate, Arthur Van Fleet, recalled that between innings of baseball games, Paul would take off his catching equipment, go to a far corner of the field to throw the discus, then come back to resume his baseball position as catcher.

He capped his glorious junior year with an academic honor—election to Phi Beta Kappa.

* * *

Near the end of his junior year, the young man suffered a most painful loss. His father died on May 17. Rev. Robeson, ailing for some time, passed away at his parsonage in Somerville at the age of seventy-two.

In a college scrapbook filled with newspaper clippings about his football exploits, Paul wrote down a single, sad line: "My dear 'Dad' departed this life May 17, 1918." For the rest of his life, he would measure his greatest achievements by thinking about "what Pop would have said."[8]

A local newspaper, the *Unionist Gazette*, noted the reverend's death in an obituary that neglected to mention he had been born a slave but commented editorially that he was "a man of strong character" and one "always interested in the rights and welfare of his people."

The family gathered for the funeral—William Jr. came from a medical school in Washington; Reeve returned for the first time from Detroit; Ben, now an army chaplain, came from his military camp in Kentucky; and Marian came from her teacher training school in Pennsylvania. It was the last time they all would be together. Paul would always remain close to Ben and Marian.

The body of Reverend Robeson was buried beside the grave of his wife, Maria Louisa, in the Princeton cemetery, across the street from the Witherspoon Street Presbyterian Church.

* * *

America's participation in World War I took place against the backdrop of the Russian Revolution of 1917, which resulted in the new Soviet Union founded under the Communist leadership of Lenin. In the summer of 1918, with the war still raging in Europe, Paul worked as a laborer in a Newark shipyard instead of going back to Narragansett. When he returned to Rutgers in the fall for his senior year, he had reached his full, mature height, a fraction over six feet, three inches, and weighed a more muscular 220 pounds.

His grades—about equally divided between As and Bs with a few Cs during his four years at Rutgers—fell off a bit in his final year and even included one D in economics. But on the football field, he was spectacular, with many sportswriters praising his fierce tackles, smashing blocks, and leaping catches. His outstanding play led the Scarlet Knights once again to a successful season. They won their first five games but suffered disappointing defeats in their final two games against powerful Great Lakes Naval Station and Syracuse.

At the end of the season, Robeson was named an all-American again. And several football experts called him the best player in the country. The authoritative Walter Camp wrote, "There never was a more serviceable end, both in attack and defense, than Robeson."

In his four seasons on the football team, Rutgers won twenty-two games, lost six, and tied three. To Paul's chagrin, the Scarlet Knights never beat Princeton in football, losing their only game to the Princeton Tigers, 22–20, despite his valiant efforts.

Turning his attention back to debating, Paul won the school's Senior Competitive Extemporaneous Speaking Contest on April 23. *The Targum* reported that he received a prize of $30 in books. In winning this contest, it added, "Robeson completes his record of four consecutive victories in public speaking contests, Freshman, Sophomore, Junior and Senior." He had continued to use the training in classic speeches that he had received from his father.

Paul added another accolade when he was selected for Cap and Skull, the college's exclusive honor society, which singled out each year "the four men who best represented the ideals of Rutgers."

Even the great Robeson of Rutgers was not completely beyond reproach. Like many students before and since, his focus faltered in that final college year, and he suffered for a while from a senior slump. It was then that he received that D in economics, the lowest grade in his academic career. But he never faltered for long.

He retained his father's enduring guidance: he must always strive for the advancement of his people, while maintaining a modest and polite demeanor that would make it easier for other Negroes to follow him.

* * *

On May 29, Paul submitted his senior thesis, which he titled "The Fourteenth Amendment: The Sleeping Giant of the American Constitution." He presented a cohesive argument, buttressed with a number of judicial decisions, contending that the amendment constituted the greatest force for protecting civil rights and "making us truly a nation."

Stressing the amendment's assurance of due process and equal protection under the law, he wrote that it made the national government the ultimate protector of "the essential rights of life, liberty, and property." "The distinctive and characteristic feature of the American Constitution is equality before the law," Paul continued. Noting its inclusive definition of citizens, he added that "the shield of the Fourteenth Amendment" provides equal protection for "persons of every race, rank, and grade."[9]

This college student, with his moderate views at the age of twenty-one, displayed considerable foresight in focusing on the amendment that civil rights lawyers would use more than three decades later to win major court cases, including the historic Supreme Court decision of 1954 that outlawed school segregation. But the pernicious virus of racism would continue to infect the nation like an epidemic of evil for much of the twentieth century.

* * *

Tall, ruggedly handsome, with a charming smile, Paul was popular with the girls he encountered at social events in the Negro communities of central New Jersey. But he had found his "one true love." She was Gerry Neale, the one who had caught his attention in the latter part of his sophomore year.

In his junior and senior years, he and Gerry saw each other as often as possible at social gatherings. He gave her his favorite sports trophies. Everyone expected them to get married when they finished school.

When Paul asked Gerry Neale to marry him after graduation, however, she said no. He was hopelessly romantic; she was coolly realistic. Gerry wanted to be a schoolteacher and lead a conventional family life. She understood that Paul was "a man of destiny" who would belong to the public, not to his family. And she did not want that kind of future.[10]

Gerry went on to marry a lawyer, Harry Bledsoe, although she always remembered Paul with affection. He never got over her rejection of him, a disappointment that haunted his heart forever. "We were meant for each other," he told a friend many years later. "I'm as sure of that today as I was back then. Gerry—she was just perfect, so sweet—the one woman in the world for me."[11]

His idealized love reflected what Stendhal called the "crystallization" of emotions that attributed a unique quality to the loved one—only she could give him true joy in life. The French novelist Marie-Henri Beyle, under the nom de plume Stendhal, published his analysis of love in 1822. Young Paul felt it just as keenly a century later.[12]

* * *

Paul Robeson enjoyed one of the most spectacular college careers in the nation's history, soaring above the terrible racism of his time. He was the quintessential scholar-athlete.[13]

Commemorating the Class of 1919, *The Targum* wrote a tribute to him, declaring, "Paul Robeson made a name and a record equaled by none." It noted that he had come to Rutgers "unheralded" in 1915, but it conveniently forgot that he had also been unwelcomed.

"For four years, Robey has been the star of football teams with enviable records. In basketball, he has played every position as the necessity arose. Again in baseball and track has his merit been shown. At the end of his junior year, a four letter man, he now leaves with the 'R' awarded to him eleven times."

The Targum added its "prophesy" for class members, predicting that by 1940 Paul would be the governor of New Jersey and "the leader of the colored race in America."[14]

* * *

On the sunny spring morning of June 10, 1919, Paul stood before the graduates, families, and dignitaries assembled for the Rutgers commencement ceremony in the Second Reformed Church in New Brunswick. He delivered the valedictory address for the sixty-nine members of his graduating class, a speech infused with patriotism and hope, which he titled "The New Idealism."

With his deep, resonant voice, using a lofty tone suitable for such an occasion, he eulogized the American soldiers who had recently fought and died in the war to attain "the triumph of right over the forces of autocracy."

"We of this less favored race," he said, "realize that our future lies chiefly in our own hands . . . that neither the old-time slavery, nor continued prejudice, need extinguish self-respect, crush manly ambition or paralyze effort."

"And may I not appeal to you who also revere [the fallen soldiers] to join with us in continuing to fight for the great principles for which they contended until in all sections of this fair land there will be equal opportunities for all . . . and until black and white shall clasp friendly hands in the consciousness of the fact that we are brethren and that God is the father of us all."[15]

It seemed fitting for this scholar-athlete that he followed the morning program by playing one last game for Rutgers in the afternoon. He took special delight in finally beating Princeton, 5–1, on the Rutgers baseball diamond. He caught a well-pitched game and contributed a hit to the victory.

Noting his graduation from Rutgers, the *New York Times* called him "one of the greatest all around athletes" and "the greatest player in collegiate football" for the past two years. This was clearly a well-deserved accolade as the young man left college.

Paul Robeson was now ready to move beyond the legendary "Robeson of Rutgers" into the larger world of New York, where a remarkable range of activities awaited him.

* * *

Taking Names

There's a man going 'round taking names,
There's a man going 'round taking names,
He has taken my mother's name
And has left my heart in pain,
There's a man going 'round taking names.

There's a man going 'round taking names, taking names,
There's a man going 'round taking names, taking names,
He has taken my father's name
And has left my heart in pain,
There's a man going 'round taking names.

Now, death is the man taking names,
Yes, death is the man taking names,
He has taken my brother's name
And has left my heart in pain,
There's a man going 'round taking names.

—arranged by Lawrence Brown

· 3 ·

Columbia and Essie

We are climbing Jacob's ladder, soldiers of the cross.

—hymn

$\mathcal{P}$aul Robeson, an earnest young man still only twenty-one years old, moved from the provincial New Jersey towns of his youth to metropolitan New York in the summer of 1919.

While still at Rutgers, he decided that the law would provide the best opportunity for him to pursue a successful career. Funds were scarce, so he spent much of the summer working as a waiter on a steamship line that carried vacationers between New York and Boston. And in the fall, he worked on the weekends as assistant to his friend Fritz Pollard, who had become the football coach at Lincoln University in Pennsylvania.

With the help of Rutgers alumni, Paul had obtained a modest scholarship to the New York University Law School in lower Manhattan. But he did not feel comfortable there and wanted to move uptown to Columbia University. The dean of Columbia's School of Law, Harlan Fiske Stone, granted his request to transfer there for the new semester that began in February 1920.

Robeson preferred the atmosphere of the stately Morningside Heights campus of Columbia University, at 116th Street, just west of Harlem. He especially enjoyed moving into Harlem—the vibrant heart of the black world in America—where he shared a small apartment on West 135th Street with a young musician named James Lightfoot. With no scholarship at Columbia, Robeson began tutoring college students for meager fees and taking part-time jobs.

He emerged as a popular figure in Harlem, the famous "Robeson of Rutgers," escorting young women and singing at parties. He appeared good-natured and unassuming, dressed in inexpensive suits that did not fit his large frame too well. He cared very little about material things.

21

His interesting young face, with its hard planes that seemed almost to have been carved from stone, would grow more rounded and softer as he aged. But a feeling of loneliness that dwelled deep within him would never go away. The death of a parent early in life can create an enduring sense of loss and longing; and so it was with Paul.

* * *

Ratification of the Nineteenth Amendment on August 26, 1920, finally gave women the right to vote. It culminated years of protest marches by women demanding this fundamental right.

In the summer of 1920, Paul Robeson got to know a young woman named Eslanda Cardozo Goode, called "Essie" by virtually everyone who knew her. Both attended summer school at Columbia that year. And Essie soon set her sights on this popular young man with a wonderful smile.[1]

Essie appeared intelligent, energetic, and assertive. Described as beautiful, with a light-olive complexion, she stood just five feet, two inches tall, more than a foot shorter than Paul, and she was a little more than two years older. She worked as a chemist in a hospital laboratory and planned to become a physician.

Paul was intent on completing law school while working at temporary jobs. With no assistance, he had to earn enough money to pay for the necessities of life. But he was young and found time for other activities too.

That summer, a neighbor of his, Dora Cole Norman, decided to stage a one-act play for the Colored Players Guild at the YWCA in Harlem. The play, written by Ridgely Torrence, was titled *Simon the Cyrenian*. It portrayed a black man who helps Christ carry the cross to the crucifixion. Mrs. Norman wanted her impressive young neighbor to play the part. With persistence, she overcame his reluctance and persuaded him to do it.

The talented black amateurs put on only three performances of the play, but they attracted the attention of Kenneth Macgowan and Robert Edmond Jones of the avant-garde Provincetown Players in Greenwich Village. The two men went backstage, complimented Robeson on his performance, and invited him to audition for their group. But he just returned to his law classes the next day.[2]

* * *

Robeson attended his law classes in the fall semester of 1920. He admired Dean Harlan Fiske Stone, who taught some of the sessions. A law student he later encountered there, William O. Douglas, would be appointed to the Supreme Court. Dean Stone would become the Supreme Court's chief justice.

That fall of 1920, Fritz Pollard decided to play professional football in the new American Professional Football Association. It consisted of a dozen rough-and-tumble teams, primarily in the Middle West, with players earning a few hundred dollars a game for playing each Sunday. Robeson coached Lincoln's college team for Pollard in 1920, although some erroneously said he played for Akron or the Hammond Pros in that first professional football season.[3]

With Pollard, the Akron Pros won all their regular games that first year. Then, they played the Buffalo All-Americans to a scoreless tie in what was arguably professional football's first play-off game. The association would turn into the better-organized National Football League two years later.

* * *

Essie Goode held a responsible job as a chemist in the surgical pathology laboratory of Presbyterian Hospital in upper Manhattan.[4]

Her mother was the former Eslanda Cardozo, a descendant of black slaves and Spanish Jews. Her father was John Goode, a lawyer, who died when Essie was four years old. Her strong-willed mother built a beauty-care business, while bringing up her three children—Essie, Frank, and John Jr.—in Washington, DC. She moved the family to New York in 1905, then to Chicago, and finally back to New York.

Essie, finishing high school at sixteen, won a scholarship to the University of Illinois, where she majored in chemistry, then transferred to Columbia for her senior year and went to work at the hospital. She now focused on Paul.

* * *

In the winter and spring of 1921, Essie made sure that she went to parties that Paul attended. They spent time together and found mutual interests; their relationship became romantic as the year unfolded. Essie gave up her plan to become a doctor and devoted herself to the task of becoming Mrs. Paul Robeson.

"Paul was so popular with everyone that it was quite a problem," she recalled. So she decided on a "campaign" to win him. Since many girls were making a fuss over this handsome football hero, she tried to appear indifferent while she pursued him—and "it worked."[5]

Essie's mother, the formidable Mrs. Goode, opposed her desire to marry this poor, young Paul Robeson. She said his skin was too dark; he lacked ambition; he could not take care of her. And when Paul asked for his brother Ben's opinion of Essie, he was told that she seemed too ambitious and that she had an irritating aristocratic manner.[6]

Life took an unexpected turn that spring, the kind that can strike young lovers. Essie became pregnant, secretly had an abortion, and did not tell Paul until a month later. He then felt angry and guilty and stopped seeing her.

It was typical of Essie to make her own decision without consulting Paul in this deeply personal matter that affected both of them. She was independent, practical, and organized in conducting her life. She denied being aggressive but said, "I have always been determined never to let anyone push me around."[7]

* * *

Essie remained determined to become Mrs. Paul Robeson. But he seemed uncertain, still yearning for Gerry Neale. He made a final effort to win Gerry, visiting her at home in Freehold, New Jersey, but to no avail. She was convinced, correctly, that he was destined to be a public figure who would not lead a normal family life.

Paul returned from Freehold to Harlem, alone and lonely. As he contemplated his future, he must have realized his need for a caring woman to share his life. He soon went to see Essie—and asked her to marry him. "It wasn't a dream," she noted in her diary, "it was a marvelous reality."[8]

They decided to elope to Greenwich, Connecticut. On arriving, they learned that Connecticut had a five-day waiting period, so they boarded a streetcar for the return trip to New York. They stopped, instead, in Port Chester, New York, where the town clerk married them quickly and quietly. It was August 17, 1921.

* * *

The couple returned to Harlem. But they kept their marriage secret and continued to live apart, Paul in the apartment he shared with Jimmy Lightfoot, and Essie with her friend Minnie Sumner. Paul would come over and play whist, a card game similar to bridge, with Essie, Minnie, and her boyfriend, William Patterson, a Harlem lawyer.[9]

This rather strange start to their marriage resulted partly from financial considerations, because Paul was still going to school, and partly from the knowledge that their families would disapprove. It was not the best of beginnings.

Their divided living arrangement continued while Paul attended law school in the fall. He also joined Fritz Pollard to play professional football for the Akron Pros in 1921 in an environment in which rowdy fans and opposing players often shouted racial epithets at the black players. The Akron team finished with a respectable 8–3–1 record for the season.

Working his way through law school by playing professional football on weekends required Robeson to take long train rides between New York and the game sites, usually in Ohio or Wisconsin. He arrived for practice on Saturday, played on Sunday, then returned to New York late that night. Two

Paul and Eslanda Robeson standing aboard the SS *Washington* arriving in New York from England on October 12, 1932. Courtesy Associated Press.

helpful classmates, Milton Rettenberg and Philip Adler, lent their notes to him so he could keep up with missed lectures.

Paul and Essie finally announced their marriage in December. She wrote to her mother, who was vacationing in Bermuda—and who was displeased. He told his brother Ben and his sister, Marian, who approved with little enthusiasm. Without further delay, Essie found their first home together, a large front room on the top floor of a private house at 321 West 138th Street in central Harlem.

* * *

Taking care of Paul became Essie's responsibility. She shopped for his clothes, which now fit him properly for the first time, and she ran their small household as well as worked at the hospital laboratory. But Paul often found himself out of sync with Essie. While she got up early and eager, he wanted to sleep until noon, then work at his part-time job as a postal clerk and stay up very late studying or talking.

"He had some personal habits I didn't like," Essie also noted, "but I was conceited enough to think, like most women, that I could change them. He's very clean, but untidy; he's very kind and generous, but thoughtless and neglectful; he could become interested in something and forget for long periods that I was there."[10]

Essie regarded Paul as a wonderful diamond in the rough that she could polish into a gleaming success. And she made progress. She became the rare person that Paul truly loved, one to whom he could express his deep feelings of affection. But he came to resent her efforts to manipulate and control him.

* * *

In March 1922, with Robeson still intent on becoming a lawyer, Dora Norman, who had induced him to participate in her production two years before, now urged him to take part in a Broadway play. A wealthy white friend of hers, Mary Hoyt Wiborg, had written a drama about plantation life in Louisiana. An English actress, Margaret Wycherly, agreed to star in this play, titled *Taboo*. Kenneth Macgowan recommended Paul for the role of a wandering minstrel.

Once again Paul resisted going on the stage, preferring to complete law school. But Essie saw the potential of a stage career for him. She suggested that he give up his dreary post office job, put off his law classes until the summer, and act in the play now. He later told an interviewer that the most important fact at the time was that "I got about $75 a week."

In an unpublished memoir, Essie observed that Paul did not want to be an actor because he had conservative views and did not consider acting a serious profession, but she recognized the limits of a law career for a Negro. "If he put his foot on the bottom rung of the ladder of the theater, he could climb to the top," she said. But he could never climb to the top of the ladder of the law. "I set my heart and mind more and more surely on a dramatic career for him."

* * *

Taboo opened on April 4 to poor reviews, although some noted Robeson's impressive stage presence and superb voice. The weak, confusing play closed after a short run. That allowed Robeson to study for his second-year law exams, which he promptly passed. He and Essie went to see other plays together; they discussed and analyzed the performances as Paul became interested in acting.

Alexander Woollcott, drama critic for the *New York Times*, had written a sharply negative review of *Taboo* and Robeson's acting debut in it. But he found Paul interesting and invited him to his Manhattan apartment for a talk. Woollcott wrote later that Robeson struck him as "someone touched by destiny."

"He was a young man on his way," Woollcott continued. "He did not know where he was going, but I never in my life saw anyone so quietly sure, by some inner knowledge, that he was going somewhere."[11]

* * *

Shortly after *Taboo* closed, chance nudged Robeson back to Broadway. He was standing on a Harlem street corner with some friends when Harold Browning joined them. Browning headed a quartet, the Harmony Kings, in a Broadway hit called *Shuffle Along*, an all-black revue. When he said the group's bass singer had suddenly left, Paul asked for a chance to replace him. Browning was skeptical but took him home to hear him sing. That did it.[12]

Robeson went to a rehearsal the next day and appeared in the show that night. The audiences greeted his singing with enthusiasm. He stayed in *Shuffle Along* for a month until the quartet's regular bass returned.

Although *Shuffle Along* contained skits reminiscent of degrading minstrel shows, with stereotyped comedians and singers in garish costumes, it won acclaim for the exhilarating music of Eubie Blake and Noble Sissle. The star was the dazzling Florence Mills.

* * *

As summer now approached, Mary Wiborg made plans to revive *Taboo*. She appeared undaunted by the play's poor reception in New York and arranged for it to go to Britain, with a new title, *Voodoo*. A legendary English actress, Mrs. Patrick Campbell, agreed to take over the starring role. They invited Robeson to join the cast in Britain. Essie urged him to accept, and this time he raised no real objection. He intended to return home in the fall for law school.

In early July, he sailed for England on his first trip abroad. Essie stayed home, supposedly to continue working in the hospital laboratory. She concealed that she was going to the hospital for difficult surgery to correct problems from an earlier operation for appendicitis. She remained in the hospital the entire time he was away.

Mrs. Campbell arranged to tour the provinces to prepare *Voodoo* for an opening in London. The tour began on July 17 in Blackpool, where it received poor notices, then went on to Edinburgh and Glasgow, receiving a better reception. Robeson enjoyed performing in the provinces. And Mrs. Campbell encouraged him to sing more songs in his role as the wandering minstrel.

From each city along the way, Paul wrote endearing letters to Essie, reporting the show's progress and declaring how much he missed her. He repeatedly expressed his love for her, using pet names they shared with each other. He suppressed the specter of Gerry Neale and adhered to his hope for a happy marriage.[13]

The next stop was Liverpool, where Paul wrote to Essie suggesting that she join him in England. Her letters to him still had not revealed that she was sick in the hospital.

Robeson went to London for a few days before the play moved on to Plymouth. He visited a Harlem acquaintance, John Payne, whose London apartment served as a social center for black visitors. There Paul met an elegant pianist and arranger named Lawrence Brown for the first time.[14]

* * *

On August 10, Essie finally wrote to Paul that she had been seriously ill with phlebitis and was still recovering in the hospital. He replied immediately with a letter that addressed her as "My own precious little wife." He implored her to take good care of herself, and he told her not to worry if she could never have a child, a possibility raised in her letter. He added, "I'll be happy with my little wife."[15]

The tour of *Voodoo* came to an inglorious end in Plymouth after a dispute between the star and the author. The planned opening in London never took place. But Paul had gained stage experience and found that he loved England.

He sailed for home as soon as possible. On arriving in New York, he went directly to the hospital to see Essie, and he stayed at her bedside for most of the next two weeks until she had recovered enough to go home. They called on her mother to help take care of her.

* * *

Robeson applied himself to his last semester of law school and to his final season of professional football in the fall of 1922.

With Fritz Pollard, he went to play for the Milwaukee Badgers, a weaker team that offered them more money. Milwaukee had a lackluster 2–4–2 record for the season. Its most notable game came on November 19, when it defeated the Oorang Indians, an Ohio team led by Jim Thorpe, the Olympic champion widely considered the greatest athlete of the century. In a 13–0 triumph over Thorpe's Indians, Robeson scored both touchdowns, recovering a fumble that he carried thirteen yards into the end zone and catching a pass that he carried twenty yards.

The powerful way that he handled himself on the football field, knocking down Indians left and right, led two boxing promoters to offer him a "big payday" to challenge Jack Dempsey for the heavyweight boxing championship. Robeson spurned the offer.

Concentrating on his studies as the year came to a close, he passed his final examinations. He had not been diligent or interested in law school, however, and received mediocre grades as a result. Columbia awarded him a law degree on February 28, 1923. Unlike at Rutgers, where he gave his valedictory speech, no ceremony marked his graduation from Columbia's law school; he simply received his law degree by mail.

Robeson first met Benjamin J. Davis Jr. in Harlem in the summer of 1923. Davis attended Amherst College, where he played left tackle on the football team, and he needed to defend himself against vicious white opponents. He said Paul "used to take me out to a lot to teach me how to protect myself in a game." Ben Davis went on to graduate from Harvard Law School. His experience with racism would propel him into the Communist Party to seek justice for black people in America. He and Paul became lifelong friends.[16]

Another prominent black figure who would later become a great Robeson friend was the renowned scholar and sociologist W. E. B. Du Bois, an influential civil rights leader for many years. Dr. Du Bois, quite short and trim, was a bit of a dandy who dressed in impeccable fashion, contrasting sharply in appearance and temperament with big, powerful Paul. But they came to share an enduring admiration and affection for each other. Robeson would always refer to Du Bois respectfully as "the doctor."

* * *

With help from Coach Sanford, Robeson joined a New York law firm headed by Louis W. Stotesbury, a Rutgers alumnus. Almost everyone at the all-white firm seemed hostile to the young black man; this difficult situation came to a climax when a stenographer refused to take dictation for him. He soon reached the conclusion that racial prejudice would severely limit any career he might have in the law. So he resigned from the law firm, his life as a lawyer finished.[17]

Another chapter of his life had ended. He had gone to law school because he thought it was the right thing to do, and he liked to finish what he started, so he did. He did not enjoy playing professional football, with its rowdy lack of sportsmanship, and he played it only to earn money for law school. His short-lived law career was over, he was married to Essie, and he looked forward to the future.

Paul Robeson became part of the Harlem Renaissance of aspiring young writers, poets, and performers, focusing his hopes on a career in the theater, where race would be less limiting, where he could aim for the stars.

* * *

Jacob's Ladder

We are climbing Jacob's ladder,
We are climbing Jacob's ladder,
We are climbing Jacob's ladder,
Soldiers of the cross.

Every round goes higher and higher,
Every round goes higher and higher,
Every round goes higher and higher,
Soldiers of the cross.

We are climbing higher and higher,
We are climbing higher and higher,
We are climbing higher and higher,
Soldiers of the cross.

—arranged by Alan Booth

· 4 ·

Provincetown Players

On my journey now, Mount Zion, my journey now.

—spiritual

$\mathcal{I}$n his quest for a career in the theater, Paul Robeson wrote a letter to
Eugene O'Neill in the fall of 1923. The Provincetown Players had recently
presented an O'Neill play, *The Emperor Jones*, with a leading black actor. The
letter asked the playwright to consider him if another part arose for a Negro.

Robeson had been relatively inactive for several months in 1923 while
he waited for something worthwhile to turn up. His wife complained that he
was lazy, just wasting time instead of aggressively taking action to start a career.
But his brother Ben understood that Paul needed to take his own time, that
he always operated on his own instincts, what his brother called "his inner
revelations."[1]

This time Robeson took the initiative, writing to O'Neill, who was not
only an innovative playwright but also a principal figure of the Provincetown
Players in Greenwich Village. Their production of *The Emperor Jones* featured
the talented black actor Charles Gilpin in the title role. Robeson had once
ignored an opportunity to audition for this group while attending law school.
But his priorities had now changed.

O'Neill replied to Robeson's letter with a friendly suggestion to keep
in touch. And Kenneth Macgowan followed a month later with a brief note
inviting Robeson to audition for O'Neill's new play, *All God's Chillun Got
Wings*. The play focuses on a black law student, named Jim Harris, who
rescues a young white woman, named Ella Downey, after she falls into pros-
titution. Jim marries Ella, but her racial prejudice drives her to insanity and
destroys his career, while he remains faithful to her.[2]

31

Robeson's audition won him the part of Jim Harris, the costarring role in the planned production for the Provincetown Players. But a series of delays postponed the start of rehearsals for some time.

This was the time of the Harlem Renaissance, which flourished in the 1920s, with many writers, poets, and actors. Among its leading figures were W. E. B. Du Bois, James Weldon Johnson, and Walter White; Langston Hughes, Countee Cullen, and Zora Neale Hurston; and Charles Gilpin, Ethel Waters, and Florence Mills.

* * *

Robeson spent a few weeks at Rutgers assisting Coach George Foster Sanford in the fall of 1923. He also gave some informal concerts. He attended several public events and parties with Essie, who continued to work at her job as a laboratory chemist for $150 a month.

To help pay their expenses, he also worked for a month in the *Plantation Revue*, a song-and-dance show starring Florence Mills at the Plantation nightclub in Harlem. He disliked this work, however, at least in part because it required him to wear the straw hat and striped overalls of a stereotypical Negro.

Rehearsals for *All God's Chillun Got Wings* were put off until April 1924. The first long delay resulted from O'Neill's agreement to wait for the play to be published in the *American Mercury* magazine. An additional delay occurred when the play's costar, Mary Blair, fell ill.

In the interim, Robeson took part in another play in March, a revival of *Roseanne*, presented by the black Lafayette Players in Harlem. The play, focusing on a heroine who saves a fallen preacher, originated on Broadway a year earlier with a white cast in black face. Robeson now portrayed the preacher with a fine actress, Rose McClendon, in the title role. It played for one week at the Lafayette in Harlem, followed by a week at the Dunbar in Philadelphia.

A *Philadelphia Record* critic disliked the play but praised the performers, describing Paul Robeson as "a strapping man with a voice that rolls out of him like a vibrant tide."

* * *

With *All God's Chillun Got Wings* still waiting to open, a major controversy flared in New York over the interracial marriage depicted in the play. Some newspapers, spearheaded by William Randolph Hearst's *American,* stirred up intense racial hostility. Hate groups spewed threats of violence, including some anonymous death threats aimed at both O'Neill and Robeson.[3]

At this time, Eugene O'Neill, who would later become America's most honored playwright, was trying to probe racism and black culture in stark dramas. His work was experimental, sometimes crude, and often controversial. A photograph taken at a rehearsal fueled the worst bigotry. Displayed in the press, the picture showed Mary Blair as Ella with Paul Robeson as Jim. The white Ella is kneeling in front of her black husband and kissing his hand. The image produced public outrage in an era when much of the country still adhered to criminal laws banning interracial marriage.

In conjunction with the long-delayed opening of *All God's Chillun Got Wings*, the Provincetown Players decided to revive *The Emperor Jones* for one week, with Robeson playing the leading role of Brutus Jones. This melodrama concerns a railroad porter who escapes from prison, flees to a Caribbean island, and imposes his dictatorial power over the superstitious islanders. They eventually turn on him, terrorizing then killing him, all amid the relentless throbbing of jungle drums.

Paul undertook the difficult task of learning the leading role in both plays at the same time. Essie helped him memorize his lines, working with him for hours, often late into the night. Paul began rehearsals for *The Emperor Jones* under the patient, thoughtful direction of Jimmy Light, who became his good friend.

* * *

The revival of *The Emperor Jones* opened on May 6, 1924. Essie went with her mother and Paul's sister, Marian, and wrote in her diary, "Paul was superb." When the final curtain closed, the sustained applause in the Provincetown Playhouse brought Robeson back for five curtain calls.[4]

Reviews in the next day's New York newspapers contained high praise for the performance of Paul Robeson, comparing him favorably to Charles Gilpin. The *Evening Post* focused on Robeson's "large and powerful voice—one rich in shadings and emotion, an organ that should play an important part in whatever success comes to the young Negro actor."

Robeson played *The Emperor Jones* for its initial one-week run while rehearsing for the opening of the second play, *All God's Chillun Got Wings*, which came a week later.

* * *

All God's Chillun Got Wings opened on May 15 at the Provincetown Playhouse in Greenwich Village.

The scene in front of the theater on MacDougal Street gave the impression that a battle might be about to begin instead of a play. Uniformed policemen stood guard outside to ward off any violence. The mayor issued a last-minute order to block traffic on the street. And the city prohibited the use of children as actors in the play.[5]

Inside the theater, both the audience and the cast seemed tense. Several burly steelworkers, who were friends of a cast member, stood guard outside the dressing rooms. With the play about to begin, the theater's manager announced to the audience that the opening scene containing some children would not be presented because the mayor's office had suddenly refused to grant the usual license for child actors to appear.

Finally, the performance went forward—successfully, without any incidents. It was, after all, just a play.

Essie noted in her diary that night, "Crowded house, applause wonderful; audience seemed gripped, moved and tense." She added the next day, "Most critics disliked the play, but all liked Paul's acting." Both Alexander Woollcott and Heywood Broun "raved about Paul."

As Essie observed, the top newspaper critics gave negative reviews to the play but lauded Robeson's performance. Broun wrote in the *World*, "Paul Robeson is a far finer actor than any white member of the cast." And Woollcott in the *Sun* said the play failed to come to life, but Robeson "superbly embodied" the lead role.

Herald Tribune critic Percy Hammond devoted almost half of his review to the mayor's interference in this play concerning "miscegenation." He observed, "Mr. Paul Robeson, a dignified and handsome negro of the earnest type, acted the black husband faithfully." He dismissed the play as the "exposition of a marriage between a stupid negro and a stupid white woman." This casual racism in the serious *Herald Tribune* indicates the racial attitudes of the time.

* * *

All God's Chillun Got Wings completed a few performances, as scheduled, and then *The Emperor Jones* reopened for two more one-week runs that began on May 19 and June 2, alternating weeks with *All God's Chillun Got Wings*.

In an article in the *World* in June, the critic Lawrence Stallings wrote that Robeson's work in *All God's Chillun Got Wings* went beyond acting and "brings genius to the piece." He also took note of "his great, taut body—the swinging grace and litheness of the man." "And who has a better voice for tragedy," he continued, "than this actor, whose tone and resonance suggest nothing so much as the dusky, poetic quality of a Negro spiritual, certainly the most tragic utterances in American life?"

George Jean Nathan gave the most glowing account of Robeson in the *American Mercury*. In terms that would be considered condescending today, despite the extravagant praise, this esteemed critic attributed Robeson's performances to his race, asserting, "The Negro is a born actor."

"Robeson, with relatively little experience and with no training to speak of, is one of the most thoroughly eloquent, impressive, and convincing actors that I have looked at and listened to in almost twenty years of professional theater-going."

Robeson as Emperor Jones in the 1933 film version of the play by Eugene O'Neill. Courtesy Bettemann/Corbis via Associated Press.

Nathan, known as one of the most powerful critics of his era, declared that Robeson's performance in both Provincetown plays delivered an "unrestrained and terrible sincerity." He said, "The effect is of a soul bombarded by thunder and torn by lightning."[6]

* * *

Essie observed that Paul happily immersed himself in the Greenwich Village environment, which was alive with artistic, intellectual, and social freedom.

"The Provincetown Players were really responsible for Paul's choice of the stage as a career," she wrote. This group of artists—writing, producing, and acting in their own plays—began at a wharf in Provincetown, Massachusetts, before moving to Greenwich Village. "They form one of the most intelligent, sincere, and non-commercial of the artistic groups in America."

She observed that Paul "fell under their spell." His friends there included Eugene O'Neill, James Light, Eleanor Fitzgerald, and Harold McGhee. At their homes, Essie added, "he had long talks with O'Neill about *Jones* and *Chillun*, about the meaning of the plays, about the purpose of the theatre."[7]

O'Neill gave a book of his plays to Robeson, with an inscription that said of Paul's performance in *All God's Chillun Got Wings*, "I found not only complete fidelity to my intent, under trying circumstances, but beyond that, true understanding and racial integrity." It was signed with "gratitude and friendship."

If Paul had been reluctant to become an actor because of his conservative attitude, as his wife contended, he adapted quickly to the congenial atmosphere of the Provincetown Players. They attracted artists and intellectuals, interesting people with a tolerant view of life and a notable absence of racial prejudice. Paul felt stimulated by and comfortable with them.

* * *

A young sculptor named Antonio Salemme, who had a studio near the Provincetown Playhouse, went to see *The Emperor Jones*. The sculptor was so impressed by Robeson's physical presence and dignity that he asked him to pose for a statue, offering him a percentage of the price if he sold the finished work.

Tony Salemme worked all summer on the life-size figure, with Paul posing nude. Paul often sang as they worked in the large studio overlooking Washington Square. When they wanted a break, Tony took Paul to museums and art galleries. And Paul took Tony to a baseball game at the Polo Grounds, where he explained the game to the sculptor.

The posing sessions went on for two years, with long interruptions for Robeson's other commitments. Completed in 1926, the statue was exhibited for a year in a San Francisco museum, but it was banned from exhibition in Philadelphia and disappeared from public view. Paul and Tony had become friends, as did Essie and Tony's wife, Betty Hardy. They took part in social gatherings and wide-ranging discussions at the sculptor's studio.

Robeson also posed during this period for a series of nude photographs taken by a prominent photographer, Nicholas Murray, who presented his subject's powerful, athletic body as a work of art. Professor Jeffrey C. Stewart observed that the photographs suggested various symbols, including classical images of Atlas and Hercules. The photographs indicate Robeson's immersion in the art and theater world of Greenwich Village at the time.[8]

* * *

Writing about the Harlem Renaissance, the historian David Levering Lewis said, "Almost everything seemed possible above 125th Street in the early twenties." One of Harlem's intellectual leaders, Walter White of the NAACP, turned his apartment at 90 Edgecombe Avenue into an interracial cultural center.[9] Paul and Eslanda Robeson became friends with Walter and Gladys White in the summer of 1924, joining their informal interracial group of artists and political activists.

Walter White wrote about an experience when he and his wife saw Paul Robeson in *The Emperor Jones*. He extolled Robeson's artistry, noting that at the end of the performance, the actor received "wave after wave of applause." Afterward, the Robesons joined the Whites outside the theater because "we wanted supper and a place to talk." But they knew of no restaurant in the area that welcomed Negroes. "So we mounted a bus and rode seven miles or more to colored Harlem, where we could be served with food without fear of insult." This exemplified the pervasiveness of racism, even in New York.[10]

* * *

On racial prejudice, Robeson shared the prevailing view of many Harlem Renaissance intellectuals that racial progress would come primarily through the artistic achievements of individual blacks, not political pressure. In *The Messenger* magazine, Robeson contended that the singer Roland Hayes was a greater "racial asset" than the people who talked about progress.

Essie quoted Paul as saying, "I am using my art for myself, for my race, for the world." He felt that "the Negro had something definite to contribute to art, particularly to music and the theatre." Paul spoke later about why he changed his career from law to the theater: "In the law I could never reach the peak; I could never be a Supreme Court judge; on the stage there was only the sky to hold me back."[11]

All God's Chillun Got Wings continued to play alternate weeks with *The Emperor Jones* through June, then played on its own for the month of July, re-opening in mid-August for two more months. It closed on October 10, 1924, after a total of one hundred performances.

Although Robeson's critical success in the two plays made him a black star, he earned a total salary of less than $2,000 from the Provincetown Players for 1924. He and Essie still depended on her salary from the laboratory to help pay their expenses. And Paul went to Rutgers for a week in October to earn a little extra money as an assistant football coach.

* * *

In late 1924, Robeson appeared in his first motion picture—a silent movie. The first "talkies" would not be made until three years later. The proposal for him to star in the film came from Oscar Micheaux, the independent black producer-director of more than thirty films with all-black casts made explicitly for black audiences. This movie was called *Body and Soul*. In it, Robeson played a double role as a corrupt, evil preacher and his good, benevolent brother.

Essie negotiated the contract with Micheaux, which paid Paul just $100 a week for three weeks of filming and 3 percent of the gross receipts after the first $40,000. The film appeared only in black movie houses, of course, and nothing indicates that Robeson ever received any money from it beyond his salary of $300.[12]

Acting in a silent film meant that Robeson could not use his greatest asset as a performer—his voice. And because Micheaux operated on a very meager budget, there were virtually no retakes. Robeson's dual performance exuded strength, but the white press did not bother to review black films.

Some film historians described it later as a brilliant movie, but in retrospect, the Robesons disliked *Body and Soul* and never spoke about it.

Another notable event in Paul's career also occurred late in 1924. Essie wrote in her diary that "Paul's first formal concert" took place on the weekend of November 1, 1924, at the Copley Plaza Hotel in Boston. It had resulted from an invitation by a socially prominent woman who had seen him on the stage. This concert attracted little notice, but Essie called it "wonderful."

* * *

When 1925 arrived, their friend Walter White introduced the Robesons to Carl Van Vechten and his wife, the actress Fania Marinoff. This sophisticated white couple gave lively parties for interesting people, regardless of race, including talented celebrities from the literary and theater worlds.

The Robesons began attending parties given by the Van Vechtens, as well as comparable parties given by the Whites. Paul often sang a few spirituals at the parties. At a Van Vechten party, they met George Gershwin, America's most talented young composer, who played his new composition "Rhapsody in Blue" on the piano; they also met Theodore Dreiser, who told Paul that he had seen *The Emperor Jones* six times.[13]

Paul and Essie maintained their friendships with several members of the Provincetown Players, including Eugene O'Neill and his wife at the time, Agnes Boulton. The Robesons became close friends with the director Jimmy Light and the stage manager Harold "Gig" McGhee and his wife, "Bert."

Paul often took friends from Greenwich Village up to Harlem to meet his black friends, attend parties, and go to popular uptown nightclubs.

In January 1925, Robeson appeared in a limited run of *The Emperor Jones* on Broadway. O'Neill's literary agent, Richard J. Madden, told him that an English producer, Sir Alfred Butt, wanted to present the play in London. Essie negotiated favorable terms for Paul to receive $300 a week, with a six-week guarantee, plus 5 percent of the gross over $100,000. The deal also included round-trip tickets on an ocean liner for both Paul and his wife.[14]

It was a few months later, while the planning for London continued, that Robeson had a fateful meeting on a Harlem street corner.

* * *

The pianist and arranger Lawrence Brown, whom Paul had met on his first trip to London, returned to the United States because his father was dying in Florida. After the funeral, he took a train to New York, then went to his new apartment in central Harlem and decided to take a walk.[15]

"There, standing on the corner of 135th Street and Seventh Avenue, all alone, in front of the bank was Paul Robeson," Brown recalled. He greeted Robeson, who promptly invited him to come along with him to visit Jimmy Light in Greenwich Village. "He said we might sing some songs."

That evening in Greenwich Village, Paul Robeson sang two of Lawrence Brown's arrangements of spirituals, "Swing Low, Sweet Chariot" and then "Every Time I Feel the Spirit." Brown, who accompanied Robeson on the piano, suddenly began to sing "as the second voice" in the latter spiritual.

"It was completely spontaneous," Brown said. Their singing the spiritual excited Jimmy Light, who said, "Why don't you fellows give a concert?"

That was the origin of their first concert and the beginning of their long career together. Lawrence Brown and Paul Robeson established an immediate rapport, personally and musically. It proved to be an enduring collaboration.

* * *

Essie wrote in her diary on March 23, 1925, "Larry and Paul making wonderful progress. I'm convinced they are a perfect combination." She added the next night, "Larry, Paul and I went down to Jimmy Light's to dinner. We threshed out the concert idea." We made an agreement for "Paul and Larry to go 50–50—and each will give me 10 per cent as agent."

Lawrence Brown—handsome, sophisticated, always immaculately dressed—had traveled extensively in Europe. He was a talented arranger and pianist. Courteous and reserved, he was considerate, self-effacing, and loyal, content to stay in the background, both as a man and a musician.

Shortly after their evening at Jimmy Light's apartment, Paul and Larry sang spirituals at a party at Van Vechten's fashionable apartment in Manhattan. Essie noted in her diary that Carl "begged for more and more songs" and offered to help arrange a public concert for them. The Provincetown Players agreed to provide their theater virtually free of charge for the event.[16]

Plans progressed for this first concert of Paul Robeson and Lawrence Brown to be held in a few weeks.

These were exciting but uncertain times for Paul and Essie, made even more difficult by the prevailing racism. The young couple had no savings and still depended on her salary as a hospital chemist to pay their bills. Paul had an amiable gentleness about him, despite his imposing size, and seemed to lack the ego and driving ambition of many young men. But he retained a quiet inner confidence. His many friends, black and white, regarded him as "Our Paul."

Paul Robeson had recently launched a new career as a stage actor, and now he was undertaking an even more uncharted career as a concert singer.

* * *

On My Journey

On my journey now, Mount Zion,
My journey now, Mount Zion,
I wouldn't take nothing, Mount Zion,
For my journey now, Mount Zion.

One day, one day, I was walking along,
Well, the elements opened
And the love come down, Mount Zion.

On my journey now, Mount Zion,
My journey now, Mount Zion,
I wouldn't take nothing, Mount Zion,
For my journey now, Mount Zion.

I went into the valley, and I didn't go to stay,
Well, my soul got happy
And I stayed all day, Mount Zion.

—arranged by Lawrence Brown

• 5 •

Voice of a People

Go down, Moses, way down in Egypt land.

—spiritual

$\mathcal{P}$aul Robeson and Lawrence Brown had only three weeks to arrange the program and hold the rehearsals for their first concert, one that would be the first of its kind and make them an enduring team.

Once the decision was made for them to give a concert, the Provincetown Players gave their full support to the project. Eleanor Fitzgerald, the company's manager, provided the Greenwich Village theater for its bare cost. Jimmy Light and Harold McGhee arranged the stage and the lights. Carl Van Vechten wrote letters to his influential friends to promote the event. Heywood Broun wrote about it in his column in the *New York World*.[1]

This would be the first formal concert consisting entirely of Negro music, spirituals for the most part. Brown said, "We chose what we felt were the most beautiful of the spirituals."[2]

* * *

On Sunday evening, April 19, 1925, Paul Robeson and Lawrence Brown stood, clearly nervous, in the wings of the Greenwich Village theater. Both men wore tuxedos. Stepping out onto the small stage, they heard sustained applause from the capacity audience, which included many of their friends, white and black.

Finally, the theater went silent. Brown sat down at the grand piano, with Robeson standing at its curve a few feet in front of him. Robeson gravely nodded his head to Brown, his signal to begin.[3]

The first notes from Brown's piano sounded the introduction of "Go Down, Moses," and then came Robeson's deep, strong voice with the spiritual's opening words:

> When Israel was in Egypt land,
> Let my people go.
> Oppressed so hard they could not stand,
> Let my people go.

They divided their program into four parts, each with four songs. The first section consisted of spirituals arranged by Harry T. Burleigh. "Go Down, Moses" was followed by "I Don't Feel No Ways Tired," then "Weepin' Mary" and "By and By," the last with Brown joining Robeson as the second voice.

Essie said the enthusiastic applause from the audience made them forgot about themselves in all this excitement, so they just sang "simply, unaffectedly, and beautifully."[4]

The second part of their program consisted of secular folk and dialect songs, beginning with one of Robeson's greatest renditions, "Water Boy," arranged by Avery Robinson. Then came "Scandalize My Name," arranged by Burleigh; "Li'l Gal," a contemporary song composed by J. Rosamond Johnson; and "Down de Lovah's Lane," by Will Marion Cook.

Both the third and fourth parts of the program contained the spirituals arranged by Lawrence Brown. They began with the hauntingly beautiful "Steal Away," followed by "I Know de Lord's Laid His Hands on Me," then "Sometimes I Feel Like a Motherless Child" and "Every Time I Feel the Spirit," with Brown's light tenor voice joining in the last one.

The final segment opened with "Nobody Knows de Trouble I Seen," followed by "I've Got a Home in-a-dat Rock," then "Swing Low, Sweet Chariot" and the lively "Joshua Fit de Battle of Jericho," with Brown again adding his voice in the final song. All would appear regularly in their repertoire.

"After each number, the applause was deafening," Essie wrote in her diary that night, reporting on "the all-Negro concert by Paul and Larry." She noted that "the boys got curtain call after curtain call" and commemorated the event in her diary with these words: "Today is one of the most significant times in our lives."[5]

The reviews in the New York newspapers the next day were rapturous. The *World* hailed "the first concert in this country made entirely of Negro music, if one may count out the chorales from Fiske." It said, "Paul Robeson's voice is difficult to describe. It is a voice in which deep bells ring."

The *Times* said, "His Negro spirituals have the ring of the revivalist, they hold in them a world of religious experience; it is a cry from the depths, this unusual humanism, that touches the heart. . . . Sung by one man, they voiced the sorrow and hopes of a people."

* * *

From the heart of the Harlem Renaissance a true renaissance figure had emerged in the person of Paul Robeson: an athlete and scholar turned actor and singer, all in a young man of great dignity and decency, with a future that seemed to glow like a burst of strong sunshine.

The tremendous success of the first concert prompted plans to follow quickly with a second one. It was held just two weeks later, on the Sunday evening of May 3, and proved equally successful.

The *Evening Post* wrote, "Last night Paul Robeson and Lawrence Brown gave their second concert of the season, and revealed once more their mastery of the songs of their people. . . . Mr. Robeson combines with a glorious rich and mellow voice a dramatic restraint and power that seems to hold untold thunder behind each song."

Essie wrote in her diary on May 3 that the second concert went very well and that the theater was sold out. Noting the remarkable success, she added, "It seems we are really launched at last."

A concert manager, James Pond, soon signed Robeson and Brown for an extensive concert tour for the following year.

* * *

James Weldon Johnson, a founder of the NAACP and an acquaintance of Robeson, explained in 1925 that the spirituals evolved when slaves in the South sought refuge in Christianity, a religion that promised compensation in a future life for the sorrows of the present one. The tribulations of the Jews in the Old Testament resonated with them.[6]

Johnson wrote that "unknown black bards" sang spirituals that came down by word of mouth from generation to generation. He praised Harry T. Burleigh, a black composer, as a pioneer who had made arrangements of this "noble music" and extended its appeal to a wider audience in recent years.

The spirituals had reached their highest point, he said, in the classic concert renditions of Roland Hayes, Paul Robeson, Marian Anderson, and Julius Bledsoe.

* * *

With Carl Van Vechten's help in 1925, Eslanda Robeson sought a $5,000 loan from Otto Kahn to relieve the financial pressure that she and Paul were under despite his recent artistic success. Kahn, a wealthy banker and patron of the arts, subsequently invited the Robesons, along with Larry Brown, for a visit that seemed more like an audition.

At 2 p.m. on Sunday, June 28, a car sent by Kahn arrived to take them to his grand Long Island estate at Cold Spring Harbor. Paul and Larry sang for the small social gathering there. That night Essie wrote in her diary, "Mr. Kahn agreed to become Paul's patron. He showed me the grounds of his estate, and we had a long talk about Paul's career."

Otto Kahn gave the Robesons a $5,000 loan, interest free, to be repaid in two years. This eased their strained finances.[7]

Two weeks later, on a summer evening in early July, Eugene O'Neill and Harold McGhee came up to Harlem to visit the Robesons for what turned out to be an all-night party. They had cocktails at the Robeson apartment, went out to dinner, then returned to the apartment, where O'Neill talked a great deal, and Paul sang several songs to his guests. Essie observed, "Gene seemed to enjoy it so much."

Paul took them all to some of Harlem's thriving nightspots, including Small's cabaret after midnight. Essie noted in her diary that they had a wonderful time, adding, "Gene and I danced quite a bit." The partying continued until dawn, when they ended with a hearty breakfast. Essie concluded, "Gene is a regular guy."

O'Neill and his wife had entertained the Robesons, along with Harold McGhee and his wife, a few weeks earlier at the playwright's country home.

* * *

On July 16, 1925, Paul Robeson and Lawrence Brown traveled to Camden, New Jersey, to make their first recordings for the Victor Talking Machine Company. They recorded five songs in their first session at the Camden studio. Essie, who went with them, reported in her diary, "The boys were very nervous."

They returned to Camden on July 27 and again on July 30 for recording sessions that proved much better. The result was eight songs that remained an important part of their repertoire.

The first records—four two-sided disks—included "Steal Away" and "Were You There," "Water Boy" and "Li'l Gal," "On My Journey" and "Sometimes I Feel Like a Motherless Child," and two songs that Larry joined in singing, "By and By" and "Joshua Fit de Battle of Jericho."

Their records proved popular, selling more than fifty thousand copies in a few months, with $1,125 going to Robeson and Brown. This success turned Robeson into a major recording artist, with offers to appear on radio.

* * *

One evening during a party at the Van Vechtens, Paul heard Essie make a remark that showed how very possessive she was of him. He kept silent but simmered with anger, and he decided to assert his freedom.[8]

As they left, they met a beautiful young woman who had just arrived. She was Freda Diamond, a tall, lively Russian Jewish girl, not yet twenty years old. Paul made an excuse to return to the party by himself and danced with Freda. The two soon began a discreet affair and would remain intimate friends for many years.

* * *

On August 5, Paul and Essie sailed for England, where he would appear in the London production of *The Emperor Jones*. Jimmy Light went as the director, with Harold McGhee as the stage manager, and they took their wives.

"They all settled down in Chelsea, where the atmosphere was somewhat like that of their beloved Village," Essie recorded in her diary. She said their life in London seemed much like home, with rounds of rehearsals, performances, and parties.

Essie clearly loved life in London. As for Paul, she said, "he felt even more at home in London than he had in America." He even became a fan of

Robeson accompanied by Lawrence Brown at the piano for a 1947 concert in Albany, New York. Courtesy Bettemann/Corbis via Associated Press.

cricket. And he dined at excellent restaurants, including those conveniently near the theater, with his white and black friends "without fear of the discrimination which all Negroes encounter in America."

One of their new friends was Emma Goldman, a noted anarchist deported from America and disillusioned with Russia, who now lived in London. After they met at a dinner party, she invited the Robesons to dinner at her apartment, where she roasted a goose for them. They took her to see Charlie Chaplin in *The Gold Rush*. Essie wrote to the Van Vechtens that Emma had "a crush on Paul."[9]

The Emperor Jones opened in London on September 10, 1925, at the Ambassadors Theatre. As usual before an opening night, Paul was nervous. Essie spent the day helping him relax by playing pinochle with him, then having a quiet dinner at home, and finally taking a taxi to the theater.

Opening night went well; Robeson took ten curtain calls. Essie wrote in her diary, "Paul was magnificent." To the Van Vechtens, she wrote, "Well darlings, we've conquered London!" The *New York Times* reported that the play "held a large audience spellbound" and predicted it would have a long run.[10]

Two weeks later, Essie noted in her diary that the big electric sign at Cambridge Circus proclaimed, "Paul Robeson in The Emperor Jones" in bright lights. She wrote, "You can see it clear down Shaftesbury Avenue to Piccadilly Circus, and it sure looks good. At last he is a star with his name in lights."

Unexpectedly, *The Emperor Jones* had only a short run in London. It closed early in October, disappointing Robeson. London's theater critics, like their counterparts in New York, praised Robeson's performance. They just did not like the play. The Robesons stayed in London for a few more weeks, enjoying plays, concerts, and the company of friends.

* * *

In early November, with cold, damp weather besetting England, Paul and Essie departed for the French Riviera to seek sunshine. They spent an interesting week in Paris first, which included a wine-and-sandwiches party given for them by Sylvia Beach, who ran the famous bookstore Shakespeare and Company. There they met Gertrude Stein, James Joyce, and Ernest Hemingway.[11]

After Paris, they traveled south to Villefranche-sur-Mer, a small town on the beautiful Mediterranean coast between Nice and Monte Carlo. They chose it because a Greenwich Village friend and writer, Glenway Westcott, lived there. He settled them into a modest, charming hotel that overlooked the harbor.

Essie wrote that it seemed like a fairyland. She added, "Colds, sinusitis, general weariness vanished before the magic of the sun." They encountered the black poet Claude McKay in Nice and had several friendly discussions with him, but Essie soon came to dislike him, considering him vulgar.

A cable from Paul's sister, Marian, arrived on November 25, 1925, reporting that their oldest brother, Bill, had died of tuberculosis in Washington, DC, at the age of forty-four. Marian, who was with him at the end, maintained contact with all the members of the family. She was the only family member who got along well with Essie.

* * *

In December, Paul and Essie returned to the United States aboard the ocean liner *Majestic* for concert tours scheduled for January and February 1926. Robeson and Brown gave well-received performances in Philadelphia, Pittsburgh, Detroit, and Indianapolis in January. Essie had quit her laboratory job to travel with them as their manager.

Their February tour began with a tedious twenty-nine-hour train ride to Chicago, where only a small audience appeared in the large hall. Robeson rewarded the people who showed up by singing his best and adding several encores. The *Herald-Examiner* hailed his as "the finest of all Negro voices and one of the most beautiful in the world."[12]

The next stops were in Milwaukee and Green Bay, Wisconsin, with sparse audiences and lots of snow.

Back in New York, they gave a successful benefit concert at the town hall for the Lower East Side Settlement House and attended a glittering party that the Van Vechtens gave in Robeson's honor.

Robeson and Brown looked forward to a concert set for March in Boston, which Larry considered his hometown. Unfortunately, a few days before going to Boston, Paul came down with a cold that failed to get better. When they arrived at their modest hotel, they again ran into a refusal to accept Negro guests. With Essie in command, they took a taxi to the expensive Copley Plaza Hotel, where they received a courteous reception.

Robeson stayed in bed all the next day before the concert but still felt sick. Essie and Larry talked him out of canceling the concert at the last minute. He went through with it, singing all the songs in the program, but his voice had never been so bad. The Boston critics were sympathetic, noting that he obviously had a cold.

At Essie's suggestion, Paul consulted Teresa Armitage, her former music teacher in Chicago. Essie told Armitage, "I've married the most beautiful voice I've ever heard, and I want you to help me with it."

Armitage recommended Frantz Proshchowsky, a prominent vocal coach, who worked briefly with Robeson to help him protect his voice from strain. Then, Robeson studied with Armitage for awhile. He also consulted Dr. John Kernan, who treated him for an inflammation of his nose and throat.[13]

In both his singing and acting, Paul Robeson relied on natural talent that he used intelligently, with virtually no formal technique or training.

* * *

Essie noted Paul's twenty-eighth birthday in her diary on April 9: "He brought home some ice cream tonight to celebrate it." It was about this time that Robeson had his first encounter with "Ol' Man River," which would later become the signature song of his career.

Shortly after composing "Ol' Man River" for *Show Boat*, Jerome Kern called Alexander Woollcott one morning to ask him for Paul Robeson's telephone number. According to Woollcott, Kern then visited the Robeson apartment and played the song on their piano while Paul sang the words from a rough manuscript. Kern persuaded him to go downtown with him to sing it for Oscar Hammerstein II, who had written the lyrics.[14]

The song was meant for Robeson, but because of a delay in the opening of *Show Boat*, he was on a concert tour and unavailable when the play reached Broadway.

Robeson took on a new play in the summer of 1926. Written by Jim Tully and Frank Dazey, it was titled *Black Boy* and portrayed the rise and fall of a boxer—reminiscent of the controversial former champion Jack Johnson. Paul's leading lady, the lovely Fredi Washington, became one of his long-lasting affairs.

Rehearsals began on August 23 in Mamaroneck, New York, followed by out-of-town tryouts. The Broadway opening took place on October 6. The play was weak and drew largely unfavorable reviews, despite praise for Robeson. Brooks Atkinson, writing in the *New York Times*, said, "Mr. Robeson's performance emerges as a fine-grained, resilient bit of characterization. His huge frame fits him well for the part of the prize fighter, and his full, deep voice has a sustaining beauty."

* * *

Black Boy closed after a few weeks, but Paul's romance with Fredi Washington continued. Essie became aware of the affair and was devastated.

Paul and Essie reached a "tacit solution" to their marital problems, according to the biography written by their son. She continued to take care of Paul and his career, while trying to ignore any affairs he might have. He preserved their social life as a married couple and continued to retain her as his manager and treasurer. They did not consider divorce for two reasons: they understood that his success depended on their teamwork, and they were emotionally dependent on each other. Their solution, though far from perfect, held them together because they still cared deeply for each other.[15]

* * *

Paul Robeson continued his concert tours with Lawrence Brown in 1927. Their most notable concert, arranged by a young black reporter named Roy Wilkins, took place in Kansas City. Robeson agreed to appear for $750, well below their normal fee, and sang to a nonsegregated audience, contrary to local custom.

A critic for the *Times Union* in Rochester, New York, wrote of a concert there that Robeson had "a voice of rare natural beauty." With his dignity, sincerity, and compelling charm, Robeson was "turning his talent—perhaps genius is the better word—to high purpose."

In a magazine interview in July 1927, Robeson talked about the pure spirituals that he had learned in his father's church and had now transformed into concert art. He spoke out, not politically but culturally. "I feel that the music of my race is the happiest medium of expression for what dramatic and vocal skill I possess," he told the YMCA magazine. "In the first place, Negro music is more and more taking its place with the music of the world. It has its own distinctive message and philosophy. Many critics say it is the only folk music of America."

"Negro music," he continued, "portrays the hopes of our people who faced the hardships of slavery. They suffered. They fled to God through their songs." The spirituals "represent the soul of my people."

* * *

Paul and Essie took a summer vacation in 1927, amid some personal tension, on the island of Martha's Vineyard, off the Massachusetts coast. She was pregnant but had not consulted him about having medical treatment to help her conceive. He felt manipulated but resigned.[16]

In September, after they returned to New York, plans were completed for a concert tour in Europe. Paul sailed for France on October 15, leaving Essie behind to have the baby. She had encouraged him to go. Aboard the ship, he wrote an extremely affectionate letter to her, saying, "You'll never know how marvelous I think you are."[17]

His tenderness toward her grew with greater distance between them.

Robeson and Brown began the concert tour in Paris on October 29, 1927, with a program of spirituals, including "Deep River" and "Swing Low, Sweet Chariot." The *New York Times* reported from Paris that the cheering audience at the sold-out performance demanded encores for fully half an hour "before the singer was allowed to leave the stage."

Back home, Paul Robeson Jr. was born on November 2, 1927, in Long Island College Hospital in Brooklyn. Essie expressed delight in her baby son, saying he looked just like his father. She had almost lost her life, however, as a result of complications during delivery.

Paul rushed home when he learned of the seriousness of her condition, sailing to New York to be with his wife—and to see his son for the first time.

* * *

Go Down, Moses (Let My People Go)

When Israel was in Egypt land,
Let my people go.
Oppressed so hard they could not stand,
Let my people go.
Go down, Moses, way down in Egypt land,
Tell old pharaoh to let my people go.

Thus spake the Lord, bold Moses said,
Let my people go.
If not I'll smite your first born dead,
Let my people go.
Go down, Moses, way down in Egypt land,
Tell old pharaoh to let my people go.

No more shall they in bondage toil,
Let my people go.
Let them come out when Egypt spoil,
Let my people go.
Go down, Moses, way down in Egypt land,
Tell old pharaoh to let my people go.

—arranged by H. T. Burleigh

· 6 ·

"Ol' Man River"

Darkies all work on the Mississippi.

—opening line of lyrics

$\mathscr{P}$aul Robeson sailed back to America aboard the SS *Mauretania*, arriving in New York on the day after Christmas of 1927, a less-than-happy holiday.

Essie remained quite ill with an abscess in her breast and severe phlebitis in her leg, and the doctors confined her to bed for weeks. The baby, Pauli, was placed in the care of his grandmother, the formidable Eslanda Goode, who would take care of him for much of his childhood. Paul still addressed his mother-in-law, deferentially, as Mrs. Goode.

In a wire to Larry Brown in Paris, Paul reported that Essie was recovering very slowly and that his return to Europe must be postponed indefinitely. He added, "Make your own plans." He had become uncertain about his future and ambivalent about his partnership with Larry, and he worried about finances.[1]

Before leaving Paris, Paul had written to Essie that he needed to expand his repertoire. He said that in order to achieve substantial financial success in Europe, "I'll need other songs, some in the language of the country or classics that they know." He suggested that work in America would be more rewarding and emphasized, "With our debts and new responsibilities we need money."[2]

Now, in January 1928, with no work at hand and finances very low, Robeson accepted a $500 advance to appear in a jazz revue scheduled to open in New York the next fall. He had no desire to sing popular music or appear in a revue, but he had no other opportunities at this point and needed the money to cover expenses. It would prove a costly decision.

51

He then received an offer to take over the role of Crown in *Porgy*, the musical play by DuBose and Dorothy Heyward. The salary of $500 a week persuaded him to accept the part, although he knew that singing above the sound of the orchestra would be hard on his voice. He struggled with this role for the next six weeks.[3]

A cheering note arrived on March 5 from the novelist Theodore Dreiser, who wrote, "When I get tired of writing, I put on one of your records—Mt. Zion or Witness or Water Boy—and let your sympathetic voice revive my failing spirits."

* * *

As his thirtieth birthday approached, Robeson faced an uncertain future. Five years had passed since he graduated from law school and made a brief attempt to begin a career as a lawyer. Since then, he had established himself as a serious actor with his performances in the O'Neill plays with the Provincetown Players. He had also won acclaim as a concert singer with his arranger and accompanist, Lawrence Brown.

Robeson was encouraged by the approval of notable friends such as Dreiser and O'Neill, as well as Harlem intellectuals like his friend Walter White. But very few parts were available in the theater for a serious black actor—and there were virtually none in the new medium of talking pictures. And his concert career seemed limited by his focus on Negro spirituals. With his wife and new baby to support, his future seemed problematic.

The important break that he needed came from the famed producer Florenz Ziegfeld, who offered him the role of Joe in the forthcoming London production of *Show Boat*. In this relatively small but significant role, he would sing just one song—"Ol' Man River"—but he would sing it three times as a recurring theme in the show.

Essie continued her recovery and resumed her role as Paul's general manager. She wrote to his European concert manager, Walter Varney, assuring him that Paul would soon be available. She also wrote to Larry Brown asking him to rejoin them for concerts in London.[4]

Robeson sailed for England in early April, with plans for his wife to follow. He was aboard ship alone on his thirtieth birthday. He wrote to Larry Brown from the ship, "I'm on this damn ocean again," and was due to open in *Show Boat* on May 3. He said he hoped they could do some concerts after the play opened.

* * *

The cast of *Show Boat* had already been rehearsing for about a week when Robeson arrived in London. He walked into the theater during a rehearsal.

Jerome Kern, who was seated at the piano on stage, rushed up, threw his arms around him, and exclaimed, "My God, Paul, it's marvelous to see you!" He led Robeson to the piano, saying he wanted to hear him sing "Ol' Man River" right then "because I had you in mind when I wrote it."

According to one of the show's stars, who recalled this scene in an interview, "Paul just walked up and put his arm on top of the piano, and this beautiful voice, this organ of a voice, came out as he sang 'Ol' Man River.' And we were all in tears."[5]

* * *

On the evening of May 3, 1928, *Show Boat* opened in London at the Royal Drury Lane Theatre with a largely British cast led by Cedric Hardwicke, Marie Burke, Edith Day, and Leslie Sarony. The musical presented two pairs of star-crossed lovers in a dramatic story line, interspersed with songs, on a paddle-wheeled riverboat that provided entertainment on the Mississippi.

Show Boat was a popular hit, filling the large Drury Lane theater with audiences that responded to the grand music of Jerome Kern and especially to Robeson's powerful singing of "Ol' Man River." Kern and Hammerstein had become the premier composer and lyricist of American musicals.

Most of the critics praised the opulent production, although some of them complained that the show was too long and complex. The reviews were unstinting in their praise of Robeson's performance. Some blacks expressed indignation, however, at the play's portrayal of stereotyped Negroes. The *London Times* complained that the theatrical boat underwent "rather heavy weather" at the Drury Lane. But it said Cedric Hardwicke was "great fun" as Captain Andy. "And Paul Robeson's melancholy song about the 'old river' is one of the two chief hits of the evening."

Shortly after the opening, Essie joined Paul in London, where she rented a furnished apartment for them in St. John's Wood, facing Regents Park, as a convenient but temporary residence.[6]

Two weeks after *Show Boat* opened, Robeson recorded "Ol' Man River" in London, the first of his five recordings of this song in Britain. Then, with Larry Brown, he recorded the traditional "Scandalize My Name" and several spirituals over the next few weeks. This was the first of the numerous records that they made in Britain.

* * *

Robeson and Brown gave their first Sunday matinee concert in the Drury Lane on July 3, attracting a large audience and superlative reviews. They then gave a series of concerts that repeatedly filled the theater on Sunday afternoons, while Robeson also appeared in the regular performances of

Show Boat. No one could recall a performer ever before giving concerts in the afternoon and playing in a major show in the evenings at the same theater.

In the *Daily Express* on July 5, 1928, the critic James Douglas wrote about hearing Robeson, whom he described as a giant in a plain tweed suit, singing Negro spirituals at the Drury Lane. He said the audience in the packed theater "sat there in a trance of noiseless ecstasy as he touched our heart-strings with his marvelous voice."

"He is more than a great actor and a great singer," Douglas went on. "He is a great man, who creates the soul of a people in bondage and shows you its true kinship with the fettered soul of man. We became like little children as we surrendered to his magical genius. . . . I have heard all the great singers of our time. No voice has ever moved me so profoundly with so many passions of thought and emotion."

When the British monarch, Queen Mary, appeared at the Drury Lane for one of the concerts, Robeson became so nervous that he started singing off-key and failed to regain his form. The Queen seemed sympathetic and returned for another concert, at which he performed up to his usual standard.

* * *

During this summer of success, the adulation of the audience became a problem for Robeson. So many people waited outside his dressing room at the Drury Lane, seeking a chance to see him, talk to him, and get his autograph, that he needed someone to protect his privacy and turn aside some of these eager fans.

The theater manager, Sir Alfred Butt, found the right man to serve as Paul's dresser, provide a buffer for him, and cater to his personal needs. He was a soft-spoken West Indian named Joseph Andrews, the same age as Paul, and he established an instant rapport with the star.

Joe Andrews became the guardian who politely monitored all who could enter the dressing room. He would remain Robeson's personal assistant and loyal confidant for twenty years.[7]

* * *

Robeson enjoyed the vibrant life of London. From the Royal Drury Lane Theatre, he could stroll down to the busy Strand and walk to historic Trafalgar Square, go up Haymarket to glittering Piccadilly Circus, then follow Shaftesbury Avenue back to the heart of the thriving theater district. Famous restaurants, such as The Ivy, welcomed him as a celebrity.

He and Essie attended parties given by some of England's leading figures, including Lord Beaverbrook, a staunch imperialist, who asked Robeson to sing at a reception he gave. Paul noted that the famous writer H. G. Wells just

Portrait of young Paul Robeson. Courtesy Bettemann/Corbis via Associated Press.

walked up and began asking him a lot of questions, and "it ended with our sitting with a group talking all night."[8]

Prominent members of the Labour Party invited Robeson to lunch at the House of Commons, a rare honor for an actor. The *New York Times* reported that former prime minister Ramsay MacDonald "talked earnestly with Mr. Robeson" at the luncheon.

"My whole social and political development was in England," Robeson said years later. He recalled how the renowned George Bernard Shaw had once "expounded on socialism" at a lunch they attended in the home of one of Larry Brown's friends. Until Shaw asked for his opinion, Robeson said, he had "never really thought about socialism."[9]

* * *

Show Boat continued as a popular hit through the summer, autumn, and winter of 1928, and the Robesons decided to stay in England even after the show closed in March 1929. Sending for her mother and baby Pauli, Essie moved the family into a house, described as a small mansion, in an exclusive neighborhood of Hampstead, overlooking the heath.

Robeson's salary for *Show Boat* was $1,200 a week, which was substantially augmented by his concerts, so he finally felt financially sound and hoped to pay his $5,000 debt to Otto Kahn. But he found himself in legal trouble for failing to fulfill his contract to appear in the scheduled jazz revue in New York for which he had accepted that $500 advance. The producer complained that Robeson's absence prevented the revue from opening, which resulted in his suspension by Actors Equity. He could not leave *Show Boat* in London, so he felt compelled to settle the dispute with the New York producer, but it cost him $8,000.

While he paid the $8,000 settlement in three installments, he had to delay his repayment of the Kahn loan. He would finally repay Kahn from the proceeds of an American concert tour two years later.[10]

* * *

In the spring of 1929, Robeson and Brown went on a European concert tour, starting April 10 in Vienna. A critic, Siegfried Geyer, wrote in *Die Stunde* the next day that Robeson embodied "the tragedy of the coloured man in the midst of a white society" that measured human worth by skin tone. The critic added that in his singing of the folk song "Water Boy," Robeson "revealed more of the true personality of his race than half a dozen learned writings and discourses."[11]

After the concert in Vienna, a young man approached Robeson, discussed music with him, and invited him to visit his home. Robeson was so impressed with his knowledge of music that he went to see him the next day and was shocked at the poverty of this cultured Jewish family. He said he had not realized the plight of the Jewish people in Europe at the time.

Robeson and Brown went from Vienna to Prague. The American minister to Czechoslovakia, unlike the ambassador in London, welcomed them cordially and invited them to supper at the American legation following their concert. Next came a concert in Budapest, where Robeson was delighted to discover an affinity between Negro music and Hungarian folk songs.

* * *

Robeson returned to London to sing at the Royal Albert Hall on April 29. And his success in London led to a tour of the provinces in the summer of 1929. Accompanied by Larry Brown, he gave a series of concerts that extended from Birmingham to Brighton and several other cities. A journalist, William R. Mitchell, described Paul's "engaging air." Referring to him by his first name, he said one feels on such "perfectly friendly terms with this giant . . . that, naturally one calls him Paul."

Robeson devoted much of his time in the fall of 1929 to studying foreign languages and beginning to prepare for a production of *Othello*. He also made several recordings, including "The Lonesome Road" and "Mighty Like a Rose," with the English bandleader Ray Noble. Robeson and Brown would leave soon for a concert tour in the United States.

Before departing, Paul and Essie went to meet an aristocratic friend, Sybil Colfax, for a late-evening drink at the famous Grill Room of the Savoy Hotel. But they were barred from entering; the hotel, favored by many rich Americans, had started barring blacks. The Robesons quietly left, but Lady Colfax complained about the incident, which was then widely reported in the press, and British authorities expressed shock at the treatment of Paul Robeson. The Savoy soon rescinded its racial policy.

* * *

Robeson returned to America for his tour in the autumn of 1929, with a concert on November 5 at Carnegie Hall in New York, followed five days later by a second concert there. The great hall was filled to overflowing for both events. Paul noted in a small diary on November 10 that Lawrence Tibbett, a Metropolitan Opera star, came backstage and said "he never enjoyed a concert so much in all his life."

In this pocket-size book, Paul confided some of his personal thoughts, providing an intriguing insight into his ideas about love, art, and God. On November 12, suffering from a cold, he wrote, "In bed and thinking how wonderful my Essie is . . . how deeply I love her . . . and her love is so great." He added, "We will do great things together."[12]

He went on to muse about art, beauty, and "a conception I'm getting about God." He referred to major figures in history, religion, and music, using his own abbreviated style for noting his thoughts. With regard to art and himself, he wrote, "Can I be artist with just negro songs? Art is creation or rather re-creation of beauty. Artist . . . brings it to others." And "we must repeat ourselves because of necessity of earning a living."

"No need of technique if not professional. Of course technique might help me grow . . . but that might not make me greater artist. Water Boy—best record—when I was untrained. . . . So O'Neill—never has developed smooth technique. But beauty and truth are there."

"Now back to God," he wrote. "Of course God doesn't watch over everyone because everyone isn't important. . . . God is interested in those beings who more closely approach him." Those who strive for beauty through art and for truth through science "show meaning of life and in small way understand God."

"So by chance [I] have some of this power—have power to create beauty. Have wife as scientist who holds me to truth necessary to create true beauty. So God watches over me and guides me. He's with me but lets me fight my own battles and hopes I'll win."

After Carnegie Hall, Robeson went on a two-month tour that included concerts in Pittsburgh, Chicago, and several other cities, as well as a triumphant return to Rutgers for a concert that ended with the audience cheering for "Robey."

* * *

Robeson returned to London in early 1930 to sing again to a gala audience at the Royal Albert Hall, although an economic depression had already made itself felt in Britain that hard winter.

Walking in London, Robeson encountered a group of out-of-work miners from South Wales who were marching along the street singing—and seeking desperately needed money for their families. One of the signs they carried proclaimed that they had walked all the way from Wales to London to petition the government for help. Their plight registered immediately with Robeson, who joined them as they marched down the London streets.

When they reached a large downtown building, Robeson climbed up the front steps and sang to the miners. He sang ballads, spirituals, and "Ol' Man River." Paul Robeson Jr. recounted the story of this event, calling it a transformative experience for those who were there.[13]

Robeson went on to raise enough money to provide the miners with a train ride home, along with food and clothing for their families in Wales's Rhondda Valley. He also donated the proceeds of one of his concerts to a relief fund for the Welsh miners. He sang in the mining communities and forged a strong bond of friendship with the miners of South Wales.

* * *

Robeson embarked on another European concert tour that took him to Vienna, Prague, Dresden, Bucharest, and Turin in early 1930. Noting the Bucharest concert in her diary, Essie said, "Queen Marie, the Princess, and the Queen of Greece attended, and the queens applauded a great deal."[14]

Then, in March, the Robesons traveled to the Swiss town of Territet, overlooking Lake Geneva, to take part in an experimental silent film titled *Borderline* being produced by an avant-garde German group. The film's esoteric plot involved the psychological entanglements of two couples, one black and one white, living a borderline existence in Switzerland. Essie took delight in her acting debut; the actors received no pay but enjoyed their time making the film.

Essie called it "one of those very advanced expressionistic things in the Russian-German manner, so it will probably be shown in Film Societies, etc." As usual, she was right.

From Switzerland, they traveled by train to Berlin, where Robeson had agreed to appear in *The Emperor Jones* at Max Reinhardt's theater for a week. James Light, who came to direct, also played the role of the emperor's side-kick. As usual, the critics liked Robeson more than they liked the play.

Both Paul and Essie loved culturally exciting Berlin, but the country's democratic government was faltering and would soon fall to the surging Nazis.

* * *

Despite their pleasant time on the Continent, the Robesons realized that their troubled marriage was on shaky ground. A new problem had arisen. Her name was Yolande Jackson.[15]

During the past year, Paul had embarked on an affair with Yolande, an adventurous young English woman from a family that was wealthy and white. Essie learned of it when she found a love letter from Yolande to Paul. This sharpened their marital tensions, which receded into the background, temporarily, as *Othello* became the focus of their attention.

The Robesons now headed back to London to prepare for *Othello*.

* * *

Ol' Man River (1928 recording)

Darkies all work on the Mississippi,
Darkies all work while the white folks play,
Pulling them boats from the dawn till sunset,
Getting no rest till the judgment day.

You and me we sweat and strain,
Body all aching and racked with pain,

>Tote that barge, lift that bale,
>You gets a little drunk and you lands in jail.
>
>I gets weary and sick of trying,
>I'm tired of living and scared of dying,
>But ol' man river, he just keeps rolling along.
>
>>—music by Jerome Kern; lyrics by
>>Oscar Hammerstein II; © 1936
>>Polygram International Publishing Inc.

Robeson deleted the hated "n-word" that opened his little-known first recording of the song in 1927; he substituted "darkies" for it in *Show Boat* in London, with the permission of Hammerstein, and did the same in the recording in 1928. He revised the opening again on later recordings to

>There's an old man called the Mississippi,
>That's the old man that I'd like to be.
>What does he care if the world's got troubles,
>What does he care if the land ain't free.

Still later, he changed the final lines of the song on his own:

>You gets a little drunk and you lands in jail.

became

>You shows a little grit and you lands in jail.

and

>I gets weary and sick of trying,
>I'm tired of living and scared of dying,

became

>I keep laughing instead of crying,
>I must keep fighting until I'm dying,
>
>And ol' man river, he just keeps rolling along.
>
>Permission to use copyrighted lyrics of "Ol' Man
>River" from Hal Leonard Corporation.

· 7 ·

Othello in London

Oh, nobody knows the trouble I've seen.

—spiritual

*T*he Robesons arrived in London in early April 1930 so that Paul could begin rehearsals for *Othello*, scheduled to open in May. Preparing to take on the difficult role, he had already studied intensely—reading all of Shakespeare, listening to recordings, and working on English pronunciation.

He would be the first black actor to star in *Othello* since Ira Aldridge, who had toured in Europe a century earlier; white actors normally played the part with their skin darkened. In an interview with the *New York Times* in April, Robeson gave his own view of *Othello*. He said, "It is a tragedy of racial conflict, a tragedy of honor rather than of jealousy." The noble hero is an alien among white people, so "he feels dishonor more deeply," and "his color heightens the tragedy."

The producer for *Othello*, Maurice Browne, cast himself in the key role of Iago. And he appointed his wife, Nellie Van Volkenburg, as the play's director. Unfortunately, neither he nor she had sufficient experience to mount a major Shakespearean production.

Van Volkenburg sat in the first row of the dress circle during rehearsals, holding a rose in one hand and a megaphone in the other. With the megaphone, she shouted her instructions to the actors on stage. The purpose of the rose remained a mystery. Essie, who went to all the rehearsals, called them dreadful and said, "Nellie doesn't know what it is all about. . . . Poor Paul is lost."[1]

The cast included Peggy Ashcroft as Desdemona, Sybil Thorndike as Emilia, Max Montesole as Cassio, and Ralph Richardson as Roderigo. Desperate over the inept direction, Robeson joined Ashcroft, Thorndike, and

Montesole in secret rehearsals at night in one of their homes. Montesole, an experienced Shakespearean actor, provided crucial assistance.[2]

* * *

Opening night on May 19, 1930, found Robeson extremely nervous. The opening exuded glamour with well-known literary, theater, and political figures among the audience filling the Savoy Theatre. Essie wore a white satin evening dress. Sir Jacob Epstein, the noted British sculptor, had sculpted a head of Robeson on display in the lobby.

Paul Robeson—with mustache and beard and garbed in a fur-trimmed robe—walked onto the stage. His first speeches seemed stiff, subdued. But he gained strength as the play proceeded, with a devious Iago duping Othello into believing that his wife has been unfaithful. In the dramatic conclusion, Othello kills his innocent wife and himself—"no way but this . . . to die upon a kiss." At the final curtain, the audience erupted in loud cheers and prolonged applause. Essie wrote to the Van Vechtens that Paul was "magnificent."[3]

The *New York Times* reported from London, "An audience at the Savoy Theatre rose for Paul Robeson tonight at the close of his first interpretation of Othello, and the curtain was raised and lowered twenty times before the frenzy of applause subsided." On his performance, it said, "For nobility of mind and rich beauty of utterance it is difficult to think the part could be better played."

London critics displayed less delight. Although several praised Robeson's performance, others said it lacked sufficient authority. Both Peggy Ashcroft as Desdemona and Sybil Thorndike as Emilia received glowing notices. But there was harsh criticism of the confused production and the incompetent Iago. The *London Times* said, "Mr Robeson plays thrillingly upon the nerves and knocks at the heart." But the *Sunday Times* appeared later with a sterner appraisal by the influential critic James Agate, who observed acidly, "Mr Robeson, alas, failed not only to show mastery of the grand style, but also to indicate any idea of its existence."

After the stinging reviews, Maurice Browne relinquished the role of Iago to his understudy. Robeson's performance improved. *Othello* ran at the Savoy Theatre for six weeks, failing to attract a wider audience. It then went on tour in the provinces. Sybil Thorndike, a great stage veteran, recalled Paul as very interesting, courteous, and modest. "He was," she said, "such a dear person."[4]

Paul Robeson did not possess the technique of a great actor, such as John Gielgud or Laurence Olivier. He imagined himself to be the character and acted accordingly in a natural manner. But he brought to the stage his own unique qualities—a majestic physical presence, an emotional power, and, of course, that magnificent voice. In plays, as in songs, he enunciated his words clearly and communicated personally with the audience.

* * *

Eslanda Robeson's first book, *Paul Robeson, Negro*, came out that spring, published in London just as *Othello* opened. Paul knew that Essie was writing the book, but he did not know—and did not ask—what it would contain. When it appeared, he was not amused.

Conveying Essie's rather fanciful view of Paul and their relationship, the book portrayed him in a patronizing fashion and injected fictitious conversations with him. Although it praised him in exalted terms, it also characterized him as lazy and dependent on his wife.

When published in New York that summer, it received mild reviews with poor sales, as it did in England. The *New York Times* said that while Mrs. Robeson was proud of her husband, she discussed his faults "with the affection of a mother for a spoiled but brilliant child." It added, "She scolds him fondly" about being lazy, procrastinating, and showing insufficient devotion to fatherhood.

Paul, who cared deeply about his privacy, resented the book's intrusion into his personal life and its distortion of his character. He apparently said nothing about it to his wife, however, at least as far as anyone ever knew.

Essie was a highly organized and determined woman who could not resist her desire to improve Paul, to make him a more successful artist and a more attentive husband. But he needed some intellectual and emotional privacy, time to study and think, excluding a wife who tried to restrict his freedom.

* * *

In an interview a month later with W. R. Titterton, a columnist and friend, Robeson stressed that his responsibility to perform as an artist came first and foremost, ahead of any obligation to his family. The interviewer then asked about his obligation to his people.

"As for men of my race," he told Titterton, "why, certainly, I would do all that I can to help them shed the last rags and tatters of old oppression. But I help them best of all by being an artist. It would be foolish, wrong, of me to be a propagandist and make speeches and write articles about what they call the Colour Question while I can sing."[5]

About this time, Robeson felt a "powerful need" to improve his mind and expand his knowledge on a wide range of subjects that included art, science, literature, and politics. This took him into a period of "intensive study" that continued for several years.[6]

While he was on tour that summer, Essie unilaterally decided to sell their Hampstead house and move into a large apartment, which she renovated at considerable expense, at 19 Buckingham Street in central London. She noted in her diary that she had found "the perfect flat . . . just for Paul and me." She sent her son with her mother to Switzerland for the healthful mountain air, while she planned to rebuild her failing marriage.

Another love letter would dash her hopeful plans. It disclosed a new romance between actors appearing together on stage, a common occurrence.

* * *

During the run of *Othello*, Robeson enjoyed an off-stage romance with his Desdemona, the beautiful, talented, twenty-two-year-old Peggy Ashcroft. She recalled many years later that she thought of their affair as probably inevitable, saying, "How could one not fall in love in such a situation with such a man." She also said Paul had encouraged her by confiding that he felt "suffocated" by his wife and needed to "express" himself outside their marriage.[7]

Essie discovered the affair on September 1 when she opened a love letter that Peggy had mailed to Paul. She wrote in her diary, "Found a letter from Peggy Ashcroft at the flat. Exactly like the one from Yolande last year. . . . I dare not think of it 'till I get away from here—my nerves are too far gone."

Essie felt betrayed and humiliated, her hopes shattered. She left London to join her mother and son in Switzerland, where she collapsed with what she termed a nervous breakdown. She roused herself to write a bitter letter to Paul, who was still on a tour of the provinces.

He replied with a letter that offered no apologies to his wife, other than to say he was sorry she had read Peggy's letter to him. He said she should not have opened his mail, adding, "You evidently don't believe your own creed—that what you don't know doesn't hurt you."

"So I see nothing but to leave you the apartment and go to an hotel. . . . I would like to get on with my work."

"I'm sure that deep down I love you very much in the way that we could love each other. It could never be wholly complete because we are too different in temperament. . . . Let's hope it will come out right."[8]

* * *

Paul and Peggy had already ended their affair in friendly fashion, and she returned to her husband, Rupert Hart-Davis, who had raised no complaint.

Essie did not realize that Yolande Jackson represented the greater threat to her marriage. Yolande was a tall, graceful, part-time actress—lovely and lively, playful and fun loving, and white. Paul seemed enchanted by her, resulting in an intense affair, one more serious than his prior romances. She appeared at a time when Paul yearned to escape the stifling control of his wife.[9]

Robeson as Othello with Peggy Ashcroft as Desdemona in London in 1930. Maurice Browne, as Iago, is watching. Courtesy Bettemann/Corbis via Associated Press.

The Robesons' convoluted relationship continued into December, when Essie returned to the London apartment while Paul remained on tour. On her birthday, she apparently dallied with the debonair Noel Coward, an English playwright and actor known for his witty style. In her diary, she wrote, "Spent birthday evening [December 15] with Noel Coward at flat, then drank to his health on Dec. 16, that being his birthday."

Paul came back to the apartment for a week, and they had what Essie described as a marvelous time going to theaters, enjoying supper with Noel Coward and a friend of his, and feeling friendly toward each other. They came to "an amicable agreement to divorce."

* * *

Writing to the Van Vechtens on December 19, Essie confided, "I had a nervous breakdown" but was all right again. Paul had "fallen in love with another girl. . . . He has not only strayed, but gone on a hike. If he wants someone else, I shant mind too much. Of course, I'll mind some, but I refuse to be tiresome."

The Robesons returned to Switzerland to spend the Christmas holiday as a family. The day after Christmas, Paul and Essie went to Paris for a few days before he sailed to America. But she became furious when Yolande called Paul from London, intruding on her precious time with him. As for Yolande, Essie now told her diary on December 27, "I made up my mind that she will never marry him as long as I live, and am able to prevent it."

The year 1930 ended with the Robeson marriage in shreds. Paul's affair with Peggy Ashcroft, Essie's book about him, the persistent tensions caused by their different temperaments, and finally the affair with Yolande Jackson became more than the marriage could bear. But Paul's career marched on.

* * *

Robeson returned to America in January 1931 for a concert tour with Lawrence Brown that began at Carnegie Hall and extended into the spring.

They appeared on January 20 at the Academy of Music in Brooklyn, where a critic said the audience was "held spellbound" by the "thrilling experience" of Robeson's singing. His rendition of "Ol' Man River" as an encore resulted in "tumultuous cheering."[10]

In Toronto on March 20, a critic wrote, "The concert by Paul Robeson in Massey Hall last night was incomparable in its beauty." The critic Pearl McCarthy observed that Robeson gave the stage a special dignity.

Returning to Carnegie Hall on March 22, Robeson sang sixteen songs on the program and nine encores, "and still the audience would not let him go," the *Evening Post* reported. Finally, he responded to "lusty shouts from all parts of the house" by reprising "Ol' Man River" and the spiritual "Steal Away."

* * *

Eslanda Robeson left London in March, sailing for New York, where, based on an entry in her diary, it seems she had an abortion. The circumstances were unclear, but Paul suspected she had an affair with the apparently bisexual

Noel Coward. Then, on a visit to Washington, she told her diary that she had "rediscovered" Grant Lucas, an old boyfriend. If Essie indulged in a romantic affair, Paul was in no position to complain.[11]

She went back to New York while Paul was performing there, and the press learned that both Robesons were in the city but not staying together. Amid rumors of an impending divorce, Essie returned to London.

Paul and Essie were living apart, anticipating their divorce, but they continued to exchange letters and visits in ways that indicated their enduring concern for each other. He urged her to write to him and said he needed her commonsense advice.

In New York, Robeson became close to Robert Rockmore, whom he knew from their past association with the Provincetown Players. Rockmore, an entertainment lawyer, also served as an agent and manager for a few special clients, such as Robeson. He became Paul's trusted friend and confidant.

* * *

In the spring of 1931, Robeson left New York and returned to London for a revival of a Eugene O'Neill play, *The Hairy Ape*, set to open in May.

Robert Rockmore produced it in London with Jimmy Light as director. The title refers to the main character, a stoker who shovels coal into a blazing furnace to power a steamship, then deteriorates under the brutal conditions. In the original production in America, he was white. Robeson now played him stripped to the waist and shouting over the noise of the ship.

Opening night on May 11, 1931, went well. As so often happened, the critics praised Robeson's performance but not the play. Some questioned why a black man was playing a role written for a white. Then a different problem arose.

Suddenly, the play closed after only five performances because Robeson suffered a bout of severe laryngitis. His wife observed that he was exhausted after his long concert tour and strenuous rehearsals for the play. He entered a nursing home for a week of complete rest.

* * *

The Robesons continued to live apart in the summer and fall of 1931. Paul's life became less orderly without his wife on hand to take care of him. In November, he was back in bed, this time with influenza. He canceled his sold-out concert at the Royal Albert Hall at the last minute, angering many of his fans.

Essie told her diary that Paul was "certainly degenerating." He seemed unable to make up his mind about his work, his marriage, or his life. "Poor fellow—I'm sorry for him."[12]

Her diary on November 29 took a different tone: "Yesterday was a red letter day for me, perhaps one of the most important in my whole life." She and Paul had talked, becoming close again, even though he might yet marry Yolanda. "We had a lovely time, slept together, and enjoyed it enormously. . . . We have something special."

In December, Essie's mother brought Pauli to London for Christmas. Paul came to the apartment and spent a happy Christmas Day with his family. Paul and Essie talked things over, however, and they agreed again to get a divorce.

* * *

Robeson sailed alone for America in early 1932. Lawrence Brown joined him for another concert tour that began in New York, with a performance at town hall. Robeson had been studying Russian music, as well as the language, and he introduced two Russian songs into the program.

Regarding his singing Russian works, he told a reporter that he found an emotional connection between them and his own Negro spirituals. He said the spirituals and many Russian folk songs stemmed from a similar life of serfdom.

In an interview, he discussed his religious beliefs, saying that God created man and gave him free will and that "the suffering of the Negro had ennobled his soul" as expressed in the spirituals. When he sang the spirituals, which carried the history of his race, he could "feel and know that God exists, and God is love."[13]

The two-month concert tour moved on to Boston and Montreal, among several other cities, drawing enthusiastic audiences and excellent reviews. The Montreal critic described Robeson as "an ebony Apollo."

In London, divorce rumors resulted in a false news story that Mrs. Robeson had filed a suit accusing Lady Edwina Mountbatten of alienation of affections. Lady Mountbatten sued the newspaper and won an apology.

* * *

On May 19, 1932, Paul Robeson appeared as Joe in a Broadway revival of *Show Boat* at the Casino Theater in New York.

Edna Ferber, whose book was the basis for *Show Boat*, opposed staging a revival so soon after the original Broadway production. She did not intend to go to opening night but changed her mind at the last minute and found herself standing in the rear of the theater just as Robeson came on stage.

"In all my years of going to the theater . . . I never have seen an ovation like that given to any figure of the stage, the concert hall or the opera," Ferber said in a letter to the critic Alexander Woollcott. She reported that the audience stood and applauded and shouted. When Robeson sang "Ol' Man River," he stopped the show, and "they called him back again and again."[14]

Brooks Atkinson's review in the *New York Times* said *Show Boat* was "still the most beautifully blended musical show we have had in this country." And he said, "Mr. Robeson has a touch of genius. It is not merely his voice, which is one of the richest organs on the stage. It is his understanding that gives 'Ol' Man River' an epic lift."

Robeson, who received $1,500 a week for *Show Boat*, also appeared on several radio shows and gave a number of press interviews in which he spoke about cultural issues but avoided politics, even though fascism was on the march in Italy and Germany.

* * *

On June 11, 1932, at a Rutgers commencement, Robeson's alma mater awarded him an honorary master of arts degree. Rutgers president Robert Clothier hailed him for bringing joy to audiences with his singing and acting.

The following month, while still appearing in *Show Boat*, Robeson gave a major outdoor concert at Lewisohn Stadium in New York, attracting a large audience and excellent reviews. The *Times* noted that the concert included "Go Down, Moses," "Deep River," and "Water Boy" and ended with "Ol' Man River." The audience gave him "a great ovation."

In London, the Associated Press reported that Mrs. Paul Robeson had filed for divorce but that she said, "We will keep on being friends." The *Times* quoted him in New York as saying that he and his wife had separated "by mutual agreement."

* * *

Paul Robeson returned to London in September 1932. Aboard the ship crossing the Atlantic, he contemplated his future. He wanted freedom to focus on his career.

In London, when Essie learned that Paul had given money to his brother Ben and his sister, Marian, as well as to Yolande, she complained in her diary, "And he has been beefing about paying me $100 a week and $500 a quarter!"

Essie decided to treat herself to a luxurious holiday in Paris. When she learned that Paul was also in Paris, without Yolande, she went to see him at his hotel on September 27. Paul told her that he was not going to marry Yolande after all. He said that she "got a lot of social pressure in London—so she has called it off." Essie noted, "We had a most delightful, pleasant talk."[15]

Back in London on October 7, Essie found Paul "ill with the flu as usual." Her diary a week later said, "Have seen a lot of Paul at the Great

Central Hotel, where he is living. He asked me to lunch and supper and has been charming."

* * *

With the country mired in the Great Depression, American voters elected Franklin D. Roosevelt, the liberal Democratic governor of New York, as president in 1932. A young singer named Bing Crosby captured the mood of the country with a somber song titled "Brother Can You Spare a Dime?" Robeson would sing in support of Roosevelt in the future.

Now, in a letter to Bob Rockmore, Paul wrote, "I am back in London because it's the only place in the world I'm really happy. I can make records, do concerts, and I have some splendid offers on the Continent."

His letter said he was "finding solace in pleasures of the mind." Reading Karl Marx for the first time was "one of the greatest treats of my life." He also enjoyed the French novelist Marcel Proust and delved into higher mathematics. This letter provided an indication of the wide range of his intellectual interests. And he informed Rockmore that he and Yolande had "decided to call it a day."[16]

All his friends had known that the frivolous Yolande Jackson did not belong in Paul's life. He finally realized it too. With Yolande banished from his life, he reconciled with Essie. Her diary for October 29 said he had invited her to his hotel for tea. After a long talk, they decided to call off the divorce and give their marriage another chance.

They were soon living together again in the apartment at 19 Buckingham Street. On December 15, her birthday, Paul took her to dinner and a play, and she had "a beautiful evening." She wrote in her diary, "I think now I can be happy with him for the rest of my life."

Essie, who cherished her position as Mrs. Paul Robeson, agreed that they could have discreet affairs. And she would continue to advise him, but Bob Rockmore would control contracts and finances.[17]

The year 1932 ended with the most troubled time of their relationship finally over. Paul and Essie had reached a reconciliation that only death would end. With Yolande Jackson, he had really acted irresponsibly for the first time in his life, causing his wife great pain and almost wrecking their marriage. His affair with the flighty and irresponsible Yolande, essentially Essie's opposite, had been a romantic fantasy. Paul had finally returned to his wife and reality.

* * *

Nobody Knows the Trouble I've Seen

Oh, nobody knows the trouble I've seen,
Nobody knows my sorrow,

Nobody knows the trouble I've seen,
Lordy, hallelujah.
Sometimes I'm up, sometimes I'm down,
Oh, yes, Lord,
Sometimes I'm almost to the ground,
Oh, yes, Lord.

—arranged by Lawrence Brown

• 8 •

Road to Moscow

Water boy, where are you hiding?

—traditional black song

$\mathcal{P}$aul and Eslanda Robeson were living together again, contentedly, in their apartment at 19 Buckingham Street as 1933 dawned in London. One of England's most talented young actresses, Flora Robson, moved into the apartment across the hall, and they quickly became friends. In her diary for January 6, 1933, Essie reported that they had talked to Flora about appearing with Paul in *All God's Chillun Got Wings*. Flora agreed to do it if they could revive the play in London.

Paul and Essie met with Andre Van Gyseghem, director of the Embassy Theatre, which presented experimental productions similar to the Provincetown Playhouse. Both the director and the theater's manager, Ronald Adams, wanted to put on the play, but they could not pay Robeson's normal salary. So he agreed to accept the theater's salary of only £10 a week, the equivalent of $50, far below his current rate. And when the management fell short of funds for the production, he contributed £100 of his own.

All God's Chillun Got Wings opened March 12, 1933, starring Paul Robeson as Jim, the law student, and Flora Robson as Ella, his doomed wife. The run was extended to three weeks, with every performance sold out. The play moved to the larger Piccadilly Theatre in the West End to run for four more weeks. The reviews extolled both the production and the players.

"In sheer emotional power," the *Morning Post* critic wrote, "there is most certainly nothing in London to compare with the acting of Mr. Paul Robeson as the Negro husband, and Miss Flora Robson as the white wife in this nightmare of Eugene O'Neill's."

Some critics thought that Robeson's acting was not yet sufficiently subtle or controlled. He felt that he had learned a lot working in this production but agreed that he still had a long way to go. Flora Robson won unanimous praise for her superlative performance.

The *News Chronicle* said Flora Robson "makes you forget she is acting," but only Paul Robeson's voice persuades you that "he is an actor of uncommon gifts." The *Sunday Times* declared that Robeson was "as firmly rooted as an oak," and "his voice is like the soughing [sighing] of the wind through the cedars."

In a letter to Alexander Woollcott, the novelist Rebecca West said of the two stars, "Both were monstrously superb."[1]

And Robeson's recording at this time of "Were You There (When They Crucified My Lord)" provided a hauntingly beautiful religious experience.

* * *

In the early spring of 1933, while *All God's Chillun Got Wings* played in the West End, several thousand Jews who had fled Nazi Germany arrived in London. A committee headed by the writer H. G. Wells sought to raise funds to help the desperate refugees. Ronald Adams said he would provide the Piccadilly Theatre for a benefit matinee of *All God's Chillun Got Wings* if the stars donated their services.

Marie Seton, a supporter of the aid project, asked Robeson to take part. He replied that as an artist he avoided political controversies. But she persuaded him, according to her account, and he began to see a parallel between the Jews of Germany and the Negroes of America. The special matinee raised £2,000, about $10,000, for the refugees.

Seton said Robeson later told her that recognizing the plight of the Jewish refugees was the beginning of his political awareness. And he said, "The white people who have been kindest to me in America have been Jewish people."[2]

* * *

The Robesons sailed to the United States in early May 1933 so that Paul could act in a film version of *The Emperor Jones*. Two independent producers, John Krimsky and Gifford Cochran, set up a company to produce the movie with a reasonable budget of $250,000. It would be released by United Artists. The director, Dudley Murphy, worked with a cast that included Dudley Digges as Smithers, the emperor's white aide, and Fredi Washington as the hero's beautiful paramour, a role she had filled off screen for Paul in the past.

To get into proper physical condition for the arduous role of Brutus Jones, Robeson engaged in workouts with Fritz Pollard, and he obtained a small part in the movie for his old football friend. Robeson was clearly the star. Later a film historian said, "His Brutus Jones was the first lead role portrayed by an African American in a mainstream motion picture, an accomplishment that would not be matched by another black actor in the United States for a quarter-century."[3]

Robeson's contract as the film's star gave him a salary of $15,000 for six weeks of work, plus his traveling expenses, and it contained a provision that he could not be required to work in the South. The jungle scenes, which would have been shot in the South, were done instead at a studio in Astoria, Queens. The director also filmed some sequences at nearby Jones Beach.

When Brutus Jones is still a chain gang prisoner in the film, he sings "Water Boy." The Robeson voice is supremely deep and pure in this song, a favorite of his fans and himself. In a memorable scene, when Brutus Jones transforms his character into the ruler of the island, he gives some serious thought to the exalted title he should bestow upon himself. With a sudden smile, he turns to Smithers and declares imperiously, "You have just had an audience with the Emperor Jones."

The movie achieved a modest profit after its release in September 1933. It also won praise for Robeson's breakthrough as a black actor playing the leading role in a "talking" picture. But the black press complained about the film's stereotypes.

The renowned photographer Edward Steichen took a series of striking pictures of Robeson in his costume for the film. Steichen's portrait of the brooding black emperor, published in *Vanity Fair*, identified Paul Robeson as *The Emperor Jones* for all time.

* * *

Paul Robeson enrolled in London University in 1933 to study African languages and also Chinese. Essie enrolled at the same time to study anthropology, with her focus on Africa. To Carl Van Vechten and his wife, she wrote, "When we get through we will know something about 'our people.'"[4]

In an article, Paul spoke of learning Swahili and other African dialects, explaining that they "come easily to me because their rhythm is the same as that employed by the American Negro in speaking English." Western man thinks in logical abstractions that produced scientific progress, he said, while Africans think in concrete symbols, the kind of thinking that built the great civilizations of the East. He said he was learning about the great African culture of art, music, and spirituality.

"Meanwhile," he said, "in my music, my plays, my films, I want to carry always this central idea: to be African." He had been giving a great deal of thought to African culture, identifying with it long before *Roots* and "black is beautiful."[5]

Professor Sterling Stuckey observed, "Robeson had systematized his thinking on the need for creative equilibrium between the spiritual and the material, between a life of *intuition and feeling* and one of *logical analysis*. In a word, he had called for a synthesis of the cultures of East and West."

A Yale philosopher, F. S. C. Northrop, presented a discourse later on the different cultures of the East and the West, emphasizing their different ways of thinking. To the technical, practical culture prevalent in America, he wrote, Negroes from Africa brought values that were "more emotive, aesthetic, and intuitive." He said Negroes possess "these values instinctively, as Paul Robeson shows in a superlative degree."[6]

In another article, Robeson rejected the idea of individual assimilation, as set forth in the melting-pot theory of America. He considered it "unthinkable" that American Negroes would "disappear into the American mass." He suggested, instead, that they could be integrated into America as "a self-respecting, solid racial unit with its spiritual roots in Africa."

* * *

Robeson said he wanted to concentrate on the folk music of the world, excluding the classical music of Europe. He believed that the traditional folk songs of different lands contained a basic similarity that transcended race and nationality and expressed the brotherhood of mankind. These were the songs he wanted to sing.

The critic W. H. Breare described Robeson's singing technique in an article for *British Musician and Musical News*. Breare said that not only does Robeson have "an extraordinary voice, but he knows how to use it so that the tones and phrases pour forth without effort, naturally, [in] the full sense of the term." He added, "His tone is always lyrical; it flows like a deep river which has not a ripple on its surface."

Lawrence Brown, who worked with him so closely for so long, described Paul as "a unique genius" more interested in knowledge than fame and success. "It seems to me," Brown said, "that if he strove in any direction, it was toward knowledge for its own sake. After the greatest ovations, Paul would go home and read or study languages—an African dialect or Russian."[7]

* * *

Robeson and Brown began a long concert tour of Britain in January 1934, part of the Harry Holt Celebrity Series. The prestigious series presented some of the world's greatest performers, including the violinist Yehudi

Robeson with his wife, Eslanda, waving from a ship arriving in New York in 1935. Courtesy Bettemann/Corbis via Associated Press.

Menuhin and the pianist Vladimir Horowitz. Paul enjoyed listening to classical music, especially Bach and Mozart. Moving beyond mainstream sites for concerts, Robeson and Brown performed in Manchester and several other industrial cities.

Besides spirituals, which he called the folk songs of his people, Robeson sang Russian, Slavic, Hebrew, English, and Scottish folk songs. He found that they all shared "a deep-lying affinity" as people's expression of basic emotions. He said he was not trying to appeal to the highbrow or the lowbrow—he was singing for "common humanity."

George Gershwin wrote to the Robesons in April that he thought Paul "admirably" suited for the role of Porgy in his planned folk opera *Porgy and Bess*. A few months later, the Chicago Opera invited him to sing in *Aida*. He turned down both of these lucrative offers because he considered his voice unsuited to operas, and he wanted to reach a broader audience.

* * *

Alexander Korda, one of Britain's most important movie producers, offered Robeson the leading role in his planned film *Sanders of the River*, based on an African adventure story by Edgar Wallace. The director would be the producer's brother, Zoltan Korda, who had spent several months in Africa to film a genuine African background for the movie.

Robeson agreed to play Bosambo, a tribal chief in a British colony, who steadfastly supports the colony's wise British commissioner, named Sanders. Leslie Banks played Sanders, dressed in a crisp white uniform complete with pith helmet. A young American Negro actress, Nina Mae McKinney, played the wife of Bosambo.

Reading the script, Robeson recognized that it presented a favorable view of British colonialism. But he felt this deficit was outweighed by his opportunity to portray an African character in a film with a real African background. And he hoped it would appeal to the general public.

Zoltan Korda filmed *Sanders of the River* at the Shepperton Studios, just outside London, during the summer of 1934. He assembled hundreds of Africans to appear as extras. Among those who became Robeson's friends on the movie set was Jomo Kenyatta, a militant foe of colonialism, who would later lead Kenya to independence.

In the film, Bosambo, wearing a loincloth that displays his physique, helps Sanders bring peace to the colony's unruly tribes. But native warriors tie Bosambo and his wife to a stake, at which point the heroic Sanders rescues them and appoints Bosambo the new king of the tribes. At the end, Bosambo sings the pulsing "Canoe Song" while the benevolent Sanders sails down the river. Even as a subservient, scantily clad native chief, Robeson imbues the film figure with at least some of the dignity of his own character.

Robeson took his son, Pauli, not quite seven years old, with him to the movie set several times during the summer when they lived together in London. "I remember him as surprisingly playful for one who appeared on the surface to be so serious," his son recalled, noting, "He taught me games of all kinds, told me stories, and stimulated my intellectual curiosity."[8]

Shortly after the filming ended, Essie accompanied Paul on another concert tour of the provinces in the autumn of 1934. They sent young Pauli with his grandmother to live in the United States for a year because they wanted the boy to be familiar with his homeland.

* * *

It was a personal invitation from Sergei Eisenstein, the renowned Russian film director, that resulted in Paul Robeson making his first visit to the Soviet Union in December 1934. Eisenstein sent an admiring letter to Robeson, asking him to come to Moscow as a guest of the Administration for Films so they could discuss making a movie together. Eisenstein gave the letter to Marie Seton, an English journalist he knew in Russia, who delivered it to Robeson in London. Arrangements were soon made for Paul and Essie to visit Russia, with Seton as their guide.[9]

The Robesons left London on December 20, crossed the English Channel, and arrived by train in Berlin the next day. They had to wait until evening to take a train to Moscow. Essie described their day in Berlin as a "nightmare" with Nazi uniforms and swastikas everywhere.

At the railroad station on the evening of December 21, when Paul was talking to Marie, who had joined them in Berlin, people "stared as though they would like to lynch him." And they felt menaced by some uniformed storm troopers who muttered racist slurs. But the Robeson party boarded the train to Moscow without further incident.[10]

Their train rolled through Poland all the next day, and when they reached the Russian border, Paul "conquered" the friendly customs officials by speaking to them in his fluent Russian, according to an entry in Essie's diary.

* * *

On December 23, they arrived at the railroad station in Moscow, where a delegation headed by Sergei Eisenstein greeted them. Eisenstein brought along Essie's brother, John Goode, who worked in Moscow as a mechanic. Her other brother, Frank, was traveling in the Soviet Union and would meet them later.

The Robesons were driven to the National Hotel at Red Square. Their suite had a "magnificent" drawing room, bedroom, and bath, Essie noted in her diary. Reporters came to interview Paul, and she added, "Sergei stayed for lunch, and we found at once, that we liked him enormously."

That evening the Robesons had dinner with Eisenstein and Seton, then they all went to the theater to see Gogol's *Government Inspector*. Afterward, Robeson and Eisenstein sat up half the night discussing languages and music and playing African records that Paul brought to Sergei as a gift.[11]

Eisenstein escorted the Robesons to a dinner party on Christmas Eve in the home of Maxim Litvinov, the Soviet foreign minister, and his wife, Ivy. Essie said, "We had a grand dinner," which included rich appetizers, soup with noodles, then turkey, followed by cake and chocolate ice cream. It turned into a merry evening with Soviet officials and their families dining and dancing.[12]

Two nights later, Eisenstein took them to a special party for Paul at Dom Kino, a huge club for people in the film industry. Essie said, "Sergei introduced Paul to the packed audience, and they applauded for a full two minutes." Paul gave a short speech in Russian, saying how at home he felt there, and he sang several songs. There was "a huge banquet."

Essie went shopping the next day and bought a warm, black, sable-lined fur coat for Paul. The week continued with a visit by Essie's brothers. And Eisenstein showed them his silent film *Battleship Potemkin* about "the naval side of the revolution."

On New Year's Eve, the Robesons went back to Dom Kino with Eisenstein for a gala midnight celebration. Essie noted in her diary, "Another colossal banquet, dancing, and everyone got drunk—home at 4 [a.m.] exhausted!"

Robeson visited a factory in Moscow and sang some spirituals to the workers early in the new year. He saw workers of different colors, from outlying areas of the vast Soviet Union, working side by side as equals. He became convinced that the Soviet government had granted equality to the country's minorities.

Both of Essie's brothers told Paul emphatically that they found no racial prejudice in the Soviet Union. They were among a number of Negroes who went there to escape American prejudice and seek a new life. This was a time when many idealistic people looked hopefully at the Russian Revolution. History had not yet caught up with the grim reality of that country.

This first visit to Moscow established Robeson's strong friendship with the Russian people. The black giant in his fur coat with his broad smile was welcomed everywhere he went, not only by public officials but by ordinary Russians on the street. He spoke to them in fluent Russian.

Marie Seton quoted him as saying to Sergei Eisenstein, "Here, for the first time in my life, I walk in full human dignity."[13]

* * *

Robeson said in an interview with the *Daily Worker* correspondent in Moscow that he felt at home in the Soviet Union. He said he knew of the

Soviet theory that all races were equal, but he had not expected such a whole-hearted welcome.

"I was not prepared," he continued, "for the endless friendliness, which surrounded me from the moment I crossed the border. . . . And this joy and happiness and friendliness, this utter absence of any embarrassment over a 'race question' is all the more keenly felt by me because of the day I spent in Berlin on the way here, and that was a day of horror—in an atmosphere of hatred, fear and suspicion."

"This is home to me," he said. "I feel more kinship to the Russian people under their new society than I ever felt anywhere else."[14]

His extravagant praise of the Soviet Union continued in another statement at the end of his visit. He said, "In Soviet Russia I breathe freely for the first time in my life. It is clear, whether a Negro is politically a Communist or not, that of all the nations in the world, the modern Russians are our best friends."

* * *

In the first wintry week of 1935, the Robesons completed their visit to Moscow. On January 6, they left for Leningrad on a train that finally arrived the next day, five hours late.

They stayed in a suite at the Astoria Hotel, visited the famous Winter Palace and Hermitage Museum, saw the opera *Boris Godunov*, and attended a concert by the great American contralto Marian Anderson at Philharmonic Hall. After the concert, they went backstage to congratulate Miss Anderson, and Essie wrote in her diary, "She is absolutely first class."

The Robesons left Leningrad after four days, traveling by train to Helsinki, Stockholm, and Copenhagen on their way back to London in that cold January 1935.

* * *

Alexander Woollcott, the famous critic who became a friend, made a defining statement about the unique quality of Paul Robeson in his 1934 book, *While Rome Burns*. Of all the people he had known, Woollcott said, Robeson was one of the few who had "greatness."

"I do not mean greatness as a football player or as an actor or as a singer," Woollcott explained. "I do not even have in mind what is, I suppose, the indisputable fact, that he is the finest musical instrument wrought by nature in our time. I mean greatness as a person." Woollcott added, "By his unassailable dignity, and his serene, incorruptible simplicity, Paul Robeson strikes me as having been made out of the original stuff of the world. In this sense is he coeval with Adam and the redwood trees of California."[15]

    Others, too, likened him to a towering tree or spoke of a voice in which deep bells rang, a voice that flowed deep as a river.

* * *

Water Boy

Water boy, where are you hiding?
If you don't come, I'm gonna tell your mammy.

There ain't no hammer that's on this mountain,
That rings like mine, boy, that rings like mine;
Done bust this rock, boy, from here to Macon,
All the way to the jail, boy, yes, back to the jail.

You jack o' diamonds, you jack o' diamonds,
Now I know you of old, boy, yes, I know you of old;
You rob my pocket, yes, you rob my pocket,
You done rob my pocket of silver and gold.

Water boy, where are you hiding?
If you don't come, I'm gonna tell your mammy,
Water boy, water boy.

—arranged by Avery Robinson

· 9 ·

Turning Left

Oh, how proud our quiet Don, quiet Don.

—Russian song

*G*ood spirits prevailed in the Robeson household after Paul and Essie returned to London from the Soviet Union in January 1935. Essie reveled in her role as Mrs. Paul Robeson. With his wife providing stability at home, Paul was working hard and looking good. Friends who saw them at this time described them as a handsome, happy couple.

With Lawrence Brown, Robeson sang at the Royal Albert Hall before they went on a concert tour of England, Scotland, Wales, and Ireland. They attracted large, enthusiastic audiences everywhere during the tour, which continued through February and March. A critic for the *Herald of Wales* stressed Robeson's popularity, observing that the huge crowd attracted by his concert "clamoured for a glimpse of him" as if a great statesman had come to town.

The premiere of *Sanders of the River* took place on April 2, 1935, at the Leicester Square Theatre. Robeson attended it with mixed feelings since he had become a firm supporter of freedom for the British colonies. He now felt embarrassed by the film's colonialist tone because its final edited version presented a more favorable view of colonialism than he had expected.[1]

Sanders of the River proved to be a smash hit, with the critics praising both the movie and Robeson. It made him a major movie star in Britain. The historian Jeffrey Richards referred to it as "the Empire genre," an action-packed outdoors adventure—also called "the British version of the American western."[2]

Robeson had achieved stardom in concerts, in plays, and now in films, with a popularity greater in Britain than in America. Despite his displeasure with how *Sanders of the River* had turned out, he now looked forward to new ventures in the movies and the theater.

* * *

The idea of establishing a small independent theater, one that could focus on new plays with a social conscience, appealed to Robeson in the spring of 1935. This idea grew from his increasing political awareness, as well as his desire to reach working-class people and to portray black culture in a positive light. An added factor was the paucity of parts for a serious black actor.

As a first step, he joined with a small group, the Arts Theatre Club, in the production of a new play in April. The play, titled *Basalik*, was written by an American, Norma Munro, under the pen name of Peter Garland. It presented a noble African chief named Basalik, who holds a British official's wife hostage to win a promise that the chief's people will be left in peace. Margaret Webster played the wife. In a tryout, it ran for just three performances, drawing reviews that derided the story and dialogue as stilted and amateurish.

The *New York Times* reported on April 8 that *Basilik* was "an interesting African play," adding, "Robeson, as always, was enthusiastically received."

* * *

Robeson moved quickly to an American play titled *Stevedore*, written by Paul Peters and George Sklar. This play, which had run successfully in New York a year earlier, concerned black dockworkers who organize to fight their white bosses and eventually confront a lynch mob after their leader is falsely accused of rape. Andre Van Gyseghem, the director of the 1933 London revival of *All God's Chillun Got Wings*, directed. Most of the play's black cast consisted of nonprofessional actors, including Lawrence Brown in a supporting role.

Stevedore, with Robeson in the lead role of a stevedore named Lonnie Thompson, ran for two weeks in May at the Embassy Theatre. It received mixed reviews that took note of its leftist theme and included high praise for Robeson's performance. Although a distinct improvement over *Basalik*, it did not attract a sufficient audience to extend its run.[3]

On May 30, 1935, the *News Chronicle* in London carried a feature article by Robeson with the headline "I Want Negro Culture." He wrote that he wanted to establish a permanent Negro theater in London. He said, "I believe that Negro culture merits an honourable place amongst the cultures of the world." In his own notebook, he wrote, "I am not a nationalist." Different cultures contain similarities "which seem to me to transcend the boundaries of nationality."[4]

* * *

In late June, Robeson and Brown began their annual summer tour of the provinces, with an itinerary of thirteen concerts. Paul scheduled the concerts a week apart to give him time for his studies, which now included politics as well as music and languages.

Essie negotiated with Universal Pictures for Paul to appear in the movie version of *Show Boat*. His contract provided a salary of $40,000, quite large at the time, and all expenses paid for both Robesons. It also gave him approval of location because he refused to work in the segregated South. But the producer rejected his demand for final approval of his part in the film, saying not even Greta Garbo had that privilege.[5]

On September 25, 1935, Paul and Essie sailed for New York, with filming of *Show Boat* to begin on November 18. Robeson had not been back for three years. Ted Poston, a journalist who interviewed him at dockside on his arrival in New York, observed that Robeson was "lavish in his praise of the Soviet Union" as he repeated his view that "only there could a Negro artist feel free."

Robeson and Brown were booked for a limited concert tour before the filming of *Show Boat* began, including concerts in New York, Princeton, Montreal, Chicago, Milwaukee, Portland, and Seattle. Albert Einstein visited Robeson in his dressing room after the concert in Princeton. Robeson also appeared on national radio in the General Motors Concert Series.[6]

* * *

First, Paul and Essie went to visit their son in Pittsfield, Massachusetts, where he was living with Grandma Goode. The youngster, not quite eight years old, had already lived in several countries, spoke fluent German, and was well ahead in schoolwork for his age. But they found him unhappy, weary of his grandmother's inflexible supervision, and sick of living away from his parents as "a black rich kid in an almost entirely white environment."

Robeson took his son on a long walk in the woods, encouraged him to talk about his feelings, and listened without interruption. He then quietly promised his son, "When you come back to London next spring, you will live with Mama and me."[7]

Young Pauli remained, at least for the time being, with his formidable grandmother, who strongly believed in education, ambition, and hard work. Nothing indicates that Essie's mother complained about having to take care of her grandson for several years.

After visiting Pauli, Robeson carried out the concert tour with Brown on their way to the West Coast.

* * *

The Robesons, with Lawrence Brown, arrived in California on schedule in November. Essie wrote to her old friend Hattie Bolling that all three had settled into "a grand flat" in Pasadena, each with a separate bedroom "so we can all live happily and comfortably, without getting under each other's heels."[8]

Filming of *Show Boat* progressed smoothly under the direction of James Whale. The cast included the two pairs of lovers played by Irene Dunne and Alan Jones, and Helen Morgan and Donald Cook, with Charles Winninger as Captain Andy and Hattie McDaniel as the Negro cook. The film emphasized the long Dunne-Jones love story. When Robeson, in the role of Joe, finished singing "Ol' Man River," the orchestra members on the set put down their instruments and applauded.

The original film version of *Show Boat* opened to excellent reviews at Radio City Music Hall in New York in January 1936. Whale told Robeson that he hoped to direct him in a starring role soon. Such a role did not turn up.

* * *

On January 12, 1936, the Robesons sailed from New York for London. Paul would once again go with Lawrence Brown on a British concert tour that extended from late January into April.

They launched the tour with a concert at the Royal Albert Hall, where Robeson sang Russian, Finnish, and English folk songs as well as Negro spirituals. The *Daily Express* said, "He placed one hand on the piano, as if for comfort, and smiled around. His voice, rich and clear, has lost none of its beauty. His singing was effortless, and every word, even on the softest note, carried to the most remote seat."[9]

After London, Leeds, and Glasgow, the tour took them to Ireland for concerts in Dublin, Cork, Limerick, and Belfast in February. The *Irish Times* said of Robeson, "Not only is he the possessor of a bass voice of exceedingly beautiful quality, but he is one of those rare singers whose vocalization is beyond reproach. He has the easy, perfect style of the true interpreter of songs."

Robeson took time in March to star in two performances of a new play called *Toussaint L'Ouverture*. The play, sponsored by the Stage Society at the Westminster Theatre, told the story of the noted Haitian revolutionary leader, who attracted Robeson's interest. It was written by C. L. R. James, a black left-wing scholar identified with the Trotskyist opposition to Stalin. He and Paul became close friends, despite political differences.

The play failed to gain sufficient support to go beyond its initial two performances. But James said that spending even a brief time with Paul Robeson amounted to a memorable experience. He described Paul's personality as "a combination of immense power and great gentleness."

Robeson holding his eight-year-old son, Pauli, who had just arrived from the United States, landing at Plymouth, England, on April 20, 1936. Courtesy Bettemann/Corbis via Associated Press.

In April, as his tour ended, Paul kept his promise to his son and brought the boy to live with him and Essie in their London apartment at 19 Buckingham Street.

His busy work schedule aside, Robeson's serious reading turned to politics. Essie informed the Van Vechtens that he was excited about a book he had just read titled *Soviet Communism: A New Civilization?* by Sidney and Beatrice Webb, prominent British socialists. Paul made numerous notes in the book's margins and also read some excerpts aloud to Essie. The focus of his studies had shifted from African culture to Soviet communism.

* * *

Essie negotiated for Paul to appear in three films to be made by major movie companies in Britain. Filming of the first one, *Song of Freedom*, began in April 1936. Produced by British Lion–Hammer Productions, it was directed by J. Elder Wills, who did some background filming in Sierra Leone.

The film's hero, played by Robeson, is a dockworker with a great voice named John Zinga; he is discovered by an impresario and becomes a famous concert star. But a carved ornament that he wears around his neck leads him to seek his roots in Africa. He travels to Africa, gains his place as a long-lost king, then returns briefly to England for a concert to raise funds for his people.

Robeson portrayed Zinga as an intelligent, idealistic man, a strong role that pleased him. And he sang the powerful "Lonesome Road." His wife in the movie was played by Elisabeth Welch, a popular black singer in Britain. She said of Paul, "I absolutely adored him."[10]

On the *Song of Freedom* set, Paul and Elisabeth often sat outdoors with their lunch trays, talking about life. He spoke of his determination to make "a better world." Sometimes there was anger or sadness in his voice, but there was also humor and laughter. She recalled working with him as a happy time. Despite a lack of good roles for black actors, she said, Paul always brought "intelligence, strength, and compassion to his characters."

Reviews for *Song of Freedom* were generally favorable, although Graham Greene described it in the *Spectator* as an "imperfect picture" notable only for "the profound beauty of Elisabeth Welch and Mr. Robeson's magnificent singing of inferior songs." Paul considered it a significant improvement over *Sanders*.

Robeson also participated briefly in a documentary film on South Africa called *My Song Goes Forth*. He sang two songs and read a prologue for the documentary, which had limited distribution.

In May 1936, Robeson was interviewed for the *Sunday Worker* by a friend, Benjamin J. Davis Jr., a black Communist Party leader from New York. Robeson contended in the interview that the Soviet Union consistently opposed racism, colonialism, and fascism. He had moved from avoiding politics to acting as an outspoken advocate of Soviet policies. He even expressed an interest in living in the Soviet Union, saying, "It's the only country in the whole world where I feel at home."

"I believe that the Soviet Union is the bulwark of civilization against both war and fascism. . . . In England they call me a Communist, because of my views, but I'm certainly not a member of the Communist Party."[11]

Essie wrote to another old Communist friend, William Patterson, about Paul's increasing interest in political issues. She said that Paul had been quietly interested in politics for a long time. He thought things out, at length, until he understood them.

* * *

Knowing what we know now, after all the revelations about the evils of Stalin, it may be difficult to understand how intelligent people could ever have supported Soviet communism. Understanding this requires recognizing two major factors in the 1930s.

First, the United States and Western Europe had fallen into the Great Depression, a deep economic disaster that exposed the faults of capitalism and left the world's major economies in ruins. Second, the young Soviet Union appeared to be a great experiment designed to end the inequities of capitalism and create a better society for masses of people.

An added factor, which greatly impressed many people, particularly people of color, involved the early leadership of Communists in fighting against racism in America, fascism in Europe, and colonialism in Africa. Robeson became a strong opponent of Franco's Fascist revolt in Spain in 1936, which Hitler and Mussolini supported, with only the Soviet Union supporting Spain's elected government. Communism's faults seemed less pronounced at that time.

An observation by the American humorist Will Rogers provides evidence that comedians can be wiser than more serious-minded thinkers. He said, "Communism is like prohibition: it's a good idea, but it won't work."[12]

* * *

The Robesons had extensive travel plans for the summer of 1936. Essie planned to take Pauli with her on a three-month trip to Africa. Paul could not take that much time away because of his movie commitments. But he intended to take a brief vacation in the Soviet Union between films.

On May 29, Paul took his wife and their eight-year-old son to Waterloo Station in London. He settled them on the boat train to Southampton. From there, they took the steamship *Winchester Castle* down the west coast of Africa to Cape Town on the tip of South Africa. Essie kept a daily diary of the journey, which included traveling by car, train, boat, and plane to Kenya, Tanganyika, Uganda, Belgian Congo, Sudan, and finally Egypt. She characterized her African trip as "one of those grand dreams come true."[13]

Before his next movie, Robeson returned to the Soviet Union to spend time with Sergei Eisenstein. He also wanted to determine if his son could go to school there. Essie's mother traveled separately to Moscow to visit her two sons. She also checked the living conditions, in case she accompanied Pauli there.

Paul returned to London as Essie and Pauli arrived from Africa. The Robesons made the decision for Pauli to go to school in Moscow, in the care of his grandmother. Robeson announced to the press that his son would go to school in the Soviet Union to be free of racism.

Young Pauli had complained in a letter from America about being the only Negro in his school and hearing racist slurs. Essie responded with a thoughtful letter noting that she and his father had similar experiences in their youth. She added, "But we were both very proud of being coloured."

* * *

Soon after his return to England, Robeson began filming *King Solomon's Mines*, another African adventure, this one without the aura of colonialism. He portrayed a worker named Umbopa, secretly an African king, who joins a group of adventurers; together they trudge through a vast desert to find "the legendary diamond mines of King Solomon."

The cast included Cedric Hardwicke as a great white hunter and a young romantic couple played by Anna Lee and John Loder, with Roland Young along for a bit of humor. When surrounded by native warriors, they use a solar eclipse to convince the natives that they are gods. They finally enter the mines, find the young woman's missing father, and escape as an erupting volcano buries the mines with boulders. Umbopa, now recognized as a king, sends the group on its way as he sings of "the mighty mountain."

Michael Balcon produced the movie at the Gaumont British Film Studios, with Robert Stevenson as the director. It had a good cast but a weak screenplay. The reviews did not take this one very seriously. The *Sunday Chronicle* called it "a thundering good version of that grand epic of one's boyhood days."

Robeson's next film, *Big Fella*, came from a novel by Claude McKay and departed from movies about Africa. Paul played a genial dockworker named Joe in the French port of Marseilles. Joe finds a young white boy missing from an ocean liner. The boy wants to stay with Joe and the colorful people of the port, but Joe reconciles him to returning with his parents on the ship to England. The film's best song was "My Curly Headed Baby."

The producer, director, and costar for *Big Fella* were the same as for *Song of Freedom*: British Lion–Hammer Productions, J. Elder Wills, and Elisabeth Welch. Essie had an acting role as a cafe owner, with Larry Brown playing a comrade in the port. This was pleasant, light fare and easily dismissed, but it presented blacks as responsible people, a rarity at the time.

During the shooting of *Big Fella*, Welch encountered a formidable Eslanda Robeson on the set. In Welch's words, "She was rather prissy, like a hospital matron, and she watched Paul like a hawk, because everybody loved him and loved being with him."[14]

* * *

In October 1936, Paul and Essie returned to the Soviet Union. This time Robeson went for a concert tour. With Lawrence Brown, he embarked on a tour of twelve concerts in Moscow, Leningrad, Kiev, and Odessa. He included some Russian songs in the concerts, all broadcast live over the national radio.

The Associated Press reported, "Soviet workers roared and pounded their approval of Paul Robeson, the American Negro singer, at a concert tonight in the Moscow Conservatory." He sang "Ol' Man River" and "Water Boy" and spoke briefly in Russian between the songs, "all but bringing down the house."

The Robesons enrolled Pauli in a "model school" in Moscow attended by the children of Soviet officials, including Stalin's daughter. Pauli, who had just turned nine, entered the equivalent of an American fifth grade, even though he did not know "a word of Russian." He found his classmates very friendly, received after-school tutoring in Russian, and adjusted quickly to the school.

When Paul and Essie returned to Moscow a month later, they were delighted with their son's progress. Paul asked his son "endless questions" about his experience.[15]

The family gathered in Moscow for New Year's Eve as 1936 turned into 1937. Paul, Essie, Pauli, and Grandma Goode were joined by one of Essie's brothers, as well as Larry Brown and their old friend William Patterson. Two weeks later, Paul and Essie departed for London, leaving their son with his grandmother comfortably settled in the Hotel National in Moscow.

* * *

The politics of Paul Robeson—his turning to communism—evolved over a few years in the 1930s. He did not join the Communist Party, but he emerged as a dedicated supporter of Soviet policies. His interest in socialism had been aroused by conversations with leftist intellectuals in England. He read Karl Marx with enthusiasm in 1932, although he had seemed reluctant to take a political position.

With his study of the language and the music of Russia, Robeson was favorably disposed toward the Soviet Union before he made his first trip there at the end of 1934. He had already spoken of feeling a kinship with the Russian people, showing more interest in culture than in politics.

That first Russian trip was an epiphany for him. The total absence of racism and the outpouring of affection that he felt in Moscow made a deep impression. And the stark contrast to the menacing hatred that he felt in Berlin gave it an added impact. His Russian visit assumed the aura of a religious experience—he refused to criticize Soviet policies, ever, almost as if to do so would be blasphemy.

Significantly, he came to believe that "scientific socialism" was superior to the capitalist system of production for private profit. He believed that a socialist society was better both economically and ethically. The Robesons' return to the Soviet Union in late 1936 and their decision to send their son to school there represented a strong endorsement of the Soviet system and its freedom from racism.[16]

The Great Depression displayed the fault lines of capitalism to a painful degree, drawing many more Americans into the U.S. Communist Party. Even so, it failed to grow into a significant political force in the United States. The historian Michael Kazin said, "Never did the Party top a hundred thousand members; due to constant turnover, its loyal core was always less than half of that." Two main socialists, Eugene Debs and Norman Thomas, ran for president several times in the first half of the century without exerting a major influence on the nation's politics.[17]

It was the Spanish Civil War—with the forces of good and evil, as he saw them, colliding in mortal combat—that strengthened Robeson's enduring devotion to the Communist-led left wing. Now the political views of Paul Robeson seemed to flow as swift and deep as the rivers in his songs.

* * *

Our Quiet Don

Oh, how proud our quiet Don,
Quiet Don, our father Don;
To the heathen he will never bow,
Never ask of others how to live.
Oh-oh-oh-oh-oh-oh.

Hear me now, our quiet Don,
Oh, quiet Don, our source of bread;
From the joyless tears of orphaned ones,
Wretched tears of widows left alone.
Oh-oh-oh-oh-oh-oh.

—from "Quiet Flows the Don" by
Ivan Dzerzhinsky, sung in English
and Russian by Robeson

• 10 •

I Have Made My Choice

Deep river, my home is over Jordan.

—spiritual

$\mathcal{P}$aul and Essie stayed at home in London for only a few days before they went to Egypt for a month to make a new movie. Paul Robeson finally set foot on the continent of Africa in January 1937 to star in *Jericho*.

In the role of Jericho Johnson, Robeson portrayed a black American soldier in World War I who rescues some soldiers trapped below deck when a torpedo hits their troop ship en route to France. He accidentally kills a sergeant during the rescue, however, and is sentenced to death in a court-martial. He makes a daring escape to North Africa and eventually becomes the leader of a desert tribe.

The film's producer, Walter Futter, and the director, Thornton Freeland, persuaded a Sudanese sheik's daughter, Princess Kouka, to play Jericho's wife. Wallace Ford played the hero's fast-talking sidekick. And Henry Wilcoxon was Captain John Mack, a white officer who relentlessly pursues Jericho into his desert kingdom but ultimately decides to leave him there in peace.

Lawrence Brown also had a small role as a soldier on the troop ship, but he did not go to Egypt because his role was limited to early scenes aboard the ship.

* * *

Much of the filming took place in the desert, not far from the famous Egyptian pyramids. On a day off from filming, Wilcoxon hired a carriage and guide to visit the Great Pyramid of Giza. Robeson and Ford joined him. At the pyramid, they climbed the steep stone exterior to the entrance, where the guide led them down a long, narrow passage to the King's Chamber, dark and huge, about 150 feet long and 150 feet wide, with a ceiling equally high.

An empty sarcophagus stood at the center of this stone chamber, deep inside the pyramid, literally silent as a tomb. When the guide started to describe the construction, Wilcoxon heard an echo, so he asked Paul to sing a few notes. They all stood, hushed in the huge chamber, as the notes echoed back like the eerily beautiful chords of an organ.

Paul began to sing Mozart's bass aria "O Isis and Osiris" from *The Magic Flute*. He sang a line, then paused while it echoed back with exquisite clarity, before he sang the next line. Wilcoxon recalled how he, Ford, and the guide "stood spellbound—not moving, hardly breathing" as they listened to the sound of Paul's voice. When the last note echoed to an end, all of them "stood silently crying."

They left the chamber, walked through the passageway, and emerged from the pyramid at dusk. They climbed into the waiting carriage and returned in virtual silence to their hotel in Cairo. The guide was so caught up in the magic of their shared experience that he refused Wilcoxon's offer to pay him.[1]

Like the grandeur of the ancient pyramid and the glory of Mozart's music, Paul Robeson embodied a sense of timeless beauty.

* * *

Filming of *Jericho* proceeded on schedule. One of its more memorable scenes focuses on Robeson, garbed in the flowing white robe and headdress of an Arab, singing the film's theme song, "My Way, Brother, Are You Going My Way?," while standing dramatically atop a sand dune silhouetted against the night sky.

When not filming, Paul and Essie frequently walked through the busy streets of Cairo, enjoying the exotic city. She wrote to the Van Vechtens that it was "great fun" to see a rich country where "the coloured folks are the bosses." As for Paul, she said he was "sweeter, dearer than ever."[2]

Jericho, called *Dark Sands* in England, drew only modest reviews when released, but it pleased Robeson because he had played an epic black hero, a positive figure, in a story with a happy ending.

* * *

Back in London after the month in Cairo, Robeson gave concerts and speeches to support Spain's Loyalists against Franco's Fascists. He also accepted an invitation from Max Yergan, now a Robeson friend, to serve as chairman of the Council on African Affairs, a new left-wing group dedicated to winning freedom for the colonies in Africa.[3]

Citing aggression taking place in Spain, China, and Ethiopia, Robeson told an interviewer that he wanted to focus beyond racism on defending democracy against "the onslaught of fascism." And he made an "irrevocable decision" to act as an ally of the Communist-led left wing because he saw it as the most effective foe of racism, poverty, and war.[4]

Paul and Essie returned to the Soviet Union in May 1937 for a four-month vacation, their first long vacation together. They stopped in Moscow to pick up their son, then went on to the summer resort of Kislovodsk, in the foothills of the Caucasus Mountains.

Robeson interrupted his vacation to visit a radio studio in Moscow to record a message for broadcast later to a London rally in support of Republican Spain. When questions arose about whether the broadcast would go through, he flew to London to appear at the rally in person.

* * *

On June 24, 1937, at the huge rally for Spanish relief at the Royal Albert Hall, Paul Robeson made a rousing speech in which he dedicated himself to "the greatest cause which faces the world today." He declared that the fight against fascism concerned everyone, saying, "There is no standing above the conflict on Olympian heights."[5]

"Fascism is no respecter of persons. It makes no distinction between combatants and non-combatants. The blood-soaked streets of Guernica, that beautiful peaceful village nestled in the Basque hills, are proof of that, as are the concentration camps full of scientists and artists."

Then, in the memorable words that would serve as his guiding principle, he said, "The artist must take sides. He must elect to fight for freedom or slavery. I have made my choice. I had no alternative."

"I stand with you in unalterable support of the government of Spain, duly and regularly chosen by its lawful sons and daughters," he went on. "For the liberation of Spain from the oppression of Fascist reactionaries is not a private matter of the Spaniards, but the common cause of all advanced and progressive humanity."

His speech evoked impassioned cheering at the rally, whose sponsors included the literary figures W. H. Auden, E. M. Forster, Sean O'Casey, H. G. Wells, and Virginia Woolf.

* * *

Robeson returned to Kislovodsk to complete his vacation. He and his wife went back to London in late August. They arranged for their son and his grandmother to leave Moscow and come to London, supposedly for a Christmas visit. In reality, Robeson feared that a war might trap them in the Soviet Union.

Essie described her mother and Pauli as "very reluctant to leave" their satisfying life in the Soviet Union. She said, "Pauli was only reconciled to leaving when I told him on the telephone that Paul and I would re-arrange our work so that we could spend a good deal of time with him every day."[6]

Back in London, Robeson immersed himself in a whirl of political activity against fascism and for the Spanish cause. He also began singing in large music halls and movie theaters that had low admission prices, making them available to working-class people. He felt a growing bond with workers, especially now that he believed the English upper class treated them with the kind of contempt that American whites reserved for Negroes.

On December 20, 1937, Robeson appeared at another huge rally at the Royal Albert Hall to raise money for victims of the Spanish Civil War. Clement Attlee, the leader of Britain's Labour Party, addressed the rally with many of the party's faithful in the audience.

It was Paul Robeson who evoked the loudest, most enthusiastic cheering when he sang a significantly altered version of "Ol' Man River." He transformed its original resigned lament into his own personal declaration of defiance by changing the song's closing lyrics.

> I gets weary and sick of trying,
> I'm tired of living and scared of dying

now became

> But I keep laughing instead of crying,
> I must keep fighting until I'm dying.

The song finished with the original ending: "And Ol' Man River, he'll just keep rolling along." Years later, when he asked Oscar Hammerstein if he objected to his changes to the lyrics, Oscar laughed and said he would keep his version, and "I could keep mine."[7]

* * *

Now Robeson made plans to go to Spain. Essie questioned why he would want to risk his life by entering a war zone. He told her, "This is our fight, my fight. If fascism wins . . . the African, the Negro, the Jew go right to the bottom of the ladder."[8]

Paul insisted on going to Spain to sing for the Loyalist troops fighting the Fascists, so Essie decided to accompany him. Her diary recorded the day-by-day details of their trip.

On Saturday, January 22, 1938, the Robesons, accompanied by a leftist writer named Charlotte Haldane, took the ferry and train from London to

Paris, then changed trains for the all-night ride to Perpignan, near the Spanish border. A Spanish lieutenant met them with a car the next morning and took them across the border for the three-hour drive to Barcelona.

They arrived at the Majestic Hotel in Barcelona in time for Sunday lunch. The press interviewed Paul and Haldane at the hotel and informed them that enemy planes had bombed Barcelona earlier that day. Next day, a Spanish official provided a big Buick sedan with a driver named Pepe and an army escort, Captain Fernando Castillo. Essie noted, "Our young captain is extremely handsome, has studied in London, and speaks English fluently."

At 5 p.m. on January 24, they left in the Buick on a five-hour drive to a coastal town near Valencia for an overnight stay in a comfortable inn. Next day, they headed for a military hospital at Benicasim. When their car stopped on the crowded road, a young Negro soldier recognized Robeson. Paul climbed out of the car and shook hands with the soldier, who "could not believe his eyes." He was one of thousands of volunteers from the United States, Britain, and other countries who had joined the International Brigade to fight with the Loyalists against the Fascists in Spain.

The Robesons resumed their drive to the hospital, where Paul sang outdoors, with no accompaniment, to the "wildly enthusiastic" soldiers who crowded around him. Essie noted, "We then went thru the wards . . . Paul singing to the patients as we went. . . . All of them asked for Ol' Man River."

From the hospital, they went to Valencia for a late lunch at the Victoria Hotel, then drove inland through several villages on their way to Albacete. At each village, "we are always stopped by heavily armed militia, who examine our driver's papers . . . and look well into the car before they allow us to pass."

About 11 p.m. that night, they arrived "worn out" at Albacete, the headquarters of the International Brigade. Essie noted, "Car moved in darkness to hotel, only candles lit, had a rather good dinner, finally."

They went to the brigade's training camp the next morning, January 26, where fifteen hundred soldiers crowded into a church. Paul simply stood at the front of the church to sing without accompaniment. Essie wrote, "Paul sang, the men shouting for songs they wanted! Ol' Man River, Water Boy, Lonesome Road, Fatherland, canoe song from Sanders of the River." Afterward, Paul signed autographs for the soldiers, and Essie accepted messages for their families.

Then, they moved on to Madrid, finally driving in the dark through the streets of the bombarded capital. They stayed at the Palace Hotel, its first two floors serving as a hospital, the upper floors still a luxury hotel. The front line, with a battle continuing, was only a mile and a half away.

Next morning, January 27, they drove through Madrid, seeing barricades everywhere. After lunch, the press interviewed Paul and Haldane. Essie said, "All during the afternoon, we hear artillery and machinegun fire, but by now,

Robeson in costume for a scene from the film *Jericho* in Egypt in 1939. Courtesy *New York Times*.

like real Madrid people, we are used to it." That night, Paul participated in a "splendid" radio broadcast.

They visited a school and a hospital the next day, and in another radio broadcast, Haldane spoke, and Paul sang. A day later, Paul sang to soldiers at barracks not far from the front line. The Robesons left Madrid that afternoon, drove to Valencia for an overnight stop, then proceeded to Barcelona.

Captain Castillo and another officer drove them north to the French border for a fond farewell on January 31. The Robesons went on to Paris to meet Larry Brown for a concert at the Spanish embassy. Paul later called the Spanish trip a "turning point" in his life, making him determined to fight fascism and return to America. Essie, who became more interested in politics, said she was "catching up" with Paul.[9]

* * *

After Robeson returned from Spain in 1938, he and Lawrence Brown went on a concert tour, focusing on working-class audiences. He felt a growing bond with the workers of Britain. And he said he would not make any more movies unless they were "socially significant."

His wife could not resist making one more move in London, taking them from their centrally situated apartment to a three-story house at Number 2 St. Albans Villas, Highgate, near Hampstead Heath. The private house, with a large garden in the rear, suited Essie more than Paul. Her mother left for America, while Pauli lived with his parents in their new home.[10]

They entertained a series of guests there. Marian Anderson, who spent an afternoon with them, spoke highly of President Roosevelt. Another visitor was Jawaharlal Nehru, leader of the Indian Congress Party, who became a friend of the Robesons. And Max Yergan spent several days discussing world affairs with Paul.

* * *

Robeson had joined the Unity Theatre, a group sponsored by the British trade unions, which took over an unused chapel in the St. Pancras area and converted it into a working-class theater. Robeson agreed to participate, with no pay, playing the role of a union organizer in an American play by Ben Bengal.

The play, *Plant in the Sun*, opened on June 14, 1938. It was directed by Herbert Marshal, a friend Robeson had first met in Moscow. It concerned a strike in an American candy factory. Robeson blended his performance with the other actors, all amateurs who held regular day jobs. Most reviews were favorable, although the *London Times* rejected the play as propaganda. The *New Statesman and Nation* called it "a rattling good play . . . [about] realities in the struggle of American labor."

Plant in the Sun ran for two months at the Unity Theatre. In the audience one evening sat Nehru, the future leader of India, who had visited the

Robeson home. The intense, austere Nehru admired Paul and described Essie as "one of the most vital and energetic women I have ever met."

Explaining why he had joined the Unity Theatre and performed without pay, Robeson told an interviewer with the London *Daily Worker*, "I've managed to get some success, but there are thousands who haven't had the chance. It's not enough for one to be able to do it. I want everyone to have the chance."[11]

* * *

When *Plant in the Sun* closed, Robeson and Brown went on a summer concert tour of the provinces, performing for large working-class audiences. Brown called it "the most successful tour we ever had."

The *Glasgow Scotsman* reported that Robeson seemed "overcome with emotion" at the warm reception he received when he sang at the city hall on August 19. It reported an "amazing crowd scene" for another Robeson performance on September 1, when "thousands of people formed into a queue, four deep and a quarter mile long, outside the concert hall."

He continued his concerts for working people and increased his political activities, particularly for Spain, throughout the rest of 1938. He told an interviewer, "I do not think my work is separate from what I believe. . . . I am definitely on the side of the labouring people because I come from labouring people. . . . I am definitely anti-fascist and I am wholeheartedly Popular Front today."[12]

* * *

Robeson and Brown began their 1939 concert tour at the Regal Cinema in Cambridge, continuing through the industrial heartland of Britain, visiting twenty-eight towns and cities, singing for large audiences all along the way. The *Birmingham Mail* reported in March, "Paul Robeson, the great negro artist, who has so sweet a compassion for the underdogs of the world, sang last night in the Birmingham Town Hall."

In America on Easter Sunday, Marian Anderson sang to seventy-five thousand people in front of the Lincoln Memorial in the capital. Eleanor Roosevelt, the president's intrepid First Lady, arranged this special concert after the haughty Daughters of the American Revolution refused to allow Miss Anderson to use their hall because she was Negro. The Robesons felt proud of their friend's concert, which happened to take place on Paul's forty-first birthday.[13]

Robeson and Brown went on a concert tour of Oslo, Copenhagen, and Stockholm in early May. They received a friendly welcome all through Scandinavia, not only for Robeson's singing but also for his strong stand against Nazi Germany, which now threatened the entire region.

* * *

Robeson sailed to New York later in May 1939 to discuss plans for a new play titled *John Henry*. He also gave a few concerts. And he appeared in a one-week revival of *The Emperor Jones*, directed by Harold McGhee, at a suburban theater in White Plains.[14]

During his six weeks in New York, he became elusive, staying secretly at McGhee's apartment. He did his best to avoid numerous requests for public appearances and dodged many old friends, which annoyed the Van Vechtens.

Essie wrote to Paul from London with the complaint, "Nobody can find you." She also wrote him a long letter analyzing the script for *John Henry* and Paul's ability to play the role. She counseled him, wisely, that he should avoid this play.[15]

Robeson returned to London in late June, in time to relax for a month and prepare for his next film, which would be his last in Britain. He also began a regimen of diet and exercise to lose some excess weight, a periodic problem for him.

* * *

In August 1939, Robeson began filming *The Proud Valley*, a story about the gritty men who do the hard, dangerous work of coal miners in South Wales. These were people for whom he had great respect and affection. Michael Balcon produced the film for Ealing Studios, with Pen Tennyson as the director.

Robeson played David Goliath, a down-at-the-heels American who hops onto a train heading for Wales in hope of finding work. He arrives in the village of Blaendy, famous for its choral singers, where some miners are practicing a song, and he spontaneously joins in their singing. The choirmaster, a miner named Dick Parry, welcomes Dave into the group and gets him a job as a coal miner. After Dick dies in a mine accident, Dave sings a beautiful rendition of the spiritual "Deep River" in honor of his fallen comrade.

The accident closes the mine, so the out-of-work miners march to London to seek help in a scene reminiscent of the time when Robeson joined a group of marching miners. The scene may have been written into the movie to reflect his experience. His character, Dave, dies heroically in the movie, which ends triumphantly with the mine opening in time to provide coal for the war effort.

Filming took place on location in the villages of South Wales, where Paul and Essie had a fine time living with the locals. He appeared quite natural in this film, saying later that it was one movie that he could be proud of making.[16]

* * *

Robeson's view of the conflict in Europe became more complicated when Stalin signed a nonaggression pact with Hitler on August 23, 1939, a shocking event. Stalin wanted time to prepare for war, and Hitler wanted to neutralize Russia; both wanted to grab a piece of Poland. William L. Shirer wrote, "For sheer cynicism, the Nazi dictator had met his match in the Soviet despot."[17]

A week later, on September 1, Hitler invaded Poland. Britain and France, honoring a treaty with Poland, declared war on Germany. World War II had begun.

With war overtaking Europe, Robeson completed *The Proud Valley* and made a series of recordings, including "Deep River," while his wife packed their possessions. He had made a total of 170 recordings while living in Britain, singing many spirituals with a power and compassion from the depth of his soul.

On September 30, 1939, less than a week after Robeson finished the film, the family sailed for America. Paul and Essie had separated for two years early in the decade; they had considered divorce, but their marriage survived, and they were together on their way home with their son.

Paul Robeson, now forty-one years old, had lived most of the past twelve years in England, where his career flourished. He had been studying and searching for something to give a deeper meaning to his life. And he found what he sought: a political commitment to fight the Fascists, with faith in the Soviet Union as the leader of this fight.

His wife remained enthralled with life in London; only the outbreak of war persuaded her to leave. Paul also loved London, but he could always feel America calling him home; he went back many times for his concert tours and plays. Now, finally, he was really returning home to America.

* * *

Deep River

Deep river, my home is over Jordan,
Deep river, Lord, I want to cross over into campground.
Deep river, my home is over Jordan,
Deep river, Lord, I want to cross over into campground.

Oh, don't you want to go to the gospel land,
That promised land, where all is peace.
Deep river, my home is over Jordan,
Oh, deep river, Lord, I want to cross over into campground.

—arranged by H. T. Burleigh

• *11* •

"Ballad for Americans"

In '76 the sky was red, thunder rumbling overhead.

—from the ballad

$\mathscr{P}$aul Robeson, with his wife and son, arrived in New York aboard the U.S. ocean liner *Washington* on October 12, 1939. In interviews with reporters at the dock, Robeson stressed his strong opposition to fascism and assailed British and French leaders as "those Munich men" who had tried to appease Hitler. The United States remained at peace and seemed to be coming slowly out of the Great Depression, while the winds of war swirled over Europe.[1]

Returning to Harlem after twelve years in London, the Robesons stayed briefly with their old friends, Hattie and Buddy Bolling, while Essie searched for an apartment. She soon settled Paul and herself into a five-room apartment on the fourteenth floor of a fashionable Harlem building at 555 Edgecombe Avenue. She placed her mother and Pauli in a three-room penthouse, one floor above the apartment. They enrolled Pauli in Fieldston, a highly regarded Ethical Culture school.[2]

Robeson felt at home in Harlem, where he could visit many friends. He also visited his brother, Benjamin, now pastor of the large Mother AME Zion Church on 137th Street. And he sometimes attended Sunday services there, singing hymns with the choir.

* * *

An opportunity of major importance presented itself to Paul Robeson just days after his return to America. Earl Robinson and John Latouche had written a patriotic piece that they called "The Ballad of Uncle Sam." It went into the show *Sing for Your Supper* produced by a federally funded theater project. They suggested the ballad for a new radio series produced by Norman

Corwin and called "The Pursuit of Happiness" on the Columbia Broadcasting System (CBS).

CBS wanted Robeson to appear on the program but considered his fee of $1,000 too high. When Corwin heard the ballad, however, he promptly agreed to pay the fee to induce him to sing on the program. Robeson then went to work with Lawrence Brown and Earl Robinson to prepare for the broadcast.

As they worked on the score, Brown noted that Paul Robeson "impressed his personality on it." He said it aroused Paul's enthusiasm because "it reflected his own great belief in what he thought was American democracy."[3]

Robeson then worked with Earl Robinson, meeting with him for several days in succession. The composer said he appreciated Robeson's painstaking approach to the music. Their only dispute, he said, involved Robeson singing in a lower pitch than the composition's original key. Robinson said of Robeson, "I never worked with a more cooperative person."[4]

The finished ballad proved to be a rousing anthem of patriotism and brotherhood, sung with a chorus and orchestra, lasting eleven minutes. It presented a brief history lesson in catchy colloquial phrases, then soared into an ode to the nation's ethnic diversity. Robeson's voice embodied the spirit of America in the ballad, singing answers to questions posed by the chorus.

* * *

In the afternoon of Sunday, November 5, 1939, less than a month after his return home, Paul Robeson stood in a CBS studio in New York and sang the dramatic composition that Norman Corwin had renamed "Ballad for Americans."

> In '76 the sky was red, thunder rumbling overhead,
> Bad King George couldn't sleep in his bed,
> And on that stormy morn, Old Uncle Sam was born.

From that opening, Robson goes on to sing of the heroic leaders and the simple workers who formed America. The chorus asks, "Are you an American?" He responds with a rapid recitation of almost twenty ethnic groups, beginning "I'm just an Irish, Negro, Jewish, Italian . . . ," ending "Czech and double check, American." He also sings of America's many religions and its varied occupations, concluding with a resounding assertion of the country's glowing future. The simple clarity of his enunciation and phrasing makes the words more meaningful.

In the CBS studio, an audience of six hundred people cheered for two minutes while the program was still on the air. They continued for several minutes after it ended. Hundreds of telephone calls and letters from listeners

Robeson with his wife and son in front of their house in Enfield, Connecticut, published in the magazine *Look* in early 1942. Photograph by Frank Bauman, Museum of the City of New York, *Look* Magazine Collection.

to the national broadcast flooded CBS with praise for the ballad and requests for the lyrics.

Robeson repeated the CBS broadcast on New Year's Day 1940. And he recorded "Ballad for Americans" for Victor Records, producing a best-selling album.[5]

Brooks Atkinson, the distinguished *New York Times* theater critic, wrote a letter to Robeson to say that his singing of "Ballad for Americans" deeply impressed him. The usually austere Atkinson expressed his appreciation for "your voice, which God gave you" and for "the fortitude and honesty of your character, which are qualities for which you are responsible yourself."[6]

* * *

Robeson agreed to star in a new play titled *John Henry,* written by Roark Bradford and based on a legendary black folk hero. Larry Brown urged Paul to go on a concert tour instead of taking on the play. Essie told him, quite accurately, that the script was inadequate. But he insisted that he wanted to get back to "American folk life." And he could be quite stubborn.

The musical drama, presenting "the steel-driving man" of the folk song, endured troubled out-of-town runs in Philadelphia and Boston. The cast included the folksinger Josh White and a chorus to back up Robeson. The singing could not overcome the desultory story.

John Henry opened on Broadway on January 10, 1940. The critics panned the play but praised Robeson's performance, a familiar phenomenon. Brooks Atkinson wrote in the *New York Times* that Robeson was "a man of magnificence who ought to be on the stage frequently in plays that suit him." He added, "For there is something heroic about this huge man with a deep voice and great personal dignity."

John Henry closed in less than a week, confirming the judgment of Essie and Larry Brown. It did little, however, to impede Robeson's progress.

* * *

On January 21, a few days after *John Henry* closed, Robeson traveled to Hamilton College in upstate New York to receive an honorary doctor of humane letters degree. Essie and Larry went with him. The honor had been proposed by Alexander Woollcott, a prominent Hamilton alumnus.

The college's president, Dr. W. H. Cowley, presented the degree to Robeson at a convocation in the college chapel. He said, "We honor you chiefly as a man—a man of tremendous stature, energy and physical dexterity; a man of brilliant mind, a man whose sensitive spirit makes possible your penetrating interpretations; and a man who, above all else, travels across the world as an exemplar of the humanity and the greatness of our democratic heritage."

Robeson responded by expressing the hope that "this troubled, war-torn world" would eventually develop into one with "a true and lasting human culture." He sang "Water Boy" and "Ol' Man River" to the cheering students.

Essie wrote a letter of thanks to Woollcott, who could not attend the ceremony, telling him, "Paul was so moved, and so proud, that he could hardly speak."[7]

* * *

Robeson renewed his close friendship with Benjamin Davis, now a black leader of the Communist Party in the United States. He also resumed working with Max Yergan on the Council on African Affairs to advocate independence for the colonies in Africa.

He rejected an invitation to take part in a benefit performance for Finland, which became a popular cause when it was invaded by its huge neighbor, the Soviet Union. But Robeson contended that the Soviet Union was conducting a "defensive war" against Finland to protect its own borders. And he again denounced "those Munich men" who appeased Hitler and vilified Stalin.[8]

After the Hitler-Stalin pact and the later Russian invasion of Finland, it became much more difficult for supporters of the Soviet Union to support its policies and actions. This was a time when Robeson certainly should have criticized Moscow. His failure to do so, with his persistent defense of Soviet policies, seriously stained his reputation.

Some old Robeson friends, including Walter White and Carl Van Vechten, sharply criticized his stalwart defense of Soviet policies. White's opposition was particularly significant because he had become the top official of the National Association for the Advancement of Colored People.

* * *

In May 1940, Robeson appeared in a *Show Boat* revival with the Los Angeles Civic Light Opera Association, which rewarded him with cheers in the theater and glowing reviews in the press. The *Chicago Defender*, a major black newspaper, reported that when Robeson appeared on the stage, the audience greeted him "like a football cheering crowd."[9] His California trip also involved flying in an airplane for the first time, an experience he enjoyed.

He began his 1940 concert tour in June at Lewisohn Stadium in New York, where he again sang "Ballad for Americans" to a large, enthusiastic audience. After the concert, the Robesons met with Eleanor Roosevelt, whom Essie described in her diary as "charming, but tired, and very gracious."

Robeson, accompanied as usual by Lawrence Brown, went on to appear in concerts across the country. In Los Angeles on July 23, he sang "Ballad for Americans" in the sold-out Hollywood Bowl for thirty thousand fans. Even so, his agent had difficulty obtaining a hotel room for him, finally persuading the luxurious Beverly Wilshire to provide a suite at $100 per night to Robeson under an assumed name.[10]

On July 28, Robeson gave a concert that attracted an enormous crowd estimated at 165,000 people in Chicago's Grant Park. He stood in the band shell of the park and opened with "Go Down, Moses" as people filled thousands of seats and overflowed onto the spacious lawns. They refused to leave at the end of the program until he sang "Ballad for Americans." The *Chicago Defender* declared, "Paul Robeson recaptured Chicago," and called him "the greatest of our living artists."

In his concerts, he frequently sang a Russian folk song or a classic piece by Mussorgsky and some folk songs of other countries, as well as his usual spirituals and now his solo version of "Ballad for Americans."

Robeson took time in the summer of 1940 to appear in a revival of *The Emperor Jones* in several cities, generating excellent reviews.

* * *

While Robeson continued to perform in America, German troops over-ran much of war-torn Europe in 1940, leaving Britain to stand alone against Nazi Germany. Prime Minister Winston Churchill stepped forward as the voice of the British lion, roaring defiance of "Hitler and his Nazi gang."

Robeson embarked on another concert tour with Brown in the fall of 1940. This time he took Clara Rockmore along as an "associate artist." Clara, a musician born in Russia, was the second wife of Paul's lawyer, Robert Rockmore. She had started her career as a violinist, but an arm injury forced her to give up that instrument. She now played an unusual musical instrument called a theremin, which involved moving her hands through a magnetic field to produce delicate sounds. It was Essie's idea for Paul to take Clara on tour with him.

Their tour began on October 6, 1940, at Carnegie Hall, where the au-dience greeted Robeson with prolonged applause. Three days later, after a concert at Rutgers, he told the audience, "I have been to many parts of the world, but the happiest days of my life were spent on this campus."

Robeson, with Lawrence Brown and Clara Rockmore, continued on their tour to Minneapolis, then to Salt Lake City and Provo, Utah, and on to the West Coast, Chicago, and several other cities, returning to New York to perform at town hall.

On stage, Clara stood next to her unusual instrument, which looked like a small cabinet plugged in like a radio, with two antennae, one that deter-mined volume and the other tone. She moved her hands through the elec-tromagnetic field to produce tones similar to a violin and cello as she played Bach, Brahms, and Ravel.

Clara, petite and pretty, often spoke Russian with Paul. They became close friends, but not romantic, as they toured together for three years. She recalled how pleased he was when reviewers praised her, an example of his generous spirit. Paul confided in Clara, allowing her to see his usually hidden pain and anger at the racism they encountered in trains, restaurants, and hotels. In public, he and Clara spoke to each other in Russian to confuse outsiders. He said, "Let them go nuts trying to figure it out."[11]

Another woman who heard Robeson's anger over racism at this time was the exquisite Lena Horne, talented but insecure, early in her career. He saw her at a Greenwich Village cabaret, where she sang in 1940 and 1941, and he offered his friendship, discussed her problems, and encouraged her. She said that "this incredible man" helped her gain self-respect as a person and per-former. Denying rumors of a romance between them, she said she regarded Paul as her helpful older brother.

Lena Horne recalled that Paul seemed hopeful about the future of the Negro people in America. She added that he was "deeply angry about what all our people suffer" but never angry at white people as a group. He helped her overcome some of her bitterness about racism.[12]

* * *

In early 1941, Eslanda Robeson went house hunting in Connecticut for a country home. She found a large colonial-style house on two acres in Enfield, which a bank wanted to sell for $19,000. The property, known as The Beeches, included a swimming pool, a billiards room, a bowling alley, and a tennis court. It had been unoccupied for some time, however, and needed substantial work.

Before buying the house, Essie required the bank to obtain assurances from the neighbors that they would not object to the Robesons moving into their white community. She then took over supervising the repairs.

The Robeson family, including Essie's mother, moved into their new home in June. Essie wrote to the Van Vechtens that they loved living in the country, adding, "Big Paul loves the quiet" and returns when he can.[13]

Paul seemed most fond of Essie when there was some distance between them. In a letter from Los Angeles that summer, he wrote, "I love you very, very much and miss you until it hurts. I do like my place so much both in Conn. and in your heart—and I feel I'm camping out until I get back to both."

When not on his frequent tours, however, he preferred New York City to Connecticut. He made an arrangement with Freda Diamond and her husband, Barry Baruch, who lived in a townhouse in Greenwich Village. They provided a private floor of their home to the restless Paul, who usually stayed there when he spent time in New York in the early 1940s.

This arrangement worked for all concerned. Paul had a refuge, hidden away from the many people who sought his attention, and he played chess with a friendly Barry. Freda said she had a happy marriage with Barry, while she also loved Paul during their long friendship.

Essie became a close friend of Freda after realizing that her position as Mrs. Paul Robeson was not in danger. She began studying for a doctoral degree in anthropology at the Hartford Seminary in Connecticut. She also took writing courses at Columbia University. And she succeeding in turning the journal of her African trip into a book titled *African Journey*.

* * *

Reviews of *The Proud Valley* lacked enthusiasm when it opened in the United States in 1941. But Robeson took pride in this one movie.

He continued his varied political activities in addition to his concerts throughout 1941. He joined several leftist leaders, including Max Yergan

Close-up of Enfield house photograph. Photograph by Frank Bauman, Museum of the City of New York, *Look* Magazine Collection.

and Congressman Vito Marcantonio, in a rally at Madison Square Garden to demand that the government free Earl Browder, the imprisoned Communist Party leader.

In Detroit, Robeson campaigned for the United Automobile Workers, part of the Congress of Industrial Organizations (CIO). He strongly endorsed the CIO branch of organized labor as the most effective force to help black workers. The autoworkers won their battle with the vehemently antiunion Henry Ford, compelling him to hold a union election and negotiate labor contracts, shortly after Robeson's appearance there in May 1941. A month later, under pressure from A. Philip Randolph, the black union leader and civil rights activist, President Roosevelt created the Fair Employment Practices Committee, which tried to eliminate discrimination against blacks seeking jobs in the growing defense industry.

Robeson appeared at a Chinese War Relief rally, cosponsored by the left-wing National Negro Congress. But Eleanor Roosevelt, an original supporter of the event, withdrew to avoid associating with extreme leftists. He also sang at the convention of the National Maritime Union (NMU) in Cleveland in the summer of 1941, where the left-wing union made him an honorary member amid prolonged applause led by NMU president Joe Curran. And with Count Basie's orchestra, he recorded an unusual jazz tribute to heavyweight champion Joe Louis in the fall.[14]

Robeson began to place his right hand lightly over his right ear to hear himself better while singing. It soon became characteristic of him to raise one large hand to the side of his face from time to time, using his long fingers to cover his ear, as he sang at concerts and rallies.[15]

* * *

On June 22, 1941, German troops invaded the Soviet Union, driving the Russians into the war on the side of the Western Allies. This transformed Russia from a Communist villain into a friendly ally, making it easier for Robeson to voice his support. Then, on December 7, 1941, Japan attacked Pearl Harbor, propelling the United States into World War II.

Robeson worked relentlessly for the war effort throughout 1942, with the United States and the Soviet Union now together in the fight against fascism. He sold war bonds, sang to troops for the USO, and participated in rallies.

In February, Robeson gave a concert in Kansas City, Missouri, where he found Negroes were confined to the balcony. After intermission, he announced he would sing the rest of the concert under protest because of the segregation in the auditorium. He said, "I have made a life-long habit of refusing to sing in Southern states or anywhere that audiences are segregated."

He attended a dinner honoring him as one of the country's leading anti-Fascists on March 23. Dorothy Parker presided at the dinner in the Biltmore Hotel in New York. One thousand people attended the sold-out event.

At Madison Square Garden on June 22, 1942, the first anniversary of the German invasion of Russia, he took part in a rally for Russian War Relief, with prominent figures that included Mayor Fiorello La Guardia, Soviet Ambassador Maxim Litvinov, and the renowned pianist Arthur Rubenstein.

This new, friendly view of the Soviet Union did not extend to J. Edgar Hoover's Federal Bureau of Investigation, which had already assigned agents to follow Robeson's activities. FBI agents monitored his mail and telephones. Hoover put him on a secret list of supposedly dangerous subversives to be seized immediately in case of a national emergency.[16]

* * *

Robeson donated his services to an independent company, Frontier Films, for a feature-length documentary, *Native Land*, released in 1942. It reenacted material from a Senate investigation about abusive attacks against unions and blacks. Robeson provided an off-camera narration.[17]

Hollywood drew Robeson to the West Coast for a Twentieth Century Fox film called *Tales of Manhattan*, also released in 1942, an episodic movie tracing the history of a formal jacket that passes from one owner to another, each with a tale to tell. The star-filled cast included Charles Boyer, Rita Hayworth, Henry Fonda, Ginger Rogers, Charles Laughton, and Edward G. Robinson. In the fifth and final episode, featuring Paul Robeson, Ethel Waters, and Eddie Anderson, the jacket, holding more than $40,000 in cash, falls from an airplane into a community of poor, naive Negroes, who shout hallelujah, share the cash, and use the jacket to dress a scarecrow.

The movie attracted a sizable audience because of its cast, but some black newspapers criticized Robeson for appearing in a stereotyped role. Robeson, who received $10,000 for playing in *Tales of Manhattan*, voiced his own displeasure with the movie in press interviews. He said he was quitting Hollywood until the movie industry started to present Negroes in a more realistic way. This was 1942. And he never made another movie.

Paul Robeson scorned Hollywood, turning down opportunities to make a great deal of money. He was that unusual celebrity who remained a regular guy devoid of pretension. For most of his career, when anyone approached him, young or old, black or white, he would easily engage the individual in friendly conversation. Neither fame nor fortune could change his character.

* * *

Ballad for Americans

In '76 the sky was red. . . .
Old Sam put on a three-cornered hat
And in a Richmond church he sat,
And Patrick Henry told him that
While America drew breath,
It was liberty or death.

Am I an American?
I'm just an Irish, Negro, Jewish, Italian,
French and English, Spanish, Russian,
Chinese, Polish, Scotch, Hungarian,
Litvak, Swedish, Finnish, Canadian,
Greek, and Turk, and Czech,
And double-check, American.

Our country's strong, our country's young,
And its greatest songs are still unsung,

From the plains and mountains we have sprung
To keep the faith with those who went before.

For I have always believed it,
And I believe it now,
And you know who I am—AMERICA!

—music by Earl Robinson; lyrics by
John Latouche; permission to use copyrighted
lyrics from Sony/ATV Music Publishing

· *12* ·

Othello on Broadway

What is America to me?

—from "The House I Live In"

$\mathscr{P}$aul Robeson and Margaret Webster began working together to present a new production of *Othello* in New York in 1942.

Webster, daughter of the notable English actors May Whitty and Ben Webster, was an experienced actress and director who had worked with the plays of Shakespeare in the past. She would direct the new *Othello* and assemble the cast to support Robeson, whom she knew from their time in London. When she looked for a New York producer, however, those she found were afraid to mount a play in which a black man loves and kills a white woman.

Without a New York producer, Robeson and Webster decided to put together their own production and try it out in summer stock theaters. They found two theaters in college towns willing to accept the play in the summer of 1942. First, they would open at the Brattle Theater in Cambridge, Massachusetts, and then move to the McCarter Theater in Princeton, New Jersey.

Webster selected a talented young couple, Uta Hagen and her husband, Jose Ferrer, for the key roles of Desdemona and Iago. Webster took on the role of Emilia herself. With a tight budget and limited time, they rehearsed for only two weeks to prepare for the opening in Cambridge.

The cast diligently worked ten hours a day during rehearsals, while both Webster and Hagen grew concerned about Robeson's acting ability. Hagen told her father, "Robeson is going to be very bad," but added, "He's an angel." Webster said Robeson depended on his intelligence and energy, not acting skill, because he knows he has "no technique." She observed that her star relied on his own feelings, not Othello's, but "fortunately his tremendous vocal resources protect him."[1]

* * *

An intense heat wave smothered Cambridge in the first week of August when *Othello* opened at the Brattle Theater. Despite all the obstacles, including the limited rehearsals and skepticism about Robeson's acting, the opening turned into a triumph. The audience, including many summer students from nearby Harvard University, applauded, cheered, and shouted bravo in an extended ovation. Boston critics praised the production, one of them calling it "a great artistic achievement." Hailing Robeson's performance, *Variety* declared that no white actor should ever presume to play this role again.

After the week in Cambridge, *Othello* moved on to Princeton's McCarter Theater, where it began a two-week run on August 17. It again drew the praise of critics and audiences in the college town where Paul was born. A backstage visitor was Albert Einstein, the Princeton resident universally regarded as the century's greatest scientist, who became a friend and admirer of Paul Robeson.

One of Robeson's cousins, Minnie Carraway, still living in Princeton at that time, went to the theater for the first time in her life. Recalling Paul's performance in *Othello*, she said, "Oh, he was wonderful." Later he walked up the street to her home. "He came right here on the porch and sat down and we talked for an hour."[2]

The out-of-town success won the respect of New York producers, now willing to bring *Othello* to Broadway. Webster selected the prestigious Theatre Guild to produce the play. Paul had a number of prior commitments, however, that prevented him from going forward with the production until next year.

* * *

Robeson spoke out repeatedly in support of the nation's war effort; he sang for the troops at military camps and participated in rallies to sell war bonds in 1942 and 1943. He also recorded a significant album titled *Songs of Free Men*, which received high praise from music critic Howard Taubman in the *New York Times*. This album included four songs in Russian—"From Border to Border," "Oh, How Proud Our Quiet Don," the Red Army's "Song of the Plains," and "Native Land"—as well as "The Peet Bog Soldiers" in German, "The Four Insurgent Generals" in Spanish, and "Joe Hill" and "The Purest Kind of a Guy" in English. He sang these politically oriented songs in a voice of compelling power. All were recorded with Lawrence Brown at the piano on January 27 and 30, 1942.[3]

In September, Robeson addressed a New York rally sponsored by the Council on African Affairs to support freedom for India from British rule. He supported freedom for all colonies, especially in Africa, but he also felt strongly about India, particularly because of his personal friendship with Jawaharlal Nehru. He told the rally that the war against Germany, Italy, and Japan was really "a war for the liberation of all peoples, all races, all colors oppressed anywhere in the world." He also traveled to California to sing and voice similar views to thousands of aircraft workers at an aviation plant and at mass rallies in San Francisco and Los Angeles in September.

Then, with Lawrence Brown and Clara Rockmore, he embarked on an unusually long concert tour that began in October 1942 and continued through the northern part of the country for six months. Robeson interrupted his tour to return to New York to lead a memorial service for his friend, Alexander Woollcott, who died in January. He read the Twenty-third Psalm at the service, held in the McMillan Theater at Columbia University.

The concert tour ended on April 5, 1943, in Mansfield, Ohio. His program included folk songs from England, France, Russia, and China, along with "Ballad for Americans." The *Mansfield Times* called the concert there "a sort of United Nations tribute."

He returned to New York in April, plagued by a persistent cold and overweight due to lack of exercise.

* * *

On May 2, with the long concert tour over, Robeson sang at a large "Labor for Victory" rally at Yankee Stadium, with Mayor Fiorello La Guardia of New York as the main speaker. Robeson told the cheering crowd of fifty-four thousand, "We are here because we believe in the dignity of man and the right to freedom of all mankind."[4]

On a rare trip into the South, he went to Georgia to receive an honorary degree, doctor of humane letters, from Morehouse College in Atlanta on June 1. The college's president, Dr. Benjamin E. Mays, said, "We are proud to be the first Negro college in the world to place its stamp of approval upon the leadership of a man who embodies all the hopes and aspirations of the Negro race and who, despite crippling restrictions, breathes the pure air of freedom."

Responding at the college's commencement ceremony, Robeson observed, "Racial and religious prejudice continue to cast an ugly shadow on the principles for which we are fighting." He said the black youth of the South held "the greatest hope of my people." And he sang several folk songs to the prolonged applause of the students.[5]

Later in June, he gave an outdoor concert for twenty-two thousand in Washington, DC, where he sang "Ballad for Americans." Lawrence Brown described the audience as equally divided between blacks and whites, sitting side by side, and they all stood up and cheered at the end. He said this crowd's reaction to the ballad was more intense than in the North because of the Jim Crow tradition in Washington.

Then came a series of meetings for six weeks in New York, Chicago, and San Francisco to support the war-effort. At the Great Lakes Naval Station, near Chicago, Robeson sang Beethoven's "Creation's Hymn" and the English folk song "Oh, No, John" to two thousand officers and enlisted men.

In an interview with the *Chicago Defender*, Robeson said India "holds the key to the entire post-war problem as it relates to race." He added, "India will be given her freedom, I have no doubt of that. Britain, regardless of her feelings in the matter, will be compelled to grant this."

Robeson appeared with the New York Philharmonic Orchestra and Robert Shaw's Collegiate Chorale before an audience of twenty thousand at a concert in Lewisohn Stadium in New York on July 1. He also sang and spoke at several union-sponsored events during that summer of 1943.

* * *

During periods of rest at home in Enfield, Paul bonded more closely with his teenage son. They had serious discussions about life, often played chess and ping pong together, and worked out with a football while Paul gave his son suggestions about how to improve his game.

Pauli asked his father what was the most important thing to him, his politics or his race. He replied, "I'm a human being first, a Negro second, and a Marxist third," adding that all three were "inseparably connected." When his son asked him why he had never joined the Communist Party, he replied that he was not willing to submit to the party's discipline. He told his son that he did what he wanted to do and said what he wanted to say; he would listen to others, "but I make my own decisions."[6]

* * *

As the summer of 1943 drew to a close, Robeson prepared to go ahead with *Othello*. He grew a beard for the role, brought his weight down to his normal 230 pounds, and accepted a salary of $1,500 a week for the play, much less than he earned as a singer, which was $2,000 or more for one concert.

With rehearsals about to begin, the Theatre Guild, as producers of the play, found fault with Jose Ferrer and Uta Hagen. They expressed anxiety about Ferrer's draft status and objected to his insistence on star billing and substantial salaries for himself and his wife—and neither would work without the other.

Robeson and Webster supported Ferrer's position, but the producers decided to bring in two replacements—Virginia Gilmore as Desdemona and

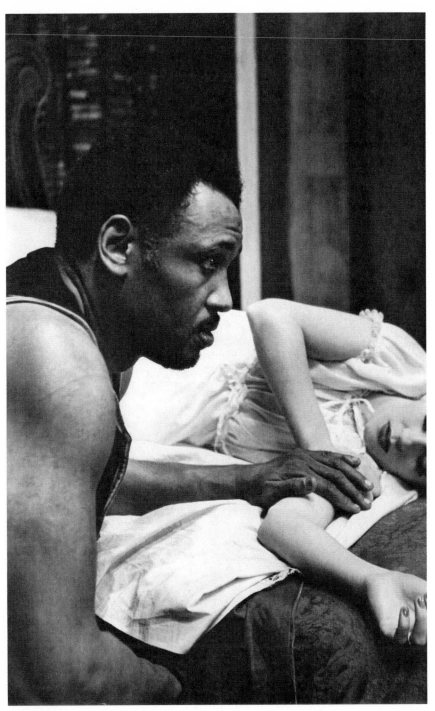

Paul Robeson as Othello with Uta Hagen as Desdemona on Broadway in 1943. Courtesy Associated Press.

Stefan Schnabel as Iago. Webster seemed satisfied. But Robeson intervened to retain the Ferrers, arranging for them to have a prominent place in advertising, short of star billing, and to receive the pay that they wanted. Revising her view of Robeson, Webster said, "This sweet, unassuming, dear, big bear of a man could crush us all." She added that he always got what he demanded, but it was "more often something for the Ferrers than for himself."[7]

The Theatre Guild tried out *Othello* for a week in New Haven, beginning on September 11, then moved to Boston and finally Philadelphia, completing more than a month of out-of-town performances before opening in New York.

* * *

On the evening of October 19, 1943, Paul Robeson opened in *Othello* at the Shubert Theater in the heart of the Broadway theater district. He presented a strong, dramatic presence on stage, with his powerful figure draped in the flowing robes of the noble but tragic Moor, the state's proud general.

Robeson said he portrayed Shakespeare's Moor as "a great Negro warrior." He added, "I am not a great actor like Jose Ferrer. All I do is feel the part. I made myself believe I am Othello, and I acted as he would act." For Paul, the play was a tragedy of honor, not of jealousy: Othello kills Desdemona because her perceived infidelity betrays him, tarnishing his sense of honor. Iago deceives him into believing that Desdemona has been unfaithful, so Othello strangles her and stabs himself.

Uta Hagen played faithful Desdemona with distinction, and Jose Ferrer played insidious Iago with a sinister flair. In his final speech in the play, which would become a virtual theme of his own life, Robeson spoke Shakespeare's words with tragic solemnity:

> Soft you, a word or two before you go.
> I have done the state some service, and they know't.
> No more of that.
>
> I pray you, in your letters,
> When you shall these unlucky deeds relate,
> Speak of me as I am, nothing extenuate,
> Nor set down aught in malice.
> Then, must you speak of one
> Who loved not wisely but too well . . .
>
> I kissed thee ere I killed thee.
> No way but this, killing myself,
> To die upon a kiss.

The opening night audience responded with an enormous ovation, applauding for twenty minutes, shouting bravo, and bringing the cast back on stage for ten curtain calls. Finally, compelled to give a brief speech, Margaret Webster said they had dreamed of such a night. Turning to Robeson, who was surrounded by the entire cast, she said, "Paul, we are all very proud of you tonight." The audience broke into another round of cheers.[8]

* * *

When *Othello* opened, Robeson was staying at the apartment of his friends Harold and Bert McGhee. They recalled that Paul beamed with pleasure when they read the reviews. Bert said, "After he had read every one of them, he said, 'Boy I'm lucky. Did you ever know such luck as I have?' It was just as though he had made his first success." She added she would never forget how Paul reacted to all the praise, how "modesty is a basic part of his character."[9]

The *World Telegram* hailed this *Othello* as "one of the most memorable events in the history of the theater." William Randolph Hearst's *Journal-American* cited "the magnificent performance of Paul Robeson in the title role." The *Herald Tribune* and the *Daily News* agreed that Robeson gave a memorable performance, although they had varied complaints. Ferrer's Iago and Hagen's Desdemona won high praise from everyone.[10]

In the *New York Times*, Louis Nichols wrote, "Excellently done both in the production and in the acting, it is the best interpretation of *Othello* to be seen here in a good many years, and one that should remain on hand for a long time to come." The *Times*, in a note alongside the review, added, "Not for several seasons has a play received the tumultuous applause that was accorded last night's presentation of Shakespeare's *Othello* starring Paul Robeson. Cries of 'bravo' echoed through the packed Shubert Theater." *Time* magazine described Robeson as "magnificent" in *Othello*. It added that he was "probably the most famous living Negro."

According to Uta Hagen, Robeson's success in *Othello* stemmed from his "great humanity" on stage. She found his performance rather conventional, but noted, "Everyone melted at his personality."[11]

Othello continued on Broadway for 296 performances, a record at the time for any production of Shakespeare in New York. It ran into the summer of 1944.

* * *

During the run of *Othello*, Robeson took time to speak out for his favorite causes: obtaining equal rights for American Negroes, winning freedom for colonial peoples, and promoting support for the Soviet Union. In November, a month after *Othello* opened, he addressed the annual *Herald Tribune* forum in New York. He asserted that three things were arousing "the bitterest resentment among black Americans": first, economic insecurity from continuing discrimination in employment; second, segregation and the inferior status of Negroes in the armed forces; and third, the South's poll tax system, which maintained "undemocratic elements in places of authority." He concluded by quoting President Roosevelt's words on the anniversary of the Atlantic Charter to the effect that "our enemies are not only Germany, Italy and Japan; they are all the forces of oppression, intolerance, insecurity and injustice which have impeded the forward march of civilization."[12]

Also in November, the longshoremen's union on the West Coast made Robeson an honorary member on the recommendation of its left-wing president, Harry Bridges. On a personal note, Essie wrote to the Van Vechtens that she considered her marriage a very good one, "with all its ups and downs, mostly ups."

* * *

On December 3, 1943, Robeson addressed the commissioner of baseball, Kenesaw M. Landis, and the owners of the major league teams at the Hotel Roosevelt in New York. At the time, organized baseball barred all black players from its teams, relegating them to their own separate, far from equal, Negro league. A group of black newspaper publishers came to the meeting with Robeson to request immediate acceptance of qualified black players.

"It is unnecessary to introduce Paul Robeson," Commissioner Landis said at the meeting. "Everybody knows him or what he's done as an athlete and an artist."

Robeson responded, "This is an excellent time to bring about an entry of Negro players into organized baseball. The time has come that you must change your attitude toward Negroes. . . . I urge you to decide favorably on this request and that action be taken this very season."[13]

It would take until 1946 for Jackie Robinson to play for Montreal in the International League and then for the Brooklyn Dodgers in 1947, finally breaking the color barrier in baseball.

* * *

With *Othello*, Robeson reached the pinnacle of his success and popularity. He received the Abraham Lincoln Medal for distinguished service in human relations in 1943, as well as the Page One Award of the New York Newspaper Guild for his performance in *Othello*. The next year he won the Donaldson Award for "outstanding achievement in the theater" and the Gold Medal of the American Academy of Arts and Sciences for the best diction in the American theater.

Robeson spoke on a national radio program in January 1944 celebrating the eightieth anniversary of the Emancipation Proclamation. Asserting that the proclamation's promise had not yet been fulfilled, he said racial progress was now linked to the outcome of the war. He declared, "Today's struggle of the Negro has become part of the world-wide struggle against fascism."[14]

The Council on African Affairs sponsored a giant party for his forty-sixth birthday in April 1944. It was attended by eight thousand people at the Seventeenth Regiment Amory on Park Avenue, with an overflow of five thousand on the street. Among the performers were Duke Ellington, Count Basie, Jimmy Durante, and Zero Mostel. Congratulatory messages came from diverse notables, including Vice President Henry Wallace, Babe Ruth, Charles Boyer, Oscar Hammerstein, Helen Hayes, Theodore Dreiser, and Earl Browder. Black educator Mary McLeod Bethune described Paul most memorably as "the tallest tree in our forest."[15]

An article by Jerome Beatty in the *American Magazine* began, "Paul Robeson, playing *Othello* this season in New York, has not only broken all American box-office records for this Shakespearean tragedy; he has established himself firmly as America's most distinguished living Negro." And the *Chicago Defender* said later in the year, "Paul Robeson is possibly now the foremost political leader of the Negro people."[16]

* * *

Othello closed in New York on July 1, 1944. The cast had a two-month summer vacation before taking the play on a cross-country tour that began in September. They performed in forty-five cities, avoiding any that segregated Negroes in the audience. The long tour continued with great success into the following spring. And the cast recorded the complete play for Columbia Records.

In a familiar pattern, Robeson engaged in an affair with his leading lady, Uta Hagen, even though her husband, Jose Ferrer, was on the road tour with them. She told biographer Martin Duberman that the affair began when she and Paul were standing in the wings one night waiting to go on stage. He suddenly caressed her, and "I got unbelievably excited."

Hagen said her husband, who was seeing another member of the cast, seemed "happy to pass me off onto Paul." Uta, who was twenty-four years old when *Othello* opened, said she idolized Paul and fell deeply in love with him. She and Paul spent hours together reading plays, listening to music, and studying things that interested him. She characterized him as brilliant and exciting, never arrogant, and "unbelievably endearing."[17]

The extended road trip of *Othello* ended in May 1945 with a month of performances at the Erlanger Theater in Chicago. Then, it reopened in New York at the City Center for three more weeks. During the entire tour,

Robeson insisted that he would perform only in theaters that were not segregated, setting a significant precedent.[18]

Robeson received another honorary doctor of humane letters degree the following month, this time from Howard University in Washington, DC.

* * *

Paul Robeson had high hopes as the Allies moved toward victory in 1945. He had strongly supported the war effort and plans to create the United Nations. He looked forward to a postwar world that would include gaining Negro rights, ending colonialism, and establishing world peace. His patriotic optimism was reflected in a new song he began to sing titled "The House I Live In." With music by Earl Robinson and lyrics by Lewis Allen, the song's sentiments recalled the earlier "Ballad for Americans."

Robeson had campaigned for the reelection of President Roosevelt in 1944. He also campaigned for his friend Benjamin Davis, the Harlem Communist, who won a seat on the New York City Council.

On April 12, 1945, President Roosevelt died suddenly. Most Americans mourned as Vice President Harry S. Truman succeeded him. The United States dropped two atomic bombs on Japan in August 1945, finally ending World War II.

Robeson had supported Roosevelt but would oppose Truman.

* * *

The House I Live In

What is America to me?
A name, a map, or the flag I see?
A certain word, "democracy"?
What is America to me?

The house I live in,
A plot of earth, a street . . .
All races, all religions,
That's America to me.

But especially the people,
That's America to me.

—music by Earl Robinson; lyrics by
Lewis Allen; permission to use
copyrighted lyrics from G. Schirmer, Inc.

· *13* ·

Confronting the President

Joshua fit de battle of Jericho.

—spiritual

*P*aul Robeson and Lawrence Brown put on army uniforms in August 1945 to travel overseas on a tour for the military-sponsored USO to sing for American soldiers shortly after the end of World War II. The five-week tour took them into France and Czechoslovakia as well as the American zone of occupied Germany. They were accompanied by some white musicians, forming the first interracial unit sent overseas to entertain the troops. Brown recalled that they gave twenty-five concerts, most of them at army bases and theaters, including a concert in "what had been Hitler's opera house in Nuremberg."

Soon after returning to the United States, Robeson received the Spingarn Medal, the most prestigious award in the Negro community. The NAACP awarded the medal annually "to the man or woman of African descent and American citizenship, who shall have made the highest achievement during the preceding year or years in any honorable field of human endeavor." The award ceremony, held in October, took place at a banquet in the Hotel Biltmore in New York. Essie sat at the table of honor with Paul and contralto Marian Anderson, arranger Harry T. Burleigh, playwright Marc Connelly, and Arthur B. Spingarn, the NAACP president. Congratulatory telegrams came from Eleanor Roosevelt and Henry Wallace.

In accepting the award, Robeson expressed his concern that America's policies seemed to be moving away from civil rights and toward colonialism, with indications of a new hostility toward the Soviet Union. He declared that black Americans expected the recent war's fight for democracy to achieve results here at home. And he said that India and other colonial lands expected to get the independence promised to them.

A prominent black newspaper, the *Pittsburgh Courier*, reported that Robeson "shocked his several hundred listeners by voicing frank and pronounced preferences for Soviet principles." It quoted him as saying, "Full employment in Russia is a fact, not a myth, and discrimination is non-existent."[1] Walter White, who presided over the Spingarn ceremony, became more and more upset by Robeson's remarks, which White regarded as excessively harsh criticism of America.

Leading the fight for India's independence was Robeson's old friend, Jawaharlal Nehru, who also expressed admiration for the accomplishments of the Soviet Union. Nehru disliked the repression and regimentation there, but he was impressed by "the reports of the great progress made by the backward regions of Central Asia under the Soviet regime."[2]

* * *

In the autumn of 1945, Robeson and Brown began a long, strenuous tour that encompassed more than a hundred concerts over several months and continued into the spring of 1946. Their concert programs included a first section devoted to English, French, Italian, and German songs, followed by selections from Mendelssohn's *Elijah* and arias from Mussorgsky, then a final group of spirituals. Paul sang encores from his Columbia album *Songs of Free Men*, which included the "Four Insurgent Generals" from the Spanish Civil War. He also frequently included the militant labor song "Joe Hill" composed by Earl Robinson.[3]

Robeson also made numerous political appearances between his concert engagements, attending rallies and union meetings. Disappointed and disillusioned with American policies after the war, as President Truman shifted to the right, Robeson spoke out with renewed vigor against lynchings and the denial of Negro rights at home, colonialism abroad, and the growing antagonism toward our recent wartime ally, the Soviet Union.

* * *

Racial violence in the form of beatings, shootings, and lynchings erupted in the South and other parts of the United States in the year after the war's end. This provided a sad return for black soldiers. But the government was focused on foreign affairs.

On March 5, 1946, Winston Churchill spoke in Fulton, Missouri, declaring that "an iron curtain" had descended in Europe, as the Soviet Union exerted control over the eastern part of the continent. His speech defined the division of Europe for the coming Cold War.

President Truman, who attended Churchill's "iron curtain" speech, soon established American policy in direct and relentless opposition to the Soviet

Union. Truman viewed this emerging Cold War as the ultimate conflict between good and evil. America had found a new enemy to oppose for the next four decades.[4]

On April 30, 1946, Robeson gave a concert in Chicago that drew rave reviews. The *News* declared, "A GREAT basso—maybe an even greater personality! That was Paul Robeson in an inspired recital at Orchestra Hall last night. It was the concluding concert of a triumphant transcontinental tour."

The *New York Times* carried an advertisement on June 3 addressed to America and the United Nations. It said 150 million Africans and most of the continent of Africa remained in "colonial subjection." In bold letters, it asked, "Will America help free Africa? Or will it seek instead a larger share of the profits squeezed out of Africa's oppressed people? America must answer!" This message was signed by Paul Robeson, chairman, and Max Yergan, executive director, of the Council on African Affairs.

* * *

Three days later, Robeson spoke at a Madison Square Garden rally for South African relief, sponsored by the Council on African Affairs. He said the American Negro had a firsthand understanding of "imperialist exploitation and oppression," for the Negro in the United States experienced "the same system of job discrimination, segregation and denial of democratic rights."

He argued that a warmongering cry of "Stop Russia" had arisen as a result of American and British policies directed against their wartime ally. "The 'Stop Russia' cry really means—stop the advance of the colonial peoples of Asia and Africa toward independence; stop the forces of the new democracy developing in Europe; stop the organized workers of America from trying to hold their ground against their profit-greedy employers; stop the Negro people from voting and joining trade unions in the South."[5]

On July 17, Robeson sang to picketers at the strike-bound Chrysler plant in Windsor, Ontario, across the border from Detroit. He also walked in their picket line, the *Canadian Press* reported, and "shook hands with every man in the line." It was one of several appearances that he made to speak and sing for labor unions that summer.

At another Madison Square Garden rally on September 12, Robeson appeared with Henry Wallace, then a member of President Truman's cabinet. Robeson vigorously denounced the wave of lynchings in the South. But it was Wallace who made headlines. He broke with Truman's "get-tough-with-Russia" policy, calling instead for a more cooperative and conciliatory foreign policy. The president compelled Wallace to resign from the cabinet a week later.

* * *

Paul Robeson, joined by W. E. B. Du Bois and others, now spearheaded a new group called the American Crusade to End Lynching. They planned a conference and a mass rally in Washington for September 23, 1946.

At Robeson's request, Albert Einstein agreed to cochair the group with him. They had become friends when Einstein attended Robeson's performances in Princeton. Einstein's fragile health precluded his making the trip to Washington, but he lent his prestige to the group. He wrote a letter to President Truman wholeheartedly endorsing the demand that "every citizen be guaranteed protection against acts of violence."[6]

The American Crusade to End Lynching convened its conference in Washington as scheduled on September 23 with fifteen hundred representatives of black as well as white organizations. It called for a strong federal program to curb mob violence. It also sent a ten-member delegation to see President Truman at the White House. Truman agreed to meet the delegation, headed by Paul Robeson and Mrs. Harper Sibley, president of the United Council of Church Women.

* * *

At 11:30 a.m., the delegation was ushered into the Oval Office to meet President Truman. Mrs. Sibley asked the president to issue a public statement denouncing lynching and to recommend federal legislation to end "the disgrace of mob violence."

President Truman responded that government action against lynching was a political matter, not a moral issue, and that the time was not right for him to speak out. He then showed some anger when Mrs. Sibley compared fascism against Jews in Europe to fascism against Negroes in America.

Robeson said it "seemed inept" for the United States to take the lead in prosecuting Nazis in the war crimes trial in Germany while the government failed to give "justice to Negroes in this country."

President Truman said Americans should not tie domestic matters to the international situation. He added that America and Britain were "the last refuge for freedom in the world."

At a critical point, Robeson told the president that the mood of Negroes in this country had changed, that returning veterans were determined to get justice, and that the government's failure to act could produce an "emergency situation."

President Truman, shaking his fist in anger, said that sounded like "a threat." Robeson assured the president that it was not a threat but a statement of fact about the attitude of the Negro people. The meeting ended with the president irritated and the delegation discouraged.[7]

* * *

Robeson in front of the Lincoln Memorial after meeting with President Harry S. Truman in 1946. Courtesy Bettemann/Corbis via Associated Press.

Reporters met the delegates outside the White House after the meeting with the president. When a reporter asked Robeson if he was a Communist, he replied, "I label myself as a violent anti-Fascist." Asked if he followed the Communist Party line, he responded, "It depends on what you mean by the Communist Party line. Right now the Communist Party is against lynching. I'm against lynching."

Standing in front of the Lincoln Memorial later that day, Robeson gave a radio address, declaring he felt "ashamed" that it was still necessary, so many years after Lincoln signed the Emancipation Proclamation, to speak of "the lynch terror and mob assaults against Negro Americans."

"People of America," he said, "we appeal to you to help wipe out this inhuman bestiality, this Ku Klux Klan hooded violence . . . as we have today appealed to the President."[8]

For Robeson, the meeting with President Truman came as a dramatic turning point. The president's refusal to act against lynchings, this most brutal violence against black people, amounted to a terrible outrage that demonstrated the worst aspect of the United States—and a sharp contrast to the Soviet Union. Lynchings had produced a profound anger in Robeson.

The press questions about whether he was a Communist signaled the direction that criticism of him would take from then on. We might consider how Paul Robeson's increasingly critical view of America might have been quite different if President Truman had responded positively at their meeting and strongly endorsed the antilynching campaign.

* * *

On October 7, 1946, Robeson was summoned to a hearing in San Francisco by the state legislature's Joint Fact-finding Committee on Un-American Activities in California, where he testified at length and under oath.[9] The committee's chairman, State Senator Jack B. Tenney, asked him if he was a member of the Communist Party, adding, "I ask it of everybody, so don't feel embarrassed."

"No, I am not embarrassed," Robeson replied. "I have heard it so much. Every reporter has asked me that. I will certainly answer it, Mr. Tenney. Only you might ask me if I am a member of the Republican or Democratic Party. As far as I know, the Communist Party is a very legal one in the United States. I sort of characterize myself as an anti-Fascist and independent. If I wanted to join any party, I could just as conceivably join the Communist Party, more so today, than I could join the Republican or Democratic Party. But I am not a Communist."

Noting that Communists controlled many countries, he said, Americans must learn to "get along with a lot of Communists." Questioned about his views on the Soviet Union, he emphasized that it had established racial equality. The questions and answers continued in a calm and courteous manner, in contrast to what he would face later in Congress.

After Robeson cited several racist incidents in the South, he was asked, "Compared to California, you don't find that sort of thing, or do you, in California?" He responded by describing how a restaurant had recently refused to serve him and some friends in Fresno, California.

"There is no solution to the Negro problem except by working it out together," Robeson told the committee. "So I will fight with the CIO and help the white workers or white liberals or any people."

* * *

In the autumn of 1946, Robeson and Brown began another long tour that included eighty-five concerts. Uta Hagen, still in love with Paul, flew to join him in some of the cities where his concerts took place that autumn. While in New York for a Christmas break, Paul went to Uta's townhouse for a Christmas Eve dinner with her. She told biographer Martin Duberman about what happened.

Uta and Paul exchanged gifts, ate dinner, and were sitting quietly in the living room, when Jose Ferrer suddenly appeared at the door. The Ferrers were separated but on friendly terms, so Uta thought that Joe, as friends called him, had come to wish her a Merry Christmas.

But Joe, accompanied by a lawyer and a detective, looked at Paul and cursed at him. Uta recalled that Paul said in a sorrowful tone, "Oh, Joe, no." Finally, Ferrer became embarrassed and left with the lawyer and the detective. He had seemed unconcerned about her affair with Paul in the past but apparently now sought an advantage in their impending divorce.

Robeson reacted in a "paranoid" way by calling some friends who came, armed with guns, and drove away with him in a limousine. The bizarre incident brought their affair to an end. They saw each other a few times afterward, Uta said, but Paul seemed remote, and the affair "just disintegrated."[10]

* * *

On December 1, 1946, from their home in Enfield, Essie wrote a forceful letter to Paul about her future and her finances. He must have received it before spending Christmas Eve with Uta Hagen. Essie began by complaining bitterly about the lawyer Robert Rockmore's control of money for her and Pauli. Then, she said, "I feel at 50, which I will be on the 15th, I'm going to start a new life."

"We shall have to have some things clear between us," she declared, enumerating four specific issues on her mind:

1. Am I to continue to be Mrs. Robeson? Yes or no.
2. You definitely want to keep the house here?
3. I can manage nicely with $100 per week household allowance.
4. I want a personal allowance, permanently . . .

"O.K. Mister . . . I've said everything that's been on my mind for some time, and I feel better for saying it, no matter how it comes out." She concluded this letter, which had the tone of an ultimatum, with the word "affectionately."

Paul, who had long left finances in the hands of Rockmore, agreed to Essie's demands. She would receive a personal allowance of $100 a week in addition to the household allowance. Paul Jr. played an intermediary role in finding out his father's intentions and conveying them to his mother. Paul Sr. remained busy with his concerts and did not visit her in Connecticut.[11]

* * *

In Harlem, Paul Robeson attended a play produced by the American Negro Theater, with a cast that included a young actor named Harry Belafonte. Talking to the actors afterward, Robeson encouraged them to perform in plays, black and white, that dramatized social issues. Belafonte recalled, "I'd found my role model" in Robeson, and "it would guide me for the rest of my life."[12]

Belafonte later began to sing popular songs without much success. Robeson urged him to sing folk songs instead, which he subsequently did, to much more acclaim. Belafonte said that Robeson and Pete Seeger "made me think I might find in folk music a way to fuse my passions for politics and art."

* * *

During the last two winter concert seasons, Robeson reached his "greatest peak" as a singer, according to Lawrence Brown. He said they did more concerts and received better receptions than ever before in the United States. Paul also recorded two albums of familiar spirituals in a voice of incomparable beauty.

Brown observed, however, that despite the quality of his singing, "He was in a terrible mood."[13] Robeson grew increasingly angry about the political issues that mattered most to him, especially lynchings in the South. This gentle man, sweet tempered by nature, turned strident in his speeches. A friend said Paul seemed to be in a controlled rage much of the time by the end of the decade.

In St. Louis in January 1947, Robeson walked on a picket line in front of the American Theater, protesting its segregation policy. And he said he planned to give up his career for two years to concentrate on campaigning against racism. He left St. Louis in a car, which suddenly had a suspicious accident on the highway—a front wheel fell off—but no one was injured.[14]

In March 1947, he gave a concert at the University of Utah in Salt Lake City. There, not far from where the union leader Joe Hill had been executed twenty years ago, Paul sang the song "Joe Hill" extolling the martyred hero. At the concert's end, Robeson walked to the front of the stage and told the stunned audience, "You've heard my final concert for at least two years, and perhaps for many more. I'm retiring here and now from concert work—I shall sing, from now on, for my trade union and college friends; in other words, only at gatherings where I can sing what I please."[15]

He was preparing to sacrifice his career on the altar of his convictions. His announcement to the audience in Salt Lake City was premature, however, because he still had some scheduled concerts to complete.

* * *

On March 12, 1947, President Truman proclaimed a policy of sending financial aid to Greece and Turkey to prevent their takeover by Communists. He called this Truman Doctrine "the turning point in America's foreign policy" to act against any aggression that threatened peace. Secretary of State George C. Marshall soon outlined a plan for substantial American aid to help Europe recover from the war. Truman lauded the Marshall Plan as a great contribution to world peace.[16]

* * *

In April 1947, a month after his appearance in Salt Lake City, Robeson arrived in Peoria, Illinois, for a concert commitment. But the concert was canceled because the House Un-American Activities Committee had just named him on a list of people "invariably found supporting the Communist Party and its front organizations." The mayor canceled a city hall reception for him.

Robeson told the press, "I have been all over the world and the only time I have seen hysteria reach these heights was in Spain under Franco and Germany under Hitler."

Next, the board of education in Albany, New York, canceled the concert that Robeson had scheduled at Livingston High School there on May 9. But black sponsors of the event sued the board of education, and a state judge ruled that Albany could not bar Robeson from singing because of his alleged sympathy for communism. He added that Robeson must refrain from making any political statements during the concert, which then went on as scheduled.

Despite the controversy, Robeson sang to a sold-out concert at Symphony Hall in Boston in July and to another at Lewisohn Stadium in New York. A Gallup Poll found that he was one of the public's fifty "favorite people."

He frequently visited the Rockmores at their summer home in Ossining, New York. Robert Rockmore remained Paul's lawyer; he and his wife, Clara, were among Paul's closest friends. He felt comfortable with them but became extremely intense when discussing politics.

Clara's teenaged nephew, Bob, listened to baseball games with Paul, who was excited and enthusiastic about Jackie Robinson, now playing for the Brooklyn Dodgers as the first black in the major leagues. Young Bob, a St. Louis Cardinals fan, rooted quietly for his own team in Paul's presence.[17]

* * *

Henry Wallace, speaking at a Madison Square Garden rally a year after his break with President Truman, observed that reactionaries labeled every liberal idea as Communist. He said "the Red-baiting" reactionaries feared democracy more than communism. "The Communist way is not my way," Wallace told the rally, but he added that suppressing ideas "demonstrated a lack of confidence in the give-and-take of the democratic process."[18]

On December 29, 1947, Henry Wallace finally announced his candidacy for president at the head of an independent third party, which would soon become the Progressive Party. He denounced the "bipartisan reactionary" foreign policy of the Democrats and the Republicans and said the voters should not have to choose "the lesser of two evils."

Noting that he favored European aid through the United Nations, Wallace said, "I fight the Truman Doctrine and the Marshall Plan, as applied, because they divide Europe into two warring camps." Historian Robert Dallek concluded that the leaders of the victorious Allies used poor judgment after World War II by engaging in competition instead of cooperation, resulting in a costly and dangerous arms race.[19]

Robeson announced that he supported Wallace in opposition to Truman, who seemed certain to be the Democratic candidate. The stage was set for an unusual political campaign in 1948.

* * *

Joshua Fit de Battle of Jericho

Joshua fit de battle of Jericho, Jericho, Jericho,
Joshua fit de battle of Jericho,
And the walls come a tumbling down.

Up to the walls of Jericho,
He marched with spade in hand,
Oh blow the ram horn, Joshua cried,
'Cause de battle am in my hand.

Then the ram horn begin to blow,
The trumpets begin to sound,
Joshua recommanded the children to shout,
And the walls come a tumbling down.

—arranged by Lawrence Brown;
sung with Brown

Campaign for Wallace

I dreamed I saw Joe Hill last night.

—Robinson/Hayes song

$\mathscr{P}$aul Robeson focused his attention and energy on the campaign to promote Henry Wallace for president in 1948. The day after Wallace announced that he would run for president on a third-party ticket, Robeson appeared with him at a Milwaukee rally to sing and express his support. Wallace's party, so new that it did not yet have a name, was simply called the New Party. It would soon be the Progressive Party.

On January 28, 1948, Robeson took part in a political meeting of the group at the McAlpin Hotel in Manhattan to form a National Wallace-for-President Committee. Elmer A. Benson, a former governor of Minnesota, was selected as the committee's chairman. Named as cochairmen were Professor Rexford Guy Tugwell, a former Roosevelt advisor; Jo Davidson, a prominent sculptor; and Paul Robeson. Wallace also named C. B. Baldwin, who had served with him in the Roosevelt administration, as his campaign manager. He chose Angus Cameron, a Boston book publisher, as treasurer.[1]

Robeson sang, spoke, and campaigned for Wallace and the Progressive Party at rallies throughout the country in the coming months.

* * *

Henry A. Wallace, a vigorous, rather rumpled man of average height with unruly silver-gray hair, had been born fifty-nine years before on a farm in Iowa. Besides editing an agricultural journal owned by his family, he invented an improved strain of corn and formed a profitable agricultural business. Liberal idealism and Christian morality infused his populist political views.[2]

Wallace served as secretary of agriculture during President Roosevelt's first two terms and then as vice president for the third term. At the insistence of conservatives, he was replaced by a party regular, Senator Harry S. Truman of Missouri, as Roosevelt's running mate in 1944. Wallace remained loyal to the president, returning to the cabinet as secretary of commerce for Roosevelt's fourth term.

After Truman became president and shifted to the right, Wallace broke away to run for president on his own. Shy and eccentric, he was a political visionary who lacked conventional political skills. Most of the news media ridiculed him as a quixotic knight jousting at political windmills, while others vilified him as a dangerous subversive because he accepted Communist support.

Wallace stated his attitude about Communists joining his campaign in a speech in February: "Any Communist who supports the independent ticket will be supporting our program, not the Communist program," he asserted. "I am not a Communist, or Socialist, or Marxist of any description, but I find nothing criminal in the advocacy of different economic and social ideas."[3]

* * *

On February 2, 1948, President Truman gave a strongly worded speech calling on Congress to act on civil rights, including antilynching legislation. He knew, however, that the Republican-controlled Congress would refuse to act. Perhaps Robeson's view of the American government would have been very different if the president had spoken out against lynching after their meeting more than a year earlier.

President Truman also issued Executive Order 9981 in 1948, finally ending segregation in the armed forces. Half a million blacks had served in segregated military units during World War II.

The broad political coalition that President Roosevelt had forged—Northern liberals, big city machines, black voters, organized labor, farmers, and Southern conservatives—seemed to be collapsing. Roosevelt, the masterful politician and inspirational leader, was gone. And his successor was no Roosevelt.

The Republicans, banished to the political wilderness for so many years, eagerly sought to recapture the White House in 1948. They had already won back both houses of Congress in the mid-term election of 1946.

Liberals split sharply over the issue of Communist influence. Wallace accepted Communist supporters, while the new Americans for Democratic Action vigorously assailed all Communists. Organized labor adopted the strongly anti-Communist position, except for a handful of leaders that included Harry Bridges of the longshoremen's union on the West Coast.

Most prominent black leaders, such as Walter White of the NAACP and Lester Granger of the Urban League, supported President Truman. But W. E. B. Du Bois joined Paul Robeson in supporting Henry Wallace.

No one, including Wallace himself, really believed that he would win the election. But he wanted to challenge the bellicose foreign policy of both major parties and carry his message of peace to the American people. And he hoped that the Progressive Party could attract enough votes to enable him to influence foreign policy or at least show that many Americans wanted friendly relations with the Soviet Union. He financed the campaign by charging admission to his rallies, frequently with Robeson as the drawing card.[4]

Most of the Democrats supported President Truman, even when they found fault with his policies. Some feared that the Progressive Party had come under the control of the Communists, while others did not want to "waste their vote" on a third-party candidate.

More than any other candidate, Wallace called for civil rights and equal justice, and when he carried his campaign into the South, he refused to speak to segregated audiences. But his main emphasis remained on urging a less hostile, more cooperative foreign policy.

Robeson took the campaign for the Progressive Party across the country, through the Middle West and on to the West Coast.

* * *

In March 1948, Robeson traveled to Hawaii for a week of concerts at the invitation of the International Longshoremen's and Warehousemen's Union. Earl Robinson accompanied him because Lawrence Brown did not want to make the long flight. The union expressed its gratitude for Robeson's appearances.

Earl Robinson remembered the Hawaiian trip and working closely with Paul for ten days as "the most exciting, the most educational, the most fulfilling time of my life." They traveled together to six of the islands and gave fifteen public concerts, performing without pay, for the union movement.[5]

In the concerts, Robeson sang Mendelssohn's "Lord God of Abraham" and an excerpt from Mussorgsky's *Boris Godunov*, as well as the spirituals "On My Journey" and "Swing Low, Sweet Chariot" in addition to "Joe Hill," "Ballad for Americans," and "Ol' Man River."

Earl found that Paul had a "winsome sense of humor" and that his voice was "a lyric instrument." He said Paul could sing anything, from love songs to the classics, adding there was "nothing on earth more tender" than Paul singing a lullaby.

At a press conference in Honolulu, Robeson spoke in favor of Henry Wallace and dismissed fears of communism, according to the *Honolulu Star-Bulletin*. He contended that President Truman had been compelled to propose

Robeson and Henry Wallace in Chicago in 1947 preparing for the 1948 campaign. Courtesy Associated Press.

a civil rights program because of pressure from Wallace's campaign and the need to justify America's position in the United Nations.

Turning to the topic of communism, Robeson said, "Either we get along with the Communists, jump in the ocean, or blow up the whole world." When asked about his own political beliefs, he described himself as "an advanced New Dealer." Robeson declared that when he returned to the mainland, he would continue to work for Wallace because "if anybody continues the New Deal traditions of Franklin Roosevelt, it is Wallace." He scoffed at suggestions that Wallace was a Communist, instead characterizing him as a "progressive capitalist."[6]

* * *

Eslanda Robeson entered the political fray by representing the Progressive Party and running, with little support, for secretary of state in Connecticut. She noted in her diary, "My work in the Wallace campaign will keep me busy."

Max Yergan, a Robeson friend and political associate for the past decade, completely reversed his political position in the spring of 1948. He turned against Robeson, assailed Communist influences, and tried unsuccessfully to take over the Council on African Affairs. Robeson rallied his supporters in the organization to oust Yergan, who became a bitter critic of his former friend.[7]

On April 9, 1948, Paul observed his fiftieth birthday without fanfare. He just kept up his campaigning for Wallace and the Progressives.

Delegates from around the country came to Chicago for the party's conference in April. Robeson introduced Wallace, who addressed the conference, and the delegates chanted, "We want Wallace!" Another chant erupted from the rear of the room: "Robeson for Vice President!" Standing on the platform, Paul looked shocked, then turned and walked out silently. He did not want to run for any political office.[8]

* * *

In Europe, the Soviet Union took two actions in 1948 that gave more credibility to American fears of Communist expansion. The Russians set up a Communist regime in Czechoslovakia in February, backed by the Red Army. In the spring, they blocked all road and rail access to Berlin in an attempt to force the Allies to leave the city, which had been divided at the end of the war. American planes then flew supplies into Berlin for more than a year until the Russians gave up the blockade.

Meanwhile, when Britain's control of Palestine ended on May 15, 1948, Zionist leaders proclaimed the new nation of Israel. The United Nations had proposed a partition of Palestine into separate Arab and Jewish states. But five Arab countries—Egypt, Syria, Jordan, Lebanon, and Iraq—declared war on Israel, a war that the Israelis won to establish their independence.

* * *

Also in April, Robeson campaigned in the Middle West, appearing with Charles P. Howard, a local NAACP leader, in Sioux City, Iowa. Officials there refused to allow him to use a school auditorium unless he signed an affidavit that he would not make any "un-American statements." He said he would not sign something other speakers were not required to sign. A black minister provided Robeson and Howard with a meeting hall. Howard, a lawyer and war veteran, was a Republican before he joined the Wallace campaign.

On May 20, Robeson addressed the International Fur and Leather Workers Union. He spoke at length, sang "Water Boy" and "Joe Hill," and closed by reading Langston Hughes's poem "Freedom Train":

> Lord, I've been awaitin' for the Freedom Train!
> Way down in Dixie the only train I see's

Got a Jim-Crow car set aside for me.
I hope there ain't no Jim-Crow on the Freedom Train.

On May 31, Robeson took time to testify before the Senate Judiciary Committee in Washington at a hearing about pending legislation known as the Mundt-Nixon Bill, which would require all Communists and Communist organizations to register with the government. The sponsors of the bill, designed to outlaw communism, were Senator Karl Mundt, a right-wing Republican from South Dakota, and Representative Richard M. Nixon, a freshman Republican from California.

The House Committee on Un-American Activities continued to hold a series of hearings in which numerous witnesses, including Eugene Dennis, the executive secretary of the Communist Party, were cited for contempt of Congress when they refused to answer questions.

At the Senate hearing, when asked to define what American Communists stood for, Robeson retorted, "For complete equality of the Negro people." Then, Senator Homer Ferguson asked him, "Are you a Communist?"

Robeson responded, "That question has become the very basis of the struggle for American civil liberties. Nineteen men are about to go to jail for refusing to answer it. I am prepared to join them. I refuse to answer it."

Replying to another question, he said he believed the best way for him to carry out his ideals was to support the third party, the Progressive Party, adding that it made him feel "infinitely more loyal to the United States." He denounced the Mundt-Nixon Bill as anti-Communist hysteria.[9]

Robeson joined some five thousand picketers in front of the White House to protest the Mundt-Nixon Bill. He marched with them to the Washington Monument, where he sang "Ol' Man River." The black *Pittsburgh Courier* called it "the most impressive march-on-Washington" in many years.

* * *

Facing the prospect of going to prison for his political beliefs, Eugene Dennis, the Communist Party leader, held a meeting in his apartment one evening with several friends and associates, including Robeson.

Dennis's son Gene, not quite six years old, went to bed early while the adults talked in somber tones that included a reference to prison. Wearing his pajamas, the child came into the living room to say goodnight to the visitors at this "scary time" in his life. Many years later, his voice choked with emotion, he recalled what happened for a documentary film titled *Children of the Left* made by Eric Stange.[10]

Robeson, who was sitting in an armchair, called the youngster to him and put him on his lap, then sang to him softly. Gene remembered "that

Robeson, with characteristic hand to ear, speaking for Wallace in 1948. Courtesy Associated Press.

wonderful feeling of being held by him, and him singing to me, and I was safe, I was safe."

This experience of the young Gene Dennis was one of many, many times when individuals in widely different circumstances—men, women, children—found their lives touched in a memorable way by the kind, thoughtful, generous spirit of Paul Robeson.[11]

* * *

In July, both the Democrats and the Republicans held their conventions in Philadelphia. The confident Republicans nominated Governor Thomas E. Dewey of New York for president, with Governor Earl Warren of California as his running mate.

The Democrats, in a contentious convention, nominated President Truman for reelection, with Senator Alben Barkley of Kentucky as his running mate. Two stalwart liberals, Mayor Hubert Humphrey of Minneapolis and former congressman Andrew Biemiller of Wisconsin, won a floor fight for a stronger civil rights plank in the party's platform.

Truman wrote in his diary on July 14, "Platform fight in dead earnest. Crackpot Biemiller from Wisconsin offers a minority report on civil rights. . . . The crackpots hope the South will bolt."[12]

Delegates from the South did bolt, walking out of the convention and forming their own States Rights Party, generally known as the Dixiecrats. They held their own convention in Birmingham, Alabama, where they selected the segregationist governor of South Carolina, J. Strom Thurmond, for president, with Mississippi governor Fielding Wright for vice president.

Later in July, the Progressive Party held its convention in Philadelphia, nominating Henry Wallace for president, with Senator Glen Taylor of Idaho for vice president. C. B. Baldwin, known as "Beanie," served as campaign manager. Eslanda Robeson took part in a committee to draft the party's liberal platform. Paul Robeson spoke and sang to a convention crowd of thirty thousand in Shibe Park, a baseball stadium illuminated with floodlights, where Wallace and Taylor gave their acceptance speeches that night.

* * *

Robeson took the Progressive Party campaign into the Deep South, where all his speeches stressed the fight for Negro rights. He faced danger more than once. In Memphis, when the authorities tried to prevent him from appearing, a black minister provided a hall for a rally. Blacks courageously provided Robeson with protection when he made appearances in South Carolina, Georgia, and Florida.

Lawrence Brown, who had been born in Florida, was most reluctant to accompany Paul on a campaign trip there. "But I didn't want to let Paul down, so I went," he told Marie Seton. He said he stayed in his room all the time except when he played for Paul.[13]

Robeson addressed a meeting of longshoremen's union on the West Coast on August 21. He ended by singing "Joe Hill" to a sustained standing ovation. The union president, Harry Bridges, told the members that Paul went to Hawaii free of charge and contributed the proceeds of his concerts there to the union.

On September 11, Robeson participated in a Progressive Party rally at Yankee Stadium. The *New York Times* said, "When the notes of 'Let My People Go' and 'Ol' Man River' washed out of the loudspeakers and shattered against the night, the crowd listened in silence, then roared applause. Robeson's bitter tirade against oppression of the Negro brought the crowd to its feet with thunderous applause."

* * *

The pompous Republican candidate, Governor Dewey, ran a lackluster campaign, staying supremely confident of victory over the Democratic president, who was under attack from all sides. All the polls and pundits shared the view that Dewey would soundly defeat Truman.

But Truman conducted an energetic "whistle-stop campaign" that took him across the country by train, stopping frequently to speak from the rear platform to welcoming crowds. He repeatedly excoriated what he called "the do-nothing Congress" of the Republicans. Supporters encouraged the feisty president by shouting to him, "Give 'em hell, Harry!"

Wallace continued to call for strong civil rights, cooperation with the Soviet Union, and proposals for peace and disarmament in the United Nations. And Robeson continued to campaign for him to the end, but the Progressive Party made little impact on the voters, including black voters.

When he joined Wallace in a radio broadcast on October 29, as the day of the election neared, Robeson dismissed President Truman's civil rights program as mere words that did nothing to deal with "the atmosphere of horror in which most Negroes live." He again praised Wallace as a courageous man and a defender of freedom.

* * *

On the night of the election, November 2, 1948, Robeson sang to hundreds of campaign workers at the Progressive Party's headquarters in New York City, while they awaited the verdict of the voters.

The voters delivered a stunning upset victory to the jubilant President Truman, who received more than 24 million votes, over 2 million more than Governor Dewey. Wallace received a disappointing total of just over 1 million votes, even a bit less than Thurmond obtained for his Dixiecrats.[14] The official count of the 1948 presidential election showed

Truman—Democrat: 24,105,812 popular votes and 303 electoral votes
Dewey—Republican: 21,970,065 popular votes and 189 electoral votes
Thurmond—Dixiecrat: 1,169,021 popular votes and 39 electoral votes
Wallace—Progressive: 1,157,172 popular votes and 0 electoral votes

His poor showing, even weaker than expected, clearly disappointed the noble but naive Wallace, who soon faded from public view. Historians could speculate in the future about how different the postwar world might have looked if Wallace, rather than Truman, had succeeded President Roosevelt.

The 1948 election was a watershed in American politics, setting the course that the country would take for more than a generation. On the international front, Truman adopted an aggressive anti-Communist policy to "contain" the Soviet Union, a policy that both Democrats and Republicans would maintain through the Cold War. The major parties tried to outdo each other in their condemnation of Communists at home, bringing on an ugly era of political intolerance. And the advent of the Dixiecrats marked the beginning of the South's mass move from the Democratic to the Republican Party.

Right-wing Republicans trumpeted their own extremism as true patriotism, disparaging the loyalty of even mainstream Truman Democrats. Two centuries earlier, Dr. Samuel Johnson observed, "Patriotism is the last refuge of a scoundrel." That seemed just as true in 1948.[15]

* * *

During the election campaign, Robeson had encountered an interesting woman, Helen Rosen, the liberal wife of a New York physician. They became fast friends, and Robeson began using the Rosen family's apartment as a safe haven in Manhattan.

After the election, Robeson traveled to Jamaica and Trinidad to give a series of successful concerts. He spoke on his return home about the people of the West Indies making progress "on the road to freedom." He added, "I am never for one moment unaware that I live in a land of Jim Crow."

The coming year would bring more controversy and serious trouble for Paul Robeson.

* * *

Joe Hill

I dreamed I saw Joe Hill last night,
Alive as you and me.
Says I, but Joe, you're ten years dead.
I never died, says he,
I never died, says he.

The copper bosses killed you, Joe,
They shot you, Joe, says I.
Takes more than guns to kill a man,

Says Joe, I didn't die,
Says Joe, I didn't die.

And standing there as big as life,
And smiling with his eyes,
Says Joe, what they could never kill,
Goes on to organize,
Goes on to organize.

From San Diego up to Maine
In every mine and mill,
Where workers strike and organize,
It's there you'll find Joe Hill,
It's there you'll find Joe Hill.

I dreamed I saw Joe Hill last night,
Alive as you and me.
Says I, but Joe, you're ten years dead.
I never died says he,
I never died says he.

—music by Earl Robinson;
lyrics by Alfred Hayes

· 15 ·

Paris and Peekskill

You call that a brother, no, no, scandalized my name.

—traditional song

$\mathcal{A}$ fateful year for Paul Robeson, the most tumultuous of his life, began with plans for a concert tour in early 1949. After the Wallace presidential campaign ended, he decided to resume his concert career. His agents scheduled a tour of eighty-five concerts in the United States, but all the dates were quickly canceled due to increasing hostility toward his politics. So he replaced the canceled American tour with a four-month concert tour of Europe that began in Britain.

Robeson, with Lawrence Brown, arrived in London in February. They had been away for ten years, but their concerts still drew enthusiastic audiences throughout Britain. Two concerts at the Royal Albert Hall filled all eight thousand seats at each performance. More sold-out concerts followed in Manchester, Birmingham, and Glasgow.

In March, at the India League conference in London, Robeson assailed racism in South Africa and all colonies. He spoke in London again in April, this time to the Committee of Colonial Peoples, which asked him to go to the World Peace Congress in Paris to express their desire for peace. He agreed.

* * *

On April 20, 1949, Paul Robeson went to Paris to speak at the World Peace Congress, attended by some two thousand delegates from many countries. Among the prominent leftist figures at this conference were W. E. B. Du Bois, Frederic Jolit-Curie, and Pablo Picasso, who painted a "peace dove" as its symbol. The speakers denounced the North Atlantic Treaty Organization, or NATO, and demanded peace with the Soviet Union.

Rousing cheers and applause greeted Robeson when he took his seat on the stage of the Salle Pleyel, the largest concert hall in Paris. He sang a few spirituals and then "Ol' Man River" to wild cheering. He also delivered a brief, extemporaneous speech in which he stressed that millions of colonial peoples throughout the world were determined to fight for peace. He also spoke some disputed words that caused a furor in the United States.[1]

"It is unthinkable that American Negroes would go to war on behalf of those who have oppressed us for generations against a country which in one generation has raised our people to the full dignity of mankind." Those were his words, as accurately as can be ascertained.[2]

According to the Associated Press report, published all over America, Paul Robeson declared that American Negroes would never fight in a war against the Soviet Union. This report aroused a firestorm of criticism, with some black leaders joining many, many whites in denouncing him.

* * *

On the evening of April 20, right after his Paris speech, Robeson had dinner with Du Bois, then flew to Oslo, Norway, for a concert the next day at the start of a Scandinavian tour. He and Lawrence Brown gave concerts in Oslo, Stockholm, and Copenhagen.

At first, Robeson did not realize that his Paris speech had created such a furor. But he soon found out. He contended in an interview in Copenhagen that his words had been "distorted out of all recognition." He said his emphasis in Paris had been "on the struggle for peace, not on anybody going to war against anybody." But the Associated Press had conveyed the thrust of his Paris speech, even if it ignored some nuance and context. He failed to understand that the press would focus on the most controversial aspect of his words.

Robeson and Brown returned to London for additional concerts there in May. They were scheduled to go on to Prague, Warsaw, and Moscow. But Larry felt exhausted and decided to go back to New York to wait for Paul to come home. To serve as his temporary accompanist, Robeson found Bruno Raikin, a white South African pianist, whom he had met in London.

Robeson and Raikin flew to Prague, where they performed before a large crowd at the International Spring Music Festival. And Paul encountered Marie Seton, who had also come to Prague. On his last night there, he talked to her about his need to fight for Negro rights at home, telling her, "I don't know if I'll live to see the end of the struggle."

"Tomorrow morning, I'm going to Warsaw and then to Moscow," he told her. "I'm going to the people I love. . . . But can you understand it? Even at this moment, I'm homesick. Even this very night, I'd rather be in America than any place on earth."[3]

Robeson singing at Peekskill, with Brown at the piano, surrounded by union men for protection against more threatened violence, on September 4, 1949. Courtesy Associated Press.

In Warsaw, Robeson sang to an enthusiastic audience in a large stadium, then at two factories in the city. He also toured the area that once contained the Warsaw Ghetto before going to Wroclaw, where he sang at a factory in the afternoon and then in a concert hall that evening.

* * *

Robeson flew to Moscow on June 4 with Peter Blackman, who served as his accompanist instead of Bruno Raikin, because Raikin had failed to get a visa. The visit to Moscow came in time to celebrate the 150th anniversary of the birth of Alexander Pushkin, the famous Russian poet of African descent, who was one of Paul's favorites. It was also the time of a Stalinist campaign against "Zionist" intellectuals, many of whom disappeared.

Robeson went to the Pushkin celebration at the Bolshoi Theatre on June 6. And he gave two acclaimed concerts, one of them outdoors in Gorky Park, where he told the crowd that he was deeply moved to be on Soviet soil again. He added, "I was, I am, always will be, a friend of the Soviet people."

When he told the authorities that he wanted to see two Jewish friends, the theater figure Solomon Mikhoels and the poet Itzik Feffer, they informed him that Mikhoels had died and that Feffer was on vacation. Mikhoels was indeed dead, but Feffer was "vacationing" in the Lubyanka prison, awaiting execution. Robeson repeatedly asked to see his missing friend.

Finally, he was informed that Feffer would visit him the day before the last Robeson concert in Moscow. And on that day, Feffer walked alone into Paul's hotel suite. The poet silently signaled Paul to indicate that the hotel rooms were bugged and that he was actually a prisoner taken to the hotel under guard. Then, speaking aloud, he said he was fine but drew a finger across his throat to show that he expected to be killed. The two friends hugged each other before Feffer left.[4]

* * *

On the evening of June 14, Paul Robeson gave what came to be known as his legendary Moscow concert of 1949. He walked onto the stage of the glittering Tchaikovsky Hall to waves of enthusiastic applause. An announcer introduced the first song on the program, the English air "Over the Mountains." Paul went on to sing "L'Amour de Moi" in French, "Beloved City" in Russian, the witty English folk song "Oh, No, John," and then his "Water Boy." The clapping and cheering for "Water Boy" continued so long and loud that he repeated the song from beginning to end.

He continued with "The Four Insurgent Generals" in Spanish, the anthem "Chi Lai" in Chinese, Monteverdi's "Let Me Die" in Italian, then his traditional "Scandalize My Name" and "Joe Hill" in English. The announcer introduced each song in turn, Robeson added his own words in Russian, and the audience responded with enthusiasm—so much so for "Joe Hill" that he sang it again.

His final songs consisted of the Negro lullaby "My Curly Headed Baby," the spiritual "Swing Low, Sweet Chariot," and then "Ol' Man River." Before singing the last one, he explained that he had changed the lyrics, saying in Russian, "We must keep fighting until we're dying for peace and freedom." Both his explanation and the song received sustained applause. He had sung fifteen songs—in English, French, Spanish, Italian, Chinese, and Russian.[5]

Now, with the program completed, he stepped forward on the stage to say he would sing just one encore. His son reported later that Robeson told the audience that he felt a deep cultural tie between the Jews of America and Russia, noting by name his two Russian Jewish friends. He then sang—in Yiddish—the "Song of the Warsaw Ghetto Rebellion." In a rousing refrain, he sang the words translated here into English:

Never say that you have reached the very end
When leaded skies a bitter future may portend;
For sure the hour for which we yearn will yet arrive
And our marching steps will thunder: we survive!

The audience cheered the conclusion of the concert. Robeson would not overtly criticize the Soviet Union or its policies, but he felt that he had made a strong symbolic statement on behalf of Russian Jews.[6]

* * *

On June 16, 1949, two days after his farewell concert, Robeson flew back to New York. He returned home just in time for his son's wedding to Marilyn Greenberg, a Jewish girl who attended Cornell University with Paul Jr.

Paul Jr. studied electrical engineering and played varsity football at Cornell. Marilyn, a leftist intellectual, initially regarded him as a "jock." But she came to know him as an intelligent, interesting young man, and they fell in love. Both were now twenty-one years old.[7]

They planned a quiet wedding ceremony to be conducted by a Congregational minister in his apartment, at 200 West 107th Street in Manhattan, on the afternoon of June 19. Paul and Essie approved of the marriage and came to the ceremony, as did Marilyn's mother, but not her father. When they arrived at the minister's address, they were confronted by reporters and photographers.

After the private ten-minute ceremony, as the small wedding group began to leave in taxicabs, they were accosted again by aggressive photographers. Incensed at the intrusion into his son's wedding, Robeson shook his fist and shouted, "I have the greatest contempt for the press—only something within me keeps me from smashing your cameras over your heads."[8]

* * *

That evening, just hours after the wedding, Robeson appeared at a large "Welcome Home" rally at the Rockland Palace in Harlem. Speakers there denounced attacks on Robeson and criticized the trial of Communist leaders.

Speaking for himself, clearly still angry, he delivered a long, passionate declaration of defiance. He asserted, "I'm looking for freedom, full freedom, not an inferior brand." He loved the Soviet people "because of their suffering and sacrifices for us, the Negro people, the progressive people, the people of the future in this world." As for the United States, "I love only part of it—the progressive part."[9]

The long day ended, at last, with a quiet party for the newlyweds at the home of Freda Diamond and Barry Baruch.

* * *

On April 4, 1949, President Truman signed the treaty that established the North Atlantic Treaty Organization, or NATO. This created the military group, led by the United States, directly opposed to the Soviet Union. The Russians successfully tested their first atomic bomb in the late summer, while nuclear scientists in America made plans for a much more powerful hydrogen bomb in the continuing arms race.

This was also the time when the Communists of Mao Tse-tung defeated the Nationalists of Chiang Kai-shek in China. The United States conducted a long, bitter, futile struggle to bar Communist China from the United Nations.

* * *

The black establishment, led by Walter White and Roy Wilkins of the NAACP, had quickly lined up against Paul Robeson after his Paris speech. They undoubtedly believed their vehemently anti-Communist rhetoric. But they also had a more personal motive: they regarded Robeson and Du Bois as their rivals and wanted to insure their own power and access to the white establishment.

Congress called on a new black hero, Jackie Robinson of the Brooklyn Dodgers, to renounce Robeson and declare black loyalty. On July 18, Robinson testified before the House Un-American Activities Committee. He began by denouncing racism, then went on to the reason for his appearance.[10]

"I've been asked to express my views on Paul Robeson's statement in Paris to the effect that American Negroes would refuse to fight in any war against Russia because we love Russia so much," Robinson said. "I haven't any comment to make on that statement except that if Mr. Robeson actually made it, it sounds very silly to me. But he has a right to his personal views, and if he wants to sound silly when he expresses them in public, that is his business and not mine. He is still a famous ex-athlete and a great singer and actor." The baseball star added that he and his family, and Negroes in general, had "too much invested in our country's welfare for any of us to throw it away because of a siren song sung in bass."

Robeson, who had spearheaded the fight to break the color barrier in baseball, spoke at a press conference in Harlem's Hotel Theresa, where reporters questioned him sharply about Jackie Robinson's testimony of the previous day. He told the reporters that he had "no quarrel" with Jackie and that Negroes should not fall for any attempt to create a feud between them.[11]

* * *

Two days after Jackie Robinson's testimony, Robeson appeared at a civil rights rally at the Mosque Theater in Newark. He sang and spoke to a cheering audience of twelve hundred fans. At the end, he stepped down from the stage and stood there for almost an hour, greeting people who lined up to shake his hand and get his autograph.

An earnest young man came up to him and said he had recently become a newspaper reporter and was troubled by Robeson's harsh criticism of the press. Paul immediately engaged him in a serious conversation, saying the press repeatedly distorted everything about him. For example, he said, on his recent tour of Scandinavia, the audiences stamped their feet, a gesture similar to applause in those countries. But the American press reported that they stamped their feet in protest.

Look at the newspapers tomorrow, he suggested, and see if they report how this large audience welcomed him; no, they will emphasize the handful of picketers outside. True to his prediction, most of the next day's newspapers ignored the large audience and focused on the fifty American Legion picketers. But the brief article in the *New York Times* reported his speech and the size of the audience before noting the picketers.[12]

* * *

In the morning of Saturday, August 27, 1949, Paul Robeson went to Grand Central Station to take a train to Peekskill for a concert there. From the station, he called his friend Helen Rosen at her summer home in Katonah, fifteen files from Peekskill, to ask about rumors of trouble. Her husband had heard reports on the radio about protesters gathering in the area. So Helen told Paul that she would meet him at the Peekskill train station. She also called a friend, Sydney Danis, who agreed to meet her there. Helen's fourteen-year-old son, John, insisted on going along, saying, "Nobody's going to hurt our Paul."

Helen Rosen told biographer Martin Duberman that when Paul arrived at the Peekskill station, they decided he should go in the Danis car. Helen said she and her son led the way in their station wagon. As they approached the concert site, the Lakeland Acres picnic grounds, they saw that a truck blocked the entrance, forcing cars to move slowly around it while a mob threw rocks at them and screamed racist and anti-Semitic epithets.

Helen got out of her station wagon, rushed up to the Danis car carrying Paul, and shouted, "Get him the hell out of here!" Danis quickly turned his car around and drove Paul to Robert Rockmore's home in Ossining.[13]

* * *

Inside the concert grounds, unaware of the violence outside, the left-wing novelist Howard Fast was checking a platform that would serve as the stage. He had arrived early in his role as a chairman of the concert. About a hundred other early arrivals, including a dozen union men, sat on chairs or sprawled on the grass awaiting the concert.[14]

Shortly after 7 p.m., Fast and some of the union men were attacked near the entrance by about three hundred protesters, many wearing American Legion caps. Fast's group retreated into the concert area, as screaming attackers rushed toward them with clubs, rocks, and bottles.

Fast's outnumbered men locked their arms together and focused on holding their defense lines against a series of attacks. Finally, after darkness fell, the state police opened a road out of the area and drove the remaining members of Fast's contingent safely away.

The rioting mob had smashed the stage to bits, set fire to the chairs, and beat up stragglers. It also put up several fiery crosses, emblematic of the Ku Klux Klan.

* * *

Sam and Helen Rosen hosted a protest meeting the next day at their Katonah house, where a committee was formed to invite Robeson to return to Peekskill. Several leftist unions promised to protect the rescheduled concert. And ten union men slept on the Rosen front porch that night to protect the family, which had received threatening telephone calls.[15]

Civil liberties groups complained about the Peekskill riot, but a Joint Veterans Council said it had only held a peaceful parade to protest against Robeson. And a Westchester County investigation resulted in no arrests.

Robeson spoke to a large rally on Tuesday, August 30, at the Golden Gate Ballroom in Harlem, protesting the Peekskill riot. He promised to return to Peekskill. The return concert was quickly set for September 4, the Sunday of the Labor Day weekend.

* * *

Early on the clear, crisp morning of September 4, groups of union men, many of them veterans, began arriving to defend the new concert site, at the Hollow Brook Golf Course, near Peekskill. The large bowl-shaped site was soon ringed by a line of twenty-five hundred union men around the perimeter.

Leon Straus, a war veteran and vice president of the International Fur and Leather Workers Union, organized the defenders. They included workers from fur, furniture, shoe, electrical, and maritime unions. They set up a small stage under an oak tree to shield Robeson, because they feared men with rifles might try to assassinate him.

Hundreds of private cars and chartered buses brought in a steady stream of concertgoers, an estimated twenty thousand of them. With no chairs, they

Paul Robeson shaking hands with W. E. B. Du Bois in Paris on June 20, 1949. Courtesy Bettemann/Corbis via Associated Press.

sat on the grass, forming a large mass that gradually filled the field in front of the stage.

At 2 p.m., the crowd sang "The Star-Spangled Banner" and listened to an invocation by a Congregational minister. Then, Pete Seeger sang a few songs, notably one that he and Lee Hays had recently written, "If I Had a Hammer." A pianist played a piece by Prokofiev. And since the concert had been arranged too quickly to print tickets, ushers collected donations from the audience.

Paul Robeson and Lawrence Brown had arrived earlier but remained in their car behind the stage for security until their turn to perform. When Robeson, with his frightened accompanist, emerged from the car and stepped onto the small stage, fifteen union volunteers surrounded them for protection.

Robeson, dressed in a dark suit, stood behind a tall microphone next to the American flag, and he began singing "Go Down, Moses," with its powerful cry of "let my people go." He continued with other favorites, including the whimsical "No, John, No." He sang for almost an hour, ending with his signature "Ol' Man River" to a standing ovation.[16]

A convoy of three cars, with union bodyguards, took Robeson and Brown safely away immediately after the concert. But when the concertgoers began leaving in cars and buses, they were attacked by young white hoodlums who screamed anti-Negro, anti-Semitic, and anti-Communist curses at them.

Pete Seeger, who followed the folksinging tradition of Woody Guthrie, the balladeer of the American Depression, gave an eyewitness account of what happened after the concert. He drove his car through the exit, where a policeman directed all cars to turn to the right onto a winding road. When each vehicle slowed to go around a bend in this road, a young white man threw rocks "as big as tennis balls" from close range, shattering windows. At each bend in the road, there stood another young man with a pile of rocks, stoning each car.

Seeger and his young family were in one of the cars. Spotting a policeman standing near one of the rock throwers, Seeger called out to him, "Officer, aren't you going to do something?" The policeman just said, "Move on, move on." Seeger became convinced that the police had participated in a deliberate plan to direct the cars along this road, through a gauntlet of flying rocks. The process continued as rocks dented vehicles, shattered windows, and injured passengers. Some cars were overturned, their occupants dragged out and beaten.

"I don't call it a riot," Pete Seeger said, recalling Peekskill. "I call it an attack, a planned attack." He said he believed that Ku Klux Klan members in the area, some of them veterans and some of them police officers, organized the attack.[17]

One thousand American Legion members had paraded earlier in the day to protest the Robeson concert. The veterans denied any part in the later violence. The police failed to intervene, according to concert organizers, but Westchester officials blamed Communist "provocations" for the violence.

* * *

A few weeks later, Robeson walked up the stone steps of the U.S. Court House at Foley Square in Lower Manhattan. He had come to testify as a witness for the eleven Communist leaders on trial for allegedly advocating the violent overthrow of the government.

Robeson, wearing horn-rimmed glasses and speaking solemnly on the witness stand, said he had known the defendants for many years. But when a defense lawyer asked if he ever heard any of them advocate violently overthrowing the government, Judge Harold R. Medina sustained the prosecutor's objection to that and other questions, effectively excluding any testimony by Robeson.

Outside, when a reporter asked why he had come to testify, he responded that the government was persecuting the defendants to silence them.[18]

Angry threats against Robeson resounded for months in many cities, with effigies of him hanged and burned in some places in the South. Essie became sufficiently concerned that she installed an alarm system in the house in Enfield. She told a reporter there that she would kill any stranger who entered the house.

Robeson wound up this tumultuous year with a tour sponsored by the Council on African Affairs, often singing and speaking in black churches, as he traveled to Washington, DC, Cleveland, Detroit, Chicago, and Los Angeles.

* * *

Scandalize My Name

I met my brother the other day, gave him my right hand,
And just as soon as ever my back was turned,
He scandalized my name.
Now do you call that a brother, no, no
You call that a brother, no, no,
You call that a brother, no, no,
Scandalized my name.

I met my sister the other day, gave her my right hand,
And just as soon as ever my back was turned,
She, too, scandalized name.
Now do you call that a sister, no, no,
You call that a sister, no, no,
You call that a sister, no, no,
Scandalized my name.

I met my preacher the other day, gave him my right hand,
And just as soon as ever my back was turned,
He scandalized my name.
Now do you call that religion, no, no,
You call that religion, no, no,
You call that religion, no, no,
Scandalized my name.

—arranged by H. T. Burleigh; first verse, traditional

· *16* ·

The Red and the Black

No more auction block for me, no more, no more.

—spiritual

 $\mathcal{P}$ aul Robeson began living a life of exile in his own country in the new decade of the 1950s. A concerted boycott curtailed his activities: concert halls closed their doors to him; stores refused to sell his recordings; all references to him were banished from the press except for the harshest criticism. Under orders from Director J. Edgar Hoover, FBI agents kept him under surveillance, intercepted his mail, and wiretapped his telephones.[1]

Robeson became the target of so much hostility that even the Communist Party suggested it might be better for him to stop speaking out and just sing for a while. He firmly rejected that idea.

Dr. Doxey A. Wilkerson, a prominent educator with radical ties at the time, observed later that Robeson was "bigger than the party." In radical circles, with their factional disputes, he avoided the jealousies that afflicted others. Wilkerson said he was "universally respected."[2]

* * *

In January 1950, Eslanda Robeson came home after a three-month trip to the People's Republic of China. She had fulfilled her husband's desire to visit China, just as she had been the one who visited Africa. She now went on a speaking tour across the United States to discuss her favorable views of communism, feminism, China, and the Soviet Union.

Paul attended a national convention of the Progressive Party in Chicago in February. The delegates elected him as cochairman of the party. Henry Wallace delivered a rather desultory speech. Robeson's speech vehemently denounced both the Democrats and the Republicans for adhering to policies that relegated black Americans to second-class citizenship. He extolled the Progressives for fighting for civil rights.

Senator Joseph R. McCarthy, a relatively unknown Wisconsin Republican, delivered a demagogic speech in February 1950, claiming that Communists riddled the federal government. He stoked the anti-Communist hysteria.

In March, Eleanor Roosevelt scheduled a discussion of "the Negro in American political life" for her Sunday afternoon television program on NBC. Her son Elliot announced the three speakers for the discussion: Adam Clayton Powell Jr., Democratic congressman from Harlem; Perry Howard, a Southern Republican; and Paul Robeson, a leader of the Progressive Party.

The inclusion of Robeson evoked an immediate avalanche of criticism. Hundreds of telephone calls poured into NBC. The American Legion and the Catholic War Veterans demanded that he be barred from speaking. William Randolph Hearst's *New York Journal-American* assailed him on its front page.[3]

Within twenty-four hours, NBC announced that Robeson would not appear on Mrs. Roosevelt's program. Even the revered Eleanor Roosevelt failed to take a stand on his exclusion. She noted that NBC had "the final say on these things." Robeson denounced NBC, although he declined to criticize Mrs. Roosevelt.

* * *

The extreme public reaction to the idea that Robeson might take part in a discussion on television indicated the overwhelming hostility directed against him in the United States. For all-too-many Americans in the mid-twentieth century, Paul Robeson represented the two things they most feared and hated: the Red and the Black, the Communist and the Negro. The full weight of the federal government and American society came down on Robeson in a relentless effort to banish him from the life of the nation.[4]

Dr. W. E. B. Du Bois, the renowned black scholar, responded to the many attacks on Robeson by saying, succinctly, "The only thing wrong with Robeson is in having too great faith in human beings."

* * *

Paul Robeson sang at Carnegie Hall on the evening of Saturday, April 15, 1950, a rare appearance celebrating an anniversary of the left-wing Yiddish newspaper *Morning Freiheit*. He opened with several Yiddish songs accompanied by a chorus. After an intermission, Vladimir Weisman played a group of classical violin pieces. Robeson returned to sing songs from his usual repertoire with Lawrence Brown at the piano.

Afterward, Robeson greeted friends and well-wishers in his backstage dressing room. He autographed the printed programs of more than a dozen people who stood in line to approach him. One of them was a high school student who asked him for a brief statement about his life, which the student wanted to use in a term paper. Robeson expressed immediate interest in the term paper and responded to the student's request in a serious tone, speaking slowly as the student wrote his words in a notebook.

"The basic mainspring of my life is the deep struggle for the freedom of my people," he told the student. "You can say that I feel a very great obligation to my people. I have many friends all over the world, but I spring from an American heritage and I feel that my fight should be here in America for my people. I feel that all people have the right to human dignity. I am fighting for the freedom and human dignity of my people and all people throughout the world."[5]

* * *

On May 28, 1950, Robeson flew to London to participate in a meeting of the World Peace Council. Twenty thousand people attended an outdoor rally to hear speeches by leaders of the peace movement. Robeson sang to them in English, Russian, and Chinese, and then he declared that fascism would never triumph in America.

He asked George Bernard Shaw, whom he had known in his early years in London, to express support for the Progressive Party. The controversial Shaw responded that using his name would lose more votes than it would gain.

His brief trip to London finished, Robeson flew back to the United States.

In Chicago on June 10, Robeson spoke to one thousand delegates attending a meeting of the National Labor Conference for Negro Rights. He urged the union members to stand together not only for the rights of workers but also for racial equality and world peace. He appealed to the white trade union members to "fight in the ranks of labor for the full equality of your Negro brothers; for their right to work in any job; to receive equal pay for equal work; for an end to Jim Crow unions."

Praising the Communists for fighting for the rights of Negroes, he assailed President Truman for portraying communism as the enemy of democracy. He said, "Our enemies are the lynchers, the profiteers . . . the atom-bomb maniacs and the war-makers."[6]

* * *

On June 24, 1950, thousands of North Korean troops swarmed over the border to invade South Korea. President Truman, with UN approval, sent American forces to Korea to defend the regime in the south.

Robeson addressed a rally on June 28 in Madison Square Garden, where he sang and spoke against President Truman's intervention in Korea. The *New York Times* reported that the arena was only half-full for the rally, sponsored by the Civil Rights Congress. Robeson warned, quite illogically, that if it succeeded in Korea, the Truman administration would eventually turn its "imperialistic designs" on Africa.

A month later, on July 28, State Department agents met with Robeson and demanded that he give them his passport. On the advice of his lawyer, Nathan Witt, he refused. Then, on August 4, the State Department canceled Robeson's passport and ordered U.S. border officials to prevent him from leaving the country. The *Herald Tribune* reflected wide approval of this action, dismissing Robeson as an "agitator."

The State Department informed his lawyer, "Robeson's travel abroad at this time would be contrary to the best interests of the United States." So Robeson requested a meeting with Secretary of State Dean Acheson. Instead, he was told that he could meet with passport officials in Washington on August 23.

At this meeting, an official told Robeson that it was "detrimental" for him to criticize the treatment of American Negroes while he was abroad. His request for a passport would be reconsidered only if he signed a statement pledging not to make any speeches overseas. He refused to give up his right to speak, and his lawyer subsequently filed a lawsuit against the State Department.

* * *

Robeson strongly supported W. E. B. Du Bois in the autumn of 1950 when the black scholar, still energetic at the age of eighty-two, decided to run for the U.S. Senate as a candidate of the American Labor Party in New York. Most black leaders supported Senator Herbert H. Lehman, the highly respected Democratic incumbent, known as a champion of civil rights.

At a Harlem rally, Robeson introduced Du Bois as "the elder statesman of our oppressed people." The election's outcome was never in doubt, however, and Senator Lehman won handily, with Du Bois obtaining a respectable 13 percent of the vote.

Du Bois and Robeson had been working together for some time, more closely since 1948 when Du Bois moved his office from the NAACP to the Council on African Affairs. Then, after the Senate election, Du Bois helped Robeson launch a new militant journal named *Freedom* at the end of 1950.

* * *

Robeson singing from a small stage, with Lawrence Brown at the piano, at the Peace Arch in 1950. Courtesy International Union of Mine, Mill, and Smelter Workers Union Archives at the University of British Columbia.

Robeson began writing a column called "Here's My Story" in *Freedom*, published monthly in Harlem. The journal, edited by Louis E. Burnham, served as the organ of the National Negro Labor Council.

In addition to Robeson's column, *Freedom* carried articles by Du Bois, Shirley Graham, Lorraine Hansberry, and other left-wing blacks. This journal, with Robeson's columns written in collaboration with Lloyd L. Brown, a leftist black journalist, continued for five years.

Robeson's first column, which briefly mentioned his early life, referred to him as "a person who fights for peace, for the admission of People's China to the U.N., for friendship with the Soviet Union, for labor's rights and for full equality for Negroes now." He said he refused to allow his personal success to be used to "explain away the injustices to fourteen million of my people."

"That explains my life. I'm looking for freedom, full freedom, not an inferior brand." He expressed pride in "my African origin." He said his feeling for the Soviet Union began with a 1934 visit when "I, for the first time, walked this earth in complete human dignity, a dignity denied everywhere in my native land."

* * *

Walter White wrote an article titled "The Strange Case of Paul Robeson" in *Ebony* magazine in early 1951. Pretending to be sympathetic, White said, "Robeson is a bewildered man who is more to be pitied than damned." He contended, quite falsely, that Robeson enjoyed luxury, neurotically resented racial slights, and did little to correct the flaws in American democracy. One could certainly censure Robeson's uncritical support of Soviet policies, but the bulk of White's criticism was specious.

Essie sent an angry response to the magazine, which refused to publish it. The *California Eagle* printed her defense of her husband, stressing his fight for Negro rights. She concluded that Paul Robeson "stands like a giant oak, like a mountain—solid."

An indication of his stature came later in 1951 at a popular Harlem nightclub called the Red Rooster. Robeson was there with some friends. So was Don Newcombe, a star pitcher for the Brooklyn Dodgers. When Robeson approached him, politely asking for an autograph for a friend, the huge black ballplayer stood up and angrily challenged him. Everyone else in the crowded club quickly rallied to Robeson's side, one saying, "Nothing is going to happen to Paul." And Newcombe backed down.[7]

When newspapers reported the incident, Essie reminded them that Paul had helped open major league baseball to black players.

* * *

Robeson continued to speak and sing at protest rallies in 1951 despite the boycott against him. He observed his fifty-third birthday on April 9. He also helped celebrate the sixtieth birthday of his friend William Patterson.

On June 10, Robeson sang at the Prince Hall Masonic Temple in a poor, predominantly black section of Newark. The program, which included a gospel singer and a choral group, raised funds for the *Freedom* journal. With Lawrence Brown at the piano, he sang a group of English, Italian, and Russian songs. He ended with three spirituals, followed by "Water Boy" as an encore. When his voice dropped deeper, deeper, and still deeper in the final notes of "Water Boy," a lovely young woman in the audience put her head in her hands and exclaimed, "Wow!"[8]

At a huge Chicago Peace Congress in July 1951, Robeson spoke about civil liberties, warning that jailing Communist opponents of American policies posed a grave threat to the First Amendment. In the lobby of his hotel there, the great jazz musician Charlie Parker noticed Paul, walked up to him, and said, "I just wanted to shake your hand. You're a great man."

Two aspiring young actors, Sidney Poitier and Harry Belafonte, went on long walks with Robeson in Harlem. As Poitier recalled, "He used to tell us not to be too radical because he never wanted us to lose our credibility."[9]

* * *

The government charged Dr. Du Bois with acting as an "unregistered foreign agent" because of his activities for the international Peace Information Center. A federal grand jury in Washington indicted him on the charge, which could have sent him to prison. But the judge handling it dismissed the faulty case in November.[10]

Besides winning his court case, the aged Dr. Du Bois found time to marry Shirley Graham and to support an unusual petition to the United Nations by his friend Paul Robeson that accused the United States of "genocide." This petition—bearing the title "We Charge Genocide"—originated with the Communist lawyer William Patterson. It presented a detailed, but dubious, statement of charges, laid out in legal style, accusing the government of "mass murder" and "institutionalized oppression" of the Negro people on the basis of race.[11]

Robeson joined Patterson in bringing the petition to the United Nations in December 1951. But the United States, with its majority of votes, prevented the UN Human Rights Commission from considering it.

* * *

On January 30, 1952, Robeson planned to give a concert in Vancouver at the invitation of the International Union of Mine, Mill, and Smelter Workers of British Columbia. A three-car caravan of union officials took him from Seattle to the border, where Americans did not normally need passports to cross into Canada. But immigration officials, on State Department orders, stopped them at the border.

The union caravan took Robeson back to Seattle. There, the next day, he sat at a desk in a union office, with a telephone in his hand, speaking and then singing "Joe Hill" over a telephone line to the union's convention in Vancouver. The convention voted to arrange a Robeson concert in the spring at the Peace Arch, a monument on the border between Canada and the United States.[12]

On the sunny afternoon of May 18, on the U.S. side of the border, Robeson climbed onto the rear of a flatbed truck, where Lawrence Brown sat at an upright piano. A few thousand listeners gathered around them. Directly across the border, a crowd estimated at thirty thousand, many of them union members who came on chartered buses from Vancouver, assembled in the Peace Arch park. They sat on the grass around the sixty-foot-high white arch, which symbolized a peaceful entrance between the two countries.

"I can't tell you how moved I am at this moment—it seems that nothing can keep me from my beloved friends in Canada," Robeson said into the public address system carrying his voice across the border. "You have known me for many years. I am the same Paul, fighting a little harder because the times call for harder struggles."

He opened the program by singing "Every Time I Feel the Spirit" with Larry Brown joining in. Then came "Joe Hill," the ballad of the mine union hero, followed by the Scottish air "Loch Lomond."

"This next song is one that comes from the very depths of the struggle of my people in America," Robeson said, introducing the spiritual "No More Auction Block." It was often heard in the AME Zion Church, he said, where first his father and then his brother Ben served as ministers. He recited the opening lines of the spiritual before singing it to the cheering audience.

He went on to sing the humorous "Oh, No, John" and the romantic "Love Will Find a Way," among other songs, and closed with "Ol' Man River."

* * *

Robeson's efforts to carry out a concert tour—before and after his Peace Arch concert—resulted in canceled dates. But black churches often came to the rescue, inviting him to sing there. He felt at home in the black churches; he had grown up singing their hymns in his father's church and understood the congregations.

Speaking at the Hartford Avenue Baptist Church in Detroit in 1952, he told the congregation, "What would my father say to me if he were alive? He would say, 'It's hard son. But don't forget I was born in slavery. And your people were not able to do anything as free people for a long time. But they struggled, they fought. . . . I escaped by the underground. So you stand your ground. You may have to stand there for a little while longer. Just keep your courage and keep your heart.'"[13]

Overseas royalties from his recordings and prudent investments by his lawyer, Robert Rockmore, provided significant income, but far less than Robeson had previously earned.

Still strongly interested in the Progressive Party, Robeson attended its nominating convention in Chicago in July 1952. He served on the committee that selected Vincent Hallinan for president and Charlotta Bass for vice president. He also campaigned for them during the summer and fall. The lackluster party received fewer than two hundred thousand votes.

* * *

Paul Robeson visited Albert Einstein at his Princeton home in October 1952 at the scientist's invitation. Accompanied by Lloyd Brown, Robeson arrived in the early afternoon and found Einstein resting on a sofa. They spent the entire afternoon discussing a wide range of topics from music to colonialism in Africa and McCarthyism at home. When Paul left the room briefly, Brown told Einstein that he felt honored to meet a great man. Einstein replied, "But you came in with a great man."[14]

In December, the Soviet Union announced the award of one of the 1952 International Stalin Peace Prizes to Paul Robeson. The prize, including a gold medal and $25,000, honored individuals for outstanding service in "the struggle against war." Robeson told the press that he accepted the prize as a part of the growing peace movement "honored by the leadership of the great scholar Dr. W. E. B. Du Bois."[15]

The State Department still rejected Robeson's request for a passport, so Soviet officials presented the peace prize to him in New York.

* * *

Soviet dictator Joseph Stalin died at his country house near Moscow on March 5, 1953. That same month Langston Hughes, sometimes called "the poet laureate of the Negro race," renounced his Soviet sympathies and testified as a "cooperating witness" before Senator Joseph McCarthy's investigating subcommittee in Washington.

On July 17, the fighting in Korea ended with an armistice that left Korea divided between north and south, as it had been before the war started.

Echoing words that Robeson had spoken fifteen years earlier, the great French writer Albert Camus published an essay in 1953 that stated, "Artists of the past could at least keep silent in the face of tyranny. The tyrannies of today are improved; they no longer admit of silence or neutrality. One has to take a stand, either for or against. Well, in that case, I am against."[16]

* * *

Eslanda Robeson was summoned by Senator McCarthy's committee on July 7, 1953. The committee, apparently wary of questioning Paul, called his wife.[17]

"You are Mrs. Paul Robeson, is that correct?" the committee counsel, Roy M. Cohn, began the questioning. She replied, "Yes, and very proud of it, too."

When asked if she was a member of the Communist Party, she refused to answer, citing the Fifth and Fifteenth amendments to the Constitution. Senator McCarthy noted politely that the Fifteenth Amendment "solely deals with your right to vote" as an American citizen.

"I don't quite understand your statement that we are all American citizens," Mrs. Robeson retorted. "I have been fighting for this for all my fifty-six years. I am a second-class citizen now, as a Negro."

Senator Stuart Symington, a Democrat, suggested, "The reason you refuse to answer . . . means there is a good chance you are a Communist . . . because of your belief that your race has not had a fair deal in the United States."

"The reason I refuse to answer the question is because . . . my opinions are my private personal affair," she responded.

When asked about people dedicated to overthrowing the government by force and violence, she replied, "I don't know anybody that is dedicated to overthrowing the government by force and violence. The only force and violence I know is what I have experienced and seen in this country, and it has not been by Communists."

After more verbal sparring, the usually bellicose Senator McCarthy turned chivalrous toward Mrs. Robeson and said he was giving her special treatment. He called her intelligent and charming, adding, "I do not propose to argue with a lady."

"Well, I think that is very nice of you, Senator McCarthy," she said, and she added, "I am a very, very loyal American."

* * *

No More Auction Block

No more auction block for me,
No more, no more,
No more auction block for me,
Many thousands gone.

No more pint of salt for me,
No more, no more,
No more pint of salt for me,
Many thousands gone.

No more driver's lash for me,
No more, no more,
No more driver's lash for me,
Oh, many thousands gone.

—arranged by Lawrence Brown

· *17* ·

You Are the Un-Americans

Oh, my soul is a witness for my Lord.

—spiritual

$\mathscr{P}$aul Robeson returned to Seattle on August 16, 1953, so that union officials could drive him to the Canadian border for his second Peace Arch concert. The crowd was smaller this time but still impressive at more than fifteen thousand. Robeson introduced Alan Booth as his accompanist, telling the crowd that Lawrence Brown sent his regards but had decided to rest in New York.

With loudspeakers again carrying his voice across the border, Robeson opened the program with three spirituals, "Didn't My Lord Deliver Daniel," "Go Down, Moses," and "Jacob's Ladder." The only song that he repeated from the first Peace Arch concert was the perennial union favorite "Joe Hill." He went on to sing "Scandalize My Name," the "Song of the Four Rivers," "Drink to Me Only with Thine Eyes," and "All Men Are Brothers," followed by the Chinese marching song "Chi Lai."

In a speech at the concert's end, he told the crowd that it was now very difficult for him to find a place to act or sing in America. Noting a recent invitation to sing for the miners in Wales, he said it was in the coal mines of Wales "where I first understood the struggle of white and Negro together."

"But I speak as one whose roots are in the soil of my land. . . . I have a right to speak out. . . . My people are determined in America to be, not second-class citizens, to be full citizens, to be first-class citizens, and that is the rock upon which I stand." He added, "It seems so simple that all people should live in full human dignity and in friendship."

"And I want you to know that I'll continue this year fighting for peace, however difficult it may be. And I want everybody in the range of my voice to hear—official or otherwise—that there is no force on earth that will make me go backwards one-thousandth part of one little inch."

A union official led the applause and called on the audience to join him in a rousing "three cheers for Paul Robeson."[1]

* * *

For several years, Paul had spent periods living restlessly in the apartment of Gig McGhee or the town house of Freda Diamond. He got together with Essie from time to time, but for the most part she had been living her own life in their house in Enfield, Connecticut.

Essie's mother died in 1953 after a long illness. Then, Essie sold the Connecticut house at the insistence of Paul's lawyer, Bob Rockmore, who cited financial needs. She stayed for a while with Paul Jr. and Marilyn in Manhattan, then moved into a residential hotel. Paul then stayed mostly at the Manhattan apartment of the Rosens or at their Westchester County house in Katonah, when he was not on the road.

Paul had developed an increasingly strong relationship with the Rosen family—Dr. Sam Rosen, his wife, Helen, and their two children, John and Judy. They provided him with the secure, comfortable environment that he needed, a haven for him to relax in, away from worldly tensions.

He particularly enjoyed his visits to their vacation home in Katonah, according to Helen, who later provided details to biographer Martin Duberman. Paul would sleep late, eat a breakfast of pancakes made by the family's housekeeper, then a late meal of fried eggs or hamburgers prepared by Helen. He also ate large amounts of corn on the cob, peanut brittle, and chocolate ice cream.

With Sam, he had long discussions about sports. He showed football plays to John. And he sang while Judy accompanied him on the piano. He walked with Helen in the woods near the house in Katonah, sometimes singing to her.[2]

Robeson also frequently visited the Du Bois town house on Grace Court in Brooklyn Heights. Du Bois and his new wife, Shirley Graham, entertained leftist friends there during much of the 1950s. Paul and the man he called "the doctor" often spent hours together discussing "the state of the world."[3]

In 1953, Dr. Du Bois and his wife held a Christmas party in their town house for the families of several UN delegates from the Soviet bloc. Robeson, with Lawrence Brown at the piano, sang to the guests in the living room. The Russian UN representative, Andre Vishinsky, asked Paul to sing "Mississippi." With a smile, he complied, singing "Ol' Man River."[4]

Speaking at a dinner for Robeson the following year, Dr. Du Bois said, "He is without doubt today, as a person, the best known American on earth. . . . His voice is known in Europe, Asia and Africa, in the West Indies and South America. . . . Only in his native land is he without honor and rights."

* * *

Paul Robeson Jr. and his wife, Marilyn, with their two young children, David and Susan, lived in a Manhattan apartment on Upper Broadway. He was an engineering graduate of Cornell University, but his name made it difficult to find work. Using his language skill, he became a translator of Russian scientific journals.

In late 1953, he and Lloyd Brown established a recording company that they called Othello Records in Harlem. They produced three albums, bringing in some royalties despite the continuing white boycott of Robeson. One album was called *Solid Rock: Favorite Hymns of My People*. It contained six church hymns sung by Robeson: "Balm in Gilead," "Jacob's Ladder," and "The Solid Rock," along with "End of My Journey," "Amazing Grace," and "Someday He'll Make It Plain." The album's back cover carried this Robeson statement: "In the churches—the main center of Negro group singing—it is the hymn rather than the spiritual that is sung by the people." Recently, he added, he sang mainly in churches.

* * *

Robeson's activities remained constricted in 1954 and 1955 as the boycott of him continued at home and the denial of his passport prevented him from traveling abroad. Writing in the January 1954 issue of *Freedom*, he declared that it was not communism but "the McCarthyite madness" that threatened America. "For McCarthyism means destruction of the constitutional rights of free speech and free press and free religion. . . . It means fear, intimidation and terror." He said that "we must reject the Big Lie" of McCarthyism that the American people are threatened by communism. He countered this with "the Big Truth" that war could destroy the world and that "different social systems must live together in peaceful cooperation and competition."[5]

* * *

On May 17, 1954, the Supreme Court handed down its historic decision in the case of *Brown v. Board of Education*, finally ruling that segregation in public schools was unconstitutional. Robeson had to be pleased.

On May 26, a group of fellow artists held a "Salute to Paul Robeson" at the Renaissance Casino in Harlem. The group included Pete Seeger, Charlie Parker, Thelonious Monk, Lorraine Hansberry, and many others. The casino drew an overflow crowd supporting Robeson's right to a passport. But the State Department rejected his application again. He vowed to take the case to the Supreme Court and hired the noted leftist lawyer Leonard B. Boudin.[6]

Robeson returned to the Northwest in August 1954 for his third Peace Arch concert. This one attracted a smaller crowd. And friends who saw him on the West Coast said he needed a rest.

In November, Robeson wrote an article for the magazine *Jewish Life* in which he presented "my heartfelt greetings to the Jewish people, who are now celebrating three centuries of life and work in this land."

"As for myself, I have always felt an especially close bond with the Jewish people." He recalled his boyhood and "the Bible stories that gave imagery to the freedom songs of my people." He said the Negro spiritual "Go Down, Moses" had been translated into Hebrew for audiences in Israel, demonstrating "the interweaving of people's cultures."

* * *

Paul moved into his brother Ben's parsonage at the Mother AME Zion Church, at 155 West 136th Street, in Harlem in late 1954. He remained there, comfortable with Ben and his wife, Frankie, for much of the following year.

In his written profile of his brother, Ben noted that in early youth Paul thought he would follow his father into the ministry. Ben said, "Who would dare assert that he is not in the ministry? His singing and acting just happen to be the means of his livelihood."

"Have you heard Paul sing 'Witness'? He is there the personification of his father with his own personality added. He is singing there for his Lord and Master; for while he may not be orthodox when it comes to church attendance, he believes and knows to whom he has committed his all."

"Here lies the heart of his singing and acting too. He visions himself breaking down the barriers that have imprisoned his race for centuries."[7]

* * *

In February 1955, Robeson appeared under subpoena before a New York State legislative committee that was investigating the fund-raising of "Communist front organizations," including the Civil Rights Congress. He testified that he was proud to be a national director of the Civil Rights Congress and that he raised money for many worthwhile groups.

While he was in Los Angeles for one of his few concerts at the time, a front wheel came off his car. It happened twice. His driver, Frank Whitley, believed that someone had tampered with the wheel, but he lacked evidence to prove it.[8]

Robeson testifying before the House Un-American Activities Committee on June 12, 1956. Courtesy Bettemann/Corbis via Associated Press.

In May, at the invitation of students, he sang and spoke at the City College of New York and at Swarthmore College in Pennsylvania. At Swarthmore, he sang songs in English, German, Russian, Yiddish, Chinese, and an African language, the college newspaper reported. It described the audience response as very enthusiastic. He also discussed his cultural views with a group of students, the report said. It noted, "He has found basic similarities in music and culture among the varied peoples he has known."

* * *

Robeson returned to the Northwest for the fourth and last of his annual Peace Arch concerts in the spring of 1955. The crowd was much smaller now.

In San Francisco to give a concert celebrating the tenth anniversary of the founding of the United Nations, he stayed for a few weeks. He wrote in his *Freedom* column of July and August 1955 that he found it exciting to meet delegates from around the world who gave "moving testimonials to mankind's longing for peace and brotherhood."

The long fight to restore his passport continued into the summer of 1955. He became optimistic because the State Department had finally conceded that he could travel to Canada. In August, he went to Washington for a hearing in the U.S. District Court. But the government's attorney argued that Robeson was "one of the most dangerous men in the world." And the judge rejected Robeson's request for restoration of his passport.[9]

The passport decision dashed his hopes for traveling overseas, where he had many invitations to perform. He suffered further disappointment when two of his favorite enterprises, the journal *Freedom* and the Council on African Affairs, ended because of deteriorating finances.

In October 1955, Robeson entered Sydenham Hospital in Harlem for a degenerative prostate condition. He underwent a difficult operation, then remained in the hospital for three weeks of recovery. And Essie suffered her own serious health problems, undergoing a mastectomy to combat breast cancer.

Instead of returning to his brother's parsonage, Paul agreed that Essie could buy a Harlem town house, at 16 Jumel Terrace, where they would live together. With her organized efficiency, she decorated their new home, supervised his diet, and returned full-time to the role of Mrs. Paul Robeson.

* * *

In December 1955, a black woman named Rosa Parks refused to give up her seat to a white person on a bus in Montgomery, Alabama, initiating a black boycott that began the civil rights movement led by Martin Luther King Jr. This certainly encouraged Robeson, although he was not asked to participate.

Two events in 1956 disillusioned many Communists in the Western world. Nikita Khrushchev gave a speech that revealed the despotic crimes of Stalin. And Soviet troops invaded Hungary to put down a democratic revolution there. But Robeson remained silent about these events.

In February 1956, Robeson left U.S. territory for the first time in six years, with the grudging assent of the State Department. He went to Canada for a convention of the mine and mill workers in Sudbury, Ontario, and then gave a sold-out concert in Toronto.

British workers arranged a tribute program for him at the Free Trade Hall in Manchester on March 11. His fans filled all five hundred seats in the hall, where a huge portrait of him dominated the stage. They listened to a tape of him speaking and singing to the workers of Manchester.[10]

* * *

At home in Harlem, Robeson began to suffer from depression. One of his physicians attributed it to an underlying arteriosclerosis. Another said the depression probably resulted from the combined stress of prostate surgery and years of political harassment. For several months, Robeson seemed obsessed with a theory of music based on the pentatonic scale, which he thought could prove the connection between different cultures. Then, he became lethargic and withdrawn.[11]

His emotional health had finally deteriorated under the relentless hostility and hatred directed against him in his own country. For much of his life, he had carried out an exhausting schedule while suffering from frequent colds. Now, physically and emotionally, he showed the results of the strain he had suffered.

Ironically, a hostile congressional committee seemed to restore his energy. He responded to its subpoena with renewed vigor and determination.

* * *

On June 12, 1956, Paul Robeson appeared under a subpoena to testify at a hearing of the House Un-American Activities Committee in Washington. Accompanying him to the capital were two lawyers, Milton H. Friedman and Leonard B. Boudin, as well as Essie and Paul Jr.

It was a combative Robeson who faced the hostile right-wing committee. He exchanged barbs with the chairman, Francis E. Walter of Pennsylvania, and the committee's staff director, Richard Arens. Ostensibly, the hearing concerned the unauthorized use of passports. But it quickly turned to communism.[12]

"Are you now a member of the Communist Party?" Arens asked him.

"Oh, please, please, please," Robeson responded. He was told to answer the question.

"What do you mean by the Communist Party?" he retorted. "As far as I know it is a legal party like the Republican Party and the Democratic Party. Do you mean . . . belonging to a party of people who have sacrificed for my people and for all Americans and workers, that they can live in dignity? Do you mean that party?"

When Arens repeated the question, Robeson replied, "Would you like to come to the ballot box when I vote and take out the ballot and see?"

"You are directed to answer the question," Chairman Walter told him. Robeson briefly consulted Friedman, the lawyer sitting beside him, and then said, "I stand upon the Fifth Amendment."

Referring to an informer's statement, Arens said, "I put it to you as a fact, and ask you to affirm or deny the fact, that your Communist Party name was John Thomas."

"I invoke the Fifth Amendment," Robeson said. "This is really ridiculous."

He said the real reason for summoning him there and for denying him a passport was "because I have struggled for years for the independence of the colonial peoples of Africa" and because "I speak out against the injustices against the Negro people of this land."

Robeson repeatedly invoked the Fifth Amendment when asked if he was a Communist, if he knew certain people, and if he had attended various meetings. He banged his fist on the table at one point and exclaimed, "This is nonsense!"

But he readily acknowledged praising the Soviet Union, and he drew the sharpest exchange of the day when he told the hostile committee, "I would say in Russia I felt for the first time like a full human being, and no colored prejudice like in Mississippi and no colored prejudice like in Washington."

"Why do you not stay in Russia?" Representative Gordon H. Scherer pointedly asked him.

"Because my father was a slave, and my people died to build this country, and I am going to stay here and have a part of it just like you," an angry Robeson declared. "And no Fascist-minded people will drive me from it. Is that clear?"

Responding to a question about his friend Benjamin Davis, he asserted, "I say that he is as patriotic an American as there can be, and you gentlemen belong to the Alien and Sedition Acts, and you are the non-patriots, and you are the un-Americans, and you ought to be ashamed of yourselves."

"Just a minute—the hearing is now adjourned!" Chairman Walter shouted, banging his gavel.

"I should think it would be," Robeson retorted. Then, Walter denied his request to read a prepared statement. And Robeson said, "You should adjourn this forever, that is what I would say."

After the committee adjourned, it voted behind closed doors to hold Robeson in contempt of Congress for refusing to answer questions, which could have sent him to prison, but the full House failed to act on it.

Congressional activities during this egregious era brought to mind an observation by Mark Twain, who once wrote, "It could probably be shown by facts and figures that there is no distinctly native American criminal class except Congress."[13]

* * *

In 1957, Robeson returned to action. He looked over the manuscript of Marie Seton's biography of him, as she requested, apparently finding no fault with it. And he worked with Lloyd Brown on writing *Here I Stand*, a book containing a description of his childhood and a declaration of his beliefs. Brown said he had to overcome Paul's "deeply private nature" to write the book.[14]

Robeson used a new transatlantic telephone service to sing an unusual concert to an audience that filled the St. Pancras Town Hall three thousand miles away in London. The hall's bare stage displayed a huge photograph of him with a British flag on one side and an American flag on the other side. He sang six songs that evoked cheers from the audience of one thousand fans. Essie told the concert's organizer that Paul was so deeply moved that "he was close to tears."[15]

The British Actors' Equity Association called for his right to come to England to perform. In a letter of support, Flora Robson, his former costar, said she had no sympathy for his politics but would "love to hear his voice, the most beautiful natural voice of this century."

On October 4, 1957, the Space Age began when the Soviet Union launched the first satellite, Sputnik, into orbit around the earth. In Arkansas, a few blacks entering a white high school needed federal troops for protection.

* * *

The year 1958 brought a growing improvement in Robeson's life. He embarked on his first real concert tour in several years, traveling across the country. And he recorded a new album for Vanguard.

Here I Stand, published in early 1958, was well received by the black press, while the white press ignored it. In this slim book, he gave a personal account of his childhood. He went on to speak of forming his worldview while living in London, discovering African culture, walking with dignity in Moscow, and developing his political philosophy.[16]

Robeson expressed his belief in "the principles of scientific socialism." He contended, "A socialist society represents an advance to a higher stage of life. . . . It is a form of society which is economically, socially, culturally, and ethically superior to a system based upon production for private profit."

He added in an interview, "I do not believe that a few people should control the wealth of any land—it should be a collective ownership in the interest of everyone." He seemed to foresee the civil rights movement when he declared that American Negroes must win their rights by taking "mass action."

* * *

On April 9, his sixtieth birthday, celebrations took place in numerous countries, including Britain, Germany, Sweden, China, Japan, Mexico, and, of course, the Soviet Union. In India, Prime Minister Jawaharlal Nehru proclaimed Paul Robeson "one of the greatest artists of our generation," who had represented, and suffered for, "the cause of human dignity."

Speaking on his friend's birthday, Dr. Du Bois said, "The persecution of Paul Robeson by the government and people of the United States during the last nine years has been one of the most contemptible happenings in modern history. Robeson has done nothing to hurt or defame this nation. He is, as all know, one of the most charming, charitable and loving of men."

Du Bois said Robeson was loved as a great artist in the Soviet Union, and he loved that land in return, as "the nation which first outlawed the color line." He said America slandered Robeson for declaring that he would not join in a war against the Soviet Union. "This, for America, was Robeson's crime."[17]

* * *

On May 9, 1958, after a dark decade, Robeson gave a concert at Carnegie Hall. With Alan Booth at the piano, he sang the English airs "Oh, No, John" and "Over the Mountain." And he sang the "Hassidic Chant," a mournful cry from the heart with a half dozen words in Hebrew from the prayer for the dead. He also sang to the music of Mussorgsky, Beethoven, Bach, and Schubert. And he sang his traditional favorites, "Water Boy," "Balm in Gilead," "Every Time I Feel the Spirit," and finally "Ol' Man River." The sold-out audience gave him several standing ovations.[18]

The concert was such a success that he returned to Carnegie Hall exactly two weeks later, on May 23, repeating the concert with some variations in the program. This time he included "Jacob's Ladder" and "Joe Hill" and ended with "The House I Live In."

Then, a month later, the Supreme Court handed down a decision in the passport case of the leftist writer Rockwell Kent, which also applied to Robeson. The 5–4 decision, written by Justice William O. Douglas, ruled that the secretary of state could not withhold a passport because of the applicant's "beliefs and associations." The Robesons were now free to travel overseas again.

* * *

Witness

Oh, my soul is a witness for my Lord . . .

Now Daniel was a Hebrew child,
Went to pray to his God for awhile.
The king at once saw Daniel descend,
Cast him into the lions' den.

The Lord sent an angel the lions for to keep,
And Daniel lay down and went to sleep.
Daniel was a witness for my Lord,
Yes, Daniel was a witness for my Lord.
Oh, Daniel was a witness for my Lord.

—arranged by Lawrence Brown

· 18 ·

His Last Hurrah

Sometimes I feel like a motherless child.

—spiritual

On the evening of July 10, 1958, with a new passport in his pocket and his wife seated beside him, Paul Robeson took off from New York on a flight to London. Paul and Essie landed the next morning at the London airport, where some two hundred friends and fans greeted them with cheers, hugs, and bouquets of flowers. The warmth of the welcome provided a sharp contrast to the past decade of hostility that Robeson had endured in his own country.

Within twenty-four hours of his arrival, the agent Harold Davison had arranged three half-hour television appearances for him at £1,000 each and also began scheduling concerts for him. And Robeson soon signed a contract to star in a major production of *Othello*, beginning April 7 the next year.

His social calendar in London included visits with many of the prominent Britons who admired him. He had tea at the House of Lords with Lord Stansgate and his son, Anthony Wedgwood Benn; lunch at the House of Commons with Aneurin Bevan and his wife, Jennie Lee; and dinner with Peggy Ashcroft.[1]

In his own country, Congress had subpoenaed him and threatened him. But here, leaders of Parliament invited him to be their honored guest. He now felt free at last—at the age of sixty, with his health in question.

* * *

He appeared on his first broadcast on July 26, singing songs from China, France, and Wales, as well as a spiritual and a Bach chorale. He also recited the closing speech of *Othello*. "This was a half hour with a fine and thoughtful artist," wrote the *London Times*. "Perhaps, his face is craggier than it was and his voice, in song, a little less miraculously smooth than we remember it."

His accompanist for the television program, Bruno Raikin, saw that Paul had definitely aged. Lawrence Brown, who came by ship rather than plane, arrived in time to accompany him in subsequent concerts.

On August 10, Robeson gave his first concert since his return to England. It was a sold-out affair at the Royal Albert Hall, with a program of folk songs and spirituals. The *Times* said, "His depth, richness and resonance of tone were a feast for the ear." It added a mild complaint that he used a microphone, which he began using to preserve his voice as he grew older.

The British publication of *Here I Stand* and Marie Seton's biography of him drew a joint review on August 14 in the *London Times*. It began, "Paul Robeson is a single-minded crusader. His mission is to secure equal social and political rights for the American Negro." The reviewer said, "All the old cliches are here."

* * *

On August 15, Paul and Essie flew to Moscow, where a cheering crowd welcomed them at the airport. Soviet television carried a film about him the next evening, followed by a live conversation with him.

Next day, Robeson gave his first concert in Russia in almost a decade, singing to eighteen thousand people who filled the Lenin Sports Stadium. He threw his arms out wide to embrace the audience as he sang a patriotic Russian song containing the words "I know no other land where people breathe so free."

It seemed that every Negro in Moscow came to the hotel to talk to Paul, according to Essie, who said the morning of August 19 was devoted to these visitors. The Robesons left that afternoon, flying to Uzbekistan for a film festival. Exhausted, Paul went to bed the next day with a cold and fever.

They then traveled aboard a Soviet steamship to Yalta, where they stayed two weeks at a rest house for government officials. At a volleyball game one afternoon, they joined Premier Nikita Khrushchev and his wife among the spectators. Khrushchev, almost a foot shorter than Robeson, laughed as he climbed onto a rock so they could speak face-to-face at the same level, and all joined in the laughter.[2]

The vacationing Khrushchev invited the Robesons to a hunting lodge for dinner with Soviet officials and their wives. Afterward, Paul and Essie left Yalta and returned briefly to Moscow before flying back to London.

* * *

On September 21, 1958, once again accompanied by Lawrence Brown, Robeson began a three-month concert tour of the British Isles.

Church officials extended an unprecedented invitation for Paul Robeson to sing at evensong in St. Paul's Cathedral on October 11. They authorized

Robeson with Premier Nikita Khrushchev at a resort near Yalta on August 30, 1958. Courtesy Bettemann/Corbis via Associated Press.

a special collection for a fund in South Africa. Four thousand people filled the historic cathedral to hear Robeson, who solemnly walked to the lectern after the sermon. He sang a series of hymns and spirituals in his deep, resonant voice, including a powerful "Jacob's Ladder." One press report said that "the nobility of his performance" brought tears to the eyes of many in the audience.

On December 1, the *London Times* reviewed a Robeson concert at the Royal Albert Hall the previous night. "Needless to say," the review reported, "Mr Robeson sang beautifully even when dragging Schubert's 'Cradle Song' along at something like half its proper speed." It said his program included "the usual collection of folk songs from almost everywhere and Mr. Robeson sang them happily in their original languages."[3]

* * *

The Robesons left London on December 29, flying to Moscow to attend a gala Kremlin party on New Year's Eve. They stayed at the Moskva Hotel. On New Year's Eve, dressed in formal attire, they set out for the party.

At the Kremlin, Soviet officials greeted an array of formally dressed guests from many countries. In a great hall with tall stone columns and brightly lit chandeliers, the guests sat at long tables for a grand banquet. Premier Khrushchev sat at the head table in the front of the room with W. E. B. Du Bois and Shirley Graham Du Bois. She described the ensuing encounter.[4]

The Robesons, arriving a bit late, sat down at a table near the door. As Paul looked around, he saw Dr. Du Bois raise a hand to greet him from the opposite side of the great hall. Then, both Robeson and Du Bois got up and began moving through the mass of tables toward each other, finally coming together in the center of the room, where the giant Robeson and the diminutive Du Bois threw their arms around each other. This brought Premier Khrushchev to his feet applauding, and everyone followed suit, standing and applauding.

After an elaborate dinner, some of Russia's most famous musicians went to a stage at the front of the hall to play for the guests. A national chorus sang, then walked across the great hall to Robeson's table and brought him back to the stage with them. On stage, he sang a Red Army anthem "The Song of the Plain" in Russian, and the chorus joined him, evoking more applause.

A gong began slowly striking the midnight hour. Robeson stood with the chorus on stage as Khrushchev rose at his table with a glass in his hand. All the guests stood up as the premier toasted the arrival of 1959.

* * *

A few days after the New Year's Eve festivities, Paul fell ill with another cold, complicated this time by bouts of dizziness. Essie also became ill; doctors suggested she go to the Kremlin hospital for treatment. A consultant who examined Paul sent him to the hospital immediately. Both Robesons entered the Kremlin Hospital on the morning of January 12, 1959.

Also on January 12, the Shakespeare Memorial Theatre announced a star-filled series of productions for its hundredth season at Stratford-upon-Avon. It said the season would open on April 7 with Paul Robeson in *Othello*. On that same day, however, the Associated Press reported from Moscow that Robeson had been admitted to the hospital. It added, "Friends said today that he has been suffering from a cold and was overtired. Mr. Robeson had to cancel a concert tonight at the Bolshoi Theatre."

Doctors found that he suffered from acute exhaustion and needed total rest. Essie also remained in the hospital for treatment of uterine bleeding. Paul's dizziness continued, so the doctors sent him to a sanatorium for government officials, and he felt much better after a month of rest there.

The *London Times*, which had previously reported that his illness would force him to withdraw from *Othello*, said on February 13, "Mr. Paul Robeson will after all be fit enough to play *Othello*."

* * *

On March 10, Robeson flew from Moscow to London, then went on to Stratford to begin rehearsals.

For his stay in Stratford, he moved into a suite of rooms in a converted farmhouse owned by an old-fashioned English lady who knew nothing about him. To her family's surprise, she became devoted to Paul, this gentle man with his great courtesy and good manners. He lived there, virtually as a member of the family, during the run of *Othello*.[5]

Tony Richardson, the noted director of the production, said he took "a traditional approach but very elaborate, with costumes inspired by Titian, and with the pace of an American musical."

The cast included Mare Ure, the young wife of playwright John Osbourne, as Desdemona, and an American actor, Sam Wanamaker, as Iago. Supporting players were Albert Finney as Cassio, Peter Woodthorpe as Roderigo, Angela Baddeley as Emilia, and Zoe Caldwell as Bianca. Ure's understudy was Vanessa Redgrave, who later married Richardson.

Rehearsals with Robeson were fascinating, but the years had taken their toll, and he now lacked the energy for the scenes of great rage, according to Tony Richardson, who said, "He gave himself with the generosity and the humility of a great and extraordinary artist." He added that the other actors loved him. "And I was very, very proud and privileged to have been able to work with Paul."[6]

On April 7, 1959, the eagerly awaited production of *Othello* opened the hundredth season of the Shakespeare Memorial Theatre, with Paul Robeson in the title role. Opening night concluded with the cheering audience calling the obviously tired star back for more than a dozen curtain calls.

The critic for the *London Times* criticized the production by Tony Richardson; he said Sam Wanamaker and Mary Ure were miscast and lacked "Mr Robeson's magnificent voice." About Robeson, he said, "His performance is occasionally exciting; it hardly ever touches the heart."

Most of the other reviews contained more praise, particularly for Robeson. The dean of the London critics, W. A. Darlington, wrote in a dispatch to the *New York Times* that Robeson's *Othello* "ranks among the best that I have ever seen."

* * *

Robeson appeared in *Othello* two or three times a week for the rest of its seven-month run, as it alternated with the other Shakespearian productions at Stratford. He also resumed an active schedule when not on stage.

In June, he sang in Trafalgar Square during a demonstration against nuclear armament. And then he made a quick two-day trip to Prague to attend the Congress of Socialist Culture.[7]

He appeared in July at London's Palladium in a midnight revue with Bob Hope, Eddie Fisher, Laurence Olivier, Peter Sellers, and other stars to aid the Actors' Orphanage.

His arduous schedule continued as he flew to Vienna to sing at an open-air concert of the World Youth Festival on the evening of August 1. The concert, which included folk dances from several countries, followed a march to ban the atomic bomb by ten thousand demonstrators carrying banners.

Back in London, the BBC featured Robeson in a series of ten Sunday evening radio broadcasts. And he took part in a television program to discuss music with the great violinist Yehudi Menuhin.

His last *Othello* appearance was November 26. He had killed Desdemona and himself performance after performance—this time with no off-stage romance.

* * *

In January 1960, the Robesons went to Moscow for three weeks to rest and undergo medical examinations. Despite his need for rest, Paul engaged in a busy schedule in Moscow, singing at a factory, appearing on both radio and television, and participating in sessions of the World Peace Council. On January 29, he sat with Premier Khrushchev in a box at the Bolshoi Theatre. Reuters reported that Robeson was called on stage to sing some songs.

Paul kept the beard he grew for *Othello*, leading Essie to complain in a letter, "Nobody likes his beard and mustache, which he still wears and likes—says it makes him look Abyssinian."

He returned to London on February 7 for a concert tour of Britain, while Essie stayed in Moscow for more medical treatment. The tour of thirty-two cities continued into the middle of May and went well. But an observer who had known him in the past found that he had aged considerably.

In an *Evening Express* interview in March, Robeson said, "If, by my singing, I can spread the brotherhood of man throughout the world, then I will have accomplished something." The interviewer, Pearl Murray, wrote, "I shall remember him for his sincerity, his humility, his energy and his dignity."[8]

On May 15, 1960, when the concert tour ended, he went to another peace demonstration by three thousand people in Trafalgar Square. London's press reported that Robeson and the leftist dean of Canterbury addressed the crowd.

* * *

Essie returned to London from Moscow in May, although her health remained problematic. Paul traveled alone to Paris and Budapest for some Communist-sponsored events in the summer.

When he gained too much weight, he underwent a strict program of injections and diets to lose forty pounds in forty days, according to Essie. His normal weight as a mature man was now about 240 pounds, but he periodically gained weight quickly and went on crash diets.

Essie joined him on a trip to East Germany for a celebration of the 150th anniversary of Humboldt University in East Berlin. The university awarded him an honorary doctor of philosophy degree. An East German peace group gave prizes to both Robesons. And East Germany's leader, Walter Ulbricht, pinned a medal on Paul.[9]

* * *

Robeson embarked on a strenuous ten-week concert tour of Australia and New Zealand, beginning in October 1960. He traveled there with Essie and Larry Brown. On arriving in Sydney, he encountered a hostile press conference, and he angrily defended his praise of the Soviet Union.

His first concert in Australia took place on the evening of October 15 at Festival Hall in Brisbane, where an audience of five thousand cheered him. The press reported a strong police presence in case of trouble, but none developed.

A few days later, Robeson went on to New Zealand for three weeks of concerts, finding a friendlier press there. He performed in an informal style, interjecting comments about his songs. In Wellington, a critic wrote that Robeson responded to the "tremendous applause" that greeted him by clapping back at the audience—then he smiled and sang, "and a legend had come true."

The rest of the concerts took place in Australia, where a music critic in Perth wrote that Robeson projected "unmistakable greatness." He is "a proud, fearless, majestic figure, but his easy, informal friendliness reaches out through song and spoken word to embrace all the members of his audience."[10]

The tour achieved artistic and financial success, earning more than the promised $100,000, which substantially augmented the family's finances.

* * *

The Robesons returned to London in December 1960. Paul said he felt tired and lonely. Clearly, he had tried to do too much after having been so restricted in America. He was worn out.

Robeson knew that Australia was his last major concert tour, just as he knew that *Othello* at Stratford was his last major stage role. He had not felt like himself for some time, not since his prostate surgery. The additional problems of arteriosclerosis and depression, along with the relentless hostility that had worn him down for a decade in America, had taken their toll.

With depleted energy, he had reached deep within himself to perform in recent years—the Carnegie Hall concerts in 1958, the *Othello* production in 1959, the Australian tour in 1960. And people constantly made demands on him. He had given his all for so long that he felt he had nothing left. He longed for a quieter, less stressful life.

In early 1961, Paul and Essie attended plays and concerts in London. But he sounded so depressed in his letters to Helen Rosen that she flew to London to see him. Helen urged him to come home to America, but Essie vehemently opposed this.[11]

Then, suddenly, Paul flew off alone to Moscow in March.

* * *

After his abrupt departure from London in March 1961, Robeson arrived alone in Moscow and talked to Essie on the telephone, sounding happy.

He sang at a factory in Moscow at the invitation of Robert Robinson, an American Negro working there who had met him during previous visits. An audience of five thousand filled the factory's large shop and applauded loudly, according to Robinson, who said Robeson "captivated the workers with his voice and his personal magnetism."[12]

After singing several songs, Robeson finished with a "mournful song" about Jewish persecution, which he sang with deep emotion in Hebrew.

Robert Robinson said he heard solid rumors the following week that Robeson had visited Premier Khrushchev at the Soviet leader's vacation villa and raised the question of anti-Semitism in the country. In an angry outburst, Khrushchev reportedly accused the stunned Robeson of meddling in the internal affairs of the Soviet Union.[13]

On the evening of March 26, 1961, a noisy party took place in Robeson's suite in his Moscow hotel. A number of visitors had come, uninvited, and some pleaded with him to help imprisoned relatives. Robeson sought seclusion in his bedroom. No verified details emerged from this party, which apparently took place shortly after his meeting with Khrushchev.

What followed was shocking.

The interpreter assigned to Robeson said she found him on the floor of his bathroom, his wrists slashed with a razor blade, on the morning of March 27. He had apparently tried to commit suicide. Doctors at a Moscow hospital diagnosed his condition as depressed and paranoid, intensified by arteriosclerosis. They treated him with tranquilizers and kept him in the hospital.[14]

Notified by Soviet officials, Robeson's wife and son rushed to Moscow. Paul Robeson Jr. was extremely suspicious that someone, possibly a CIA agent, had drugged his father at the party and precipitated the attempted suicide. He said his father told him only that "someone close" to him had harmed the Soviet Union. That enigmatic comment was all he said on the subject.

Robeson as Othello with Mary Ure as Desdemona at Stratford in 1959. Courtesy Associated Press.

Paul Jr. questioned Soviet authorities but learned nothing more. He soon felt ill himself, began hallucinating, and spent some time with his father in the same sanatorium. He flew home to New York in early June. Coincidentally, Ernest Hemingway committed suicide a month later after complaining that the FBI had been hounding him with incessant surveillance.[15]

* * *

Facts about Robeson's suicide attempt remain obscure. He suffered from depression, exhaustion, and arteriosclerosis, with dizzy spells. But something had to trigger what happened. He hinted at damaging words by someone close to him, possibly one of Essie's brothers or perhaps a provocation at the hotel party; and the Khrushchev incident, if true, certainly would deeply distress him since he had sacrificed so much for the Soviet Union.

Whatever the cause, the result was Robeson's tragic collapse and a long convalescence.

One could certainly sympathize with his son's difficulty in understanding his father's attempt to kill himself. Depression can devastate the human spirit, and a decade of the most extreme hostility in his own homeland surely had a depressing impact on Robeson. Perhaps killing himself so often on stage in *Othello* helped to prepare him for attempting to commit suicide in reality. But it is painful to accept that such an extraordinary man wanted to end his own life.

* * *

In June 1961, after their son left, Essie accompanied Paul back to London. He soon became depressed, however, and she took him back to the Moscow sanatorium for three months. Returning to London again, he seemed deeply troubled.

Essie called Helen Rosen, who flew immediately to London. They then arranged for Paul to enter the Priory, a noted psychiatric nursing home in southwest London. There, he underwent electric-shock treatments and took heavy medication for depression. For a month, Essie and Helen stayed together in the Robeson apartment in London; together they visited him every day at the Priory.[16]

Writing to a friend, Essie reported that Paul was slowly recovering in a nursing home. She said that "exhaustion is a very, very difficult thing" to get over. "The long years of doing too much in too many places has taken its toll."[17]

Robeson continued his convalescence at the Priory for almost two years. He improved and sometimes went back to the apartment with Essie for weekend visits to the theater. And he received many congratulatory messages on his sixty-fifth birthday in April 1963.

* * *

Essie made a quick trip to East Berlin to check out an acclaimed clinic, then decided to take Paul there. Wearing a dark suit and gray hat, Paul boarded a Polish airliner at the London airport on Sunday, August 25. His fiercely protective wife accompanied him on the flight to East Berlin.

London's *Sunday Telegraph* carried a sensationalistic article that day suggesting Robeson was being "smuggled" behind the Iron Curtain to silence him because he was "disillusioned" with communism. A reporter got on the same flight and tried to interview Robeson, who called the article a "vicious misrepresentation."[18]

When they arrived at the airport in East Berlin, a tired-looking Robeson left the plane with his wife. They climbed into a car awaiting them next to the plane and were whisked away. The next day, Robeson gave a statement to the East German press service, saying he had accepted a "cordial invitation" to visit the German Democratic Republic and stay in a convalescent home. His wife added that he was suffering from "circulatory trouble."

At the Buch Clinic, East German doctors sharply reduced the drugs that Robeson had been given in England. He remained at the clinic for almost four months, recovering while Essie protected him. She delayed telling him for some time that both his brother Ben and his friend Bob Rockmore had died.[19]

Finally, after more than five years abroad, half of this time in hospitals and nursing homes, Paul decided to go home. On December 18, he and Essie flew from Berlin to London, collected their things, and said goodbye to friends. His agent said Robeson was retiring.

The Robesons flew from London to New York on December 22, 1963.

* * *

"Sometimes I Feel Like a Motherless Child"

Sometimes I feel like a motherless child,
Sometimes I feel like a motherless child,
Sometimes I feel like a motherless child,
A long way from home, a long way from home,
Oh my brother, a long way from home,
A long way from home.

Sometimes I feel like I'm almost gone,
Sometimes I feel like I'm almost gone,
Sometimes I feel like I'm almost gone,
A long way from home, a long way from home,
Oh my brother, a long way from home,
A long way from home.

—arranged by Lawrence Brown

· 19 ·

Home to Harlem

Swing low, sweet chariot, coming for to carry me home.

—spiritual

$\mathcal{A}$ British jetliner landed at New York's Idlewild Airport at 3:35 p.m. on December 22, 1963, bringing Paul Robeson back to America for the first time in five and a half years.

Dressed in a gray overcoat and broad-brimmed hat and wearing large horn-rimmed glasses, Robeson appeared thin and subdued as he and Essie walked out of the international arrivals building. Paul Robeson Jr. waited there with his wife, Marilyn, and their two children, twelve-year-old David and ten-year-old Susan.

"Hello, Dad," Paul Jr. said, as he hugged his father and kissed him on the cheek. Hugging him back, Paul Sr. replied softly, "Hello there, Chappie."

When reporters asked how he felt, Robeson replied, "Very glad to be back." Asked what he planned to do, he said, "I'm going to rest for a while." And asked if he would take part in the civil rights struggle, he said, "I've been a part of it all my life." When asked about some press reports that he had become "disillusioned" with communism, Essie retorted that the reports were "stupid" and that her husband thought communism was "terrific."[1]

Robeson rode away in a car with his son and two men identified by Essie as physicians. Then, Essie and Marilyn shifted suitcases from two luggage carts into another car, and they rode away with the two children. Essie was heard gushing over her grandchildren, "My David, my Suzy, they've grown up."

The Robesons had refused to say where they were going, but they headed for their Harlem home at 16 Jumel Terrace.

On the flight to America, Paul Robeson had jotted down some brief notes that included these words: "It is a profound satisfaction, and indeed a form of medicine, to see my Negro people in motion well on their way to achieve their Constitutional rights after 200 years of denial and postponement."[2]

* * *

Little more than a year earlier, the United States had challenged the Soviet Union for installing missile bases in Cuba, and Khrushchev had withdrawn the missiles, stepping back from the brink of nuclear war. And President John F. Kennedy was assassinated in Dallas just a month before Robeson came home.[3]

Paul and Eslanda Robeson lived together, quietly, in their Harlem home during the opening months of 1964. She was once again in charge of the house, and part of her job was to protect him by turning away visitors. She had often played this role of gatekeeper for him, acting as his official naysayer, rejecting the requests of people who wanted to see him. Those she rejected resented her, of course, failing to recognize that she usually carried out his wishes, sometimes with more vigor than necessary.

Essie took pride in being organized, intelligent, and disciplined. She also relied on her personality, her style, and strove to be charming. Many people found her pretentious, however, in contrast to her husband's unassuming manner. Some believed that she was the more radical of the two and that she prodded him to the left; they misunderstood her and underestimated him. Paul Robeson was always his own man, though now aged and ill.

* * *

Robeson's doctors found him thin, depressed, and suffering from insomnia. Paul Jr. visited his father almost every day. Lloyd Brown and Ben Davis were among the few friends welcomed as visitors from time to time.

In the first public appearance by either of the Robesons since their return, Essie received a standing ovation when she attended a Carnegie Hall tribute in February to W. E. B. Du Bois, who had died in Ghana at the age of ninety-three.

Essie wrote a letter addressed to "Dear Friends" on February 27, 1964, reporting Paul's progress. She said he was eating well and gaining weight. He discusses sports with Pauli, and "he reads *The Times* every morning, for an hour or more, in detail."[4]

In unpublished notes, Robeson made some observations about race relations, redefining an earlier view and emphasizing the bond between the races. He wrote, "I do not believe the Negro is essentially different from the white man, that the European, the Asian, the African is a different species of humanity. I believe we are all members of one wonderful human family, with a common origin, a common culture with a wealth of art and music, a common purpose, a common destiny."[5]

Essie went to the West Coast on a two-week lecture tour in the spring of 1964. In her absence, Paul stayed with his sister, Marian, in Philadelphia, where he continued to improve, eating and sleeping more regularly. In June, having returned to Harlem, he went to a baseball game with his son. Essie observed, "Paul is so much better."

* * *

On August 22, 1964, Benjamin Davis Jr. died of cancer. Robeson spoke in public for the first time since his return, delivering a brief speech at a memorial service for his "beloved comrade." He noted his friend's career as a lawyer, as a leader of the Communist Party, and as Harlem's elected member of the city council, "where he led the fight for justice and equality for our people."

"For me, this has been a time of deep sorrow," Robeson added, referring to two other recent deaths. "For Ben Davis now goes to join another Ben I have lost—my beloved older brother; he also joins his colleague Dr. W. E. B. Du Bois, one of our very great Americans."[6]

Two days later, Robeson issued a written statement to the black press, explaining that he had not given any interviews since his return home from Europe some eight months before. He now wanted to say a few words to the many people who had been "wondering what has happened to me." "The fact is, I have been resting and recovering my health and strength after a rather prolonged illness," he said. But he wanted to assure well-wishers that he was feeling better and was "on the road to recovery."

"While I must continue my temporary retirement from public life, I am of course deeply involved with the great upsurge of our people. Like all of you, my heart has been filled with admiration for the many thousands of Negro Freedom Fighters and their white associates who are waging the battle for civil rights throughout the country and especially in the South."

He again expressed his sorrow at "the loss of persons who, for many long years, were near and dear to me"—his brother Ben, his colleague Dr. Du Bois, and his friend Ben Davis.[7]

* * *

In November 1964, Robeson attended a Soviet reception at the United Nations Headquarters in New York. He also went to an American-Soviet friendship celebration at Carnegie Hall, where the audience gave him a sustained standing ovation.

When Lorraine Hansberry died of cancer in early 1965, Robeson went to the funeral and delivered the eulogy in a compelling voice, lauding her "feeling and knowledge of the history of our people." Hansberry, who had worked with Robeson as a secretary and writer on his *Freedom* publication, had become a talented playwright who wrote *A Raisin in the Sun*. She died of cancer at the age of thirty-four.[8]

Malcolm X, a charismatic Black Muslim leader who had praised Robeson for questioning why black people would fight for a country that mistreated them, sought out Paul Robeson Jr. at the Hansberry funeral in New York. He said he would like to meet Robeson. But this overture died with him some weeks later when he was assassinated by gunmen from a rival faction.

A surge of black anger against white society's relentless racism produced widespread rioting and a relatively small but assertive "black nationalism" movement in America of the 1960s. Historian C. Vann Woodward said the movement's varied leaders shared "an antipathy toward 'integration' and 'nonviolence'—the two ideals [of] the civil rights movement." Malcolm X had been "the most powerful voice" of these blacks who wanted to create a separate society of their own, one that they could protect by force of arms. More recently, however, Malcolm X had modified his views, becoming less militant.[9]

* * *

Early in 1965, Robeson wrote an article on the legacy of Dr. Du Bois in the journal *Freedomways*, praising him as a distinguished historian and a social scientist who worked for civil rights at home and for freedom of the colonies in Africa. Robeson and Du Bois valued black culture, not black nationalism.

"We often talked about the wealth and beauty of our folk heritage, particularly about Negro music which he loved and found deeply moving," Robeson recalled. "He often stressed the importance of this special contribution to American culture. We had interesting discussions about the likeness of our Negro folk music to many other folk musics throughout the world."

He also described Du Bois as "a strong supporter of socialism as a way of life" and as a friend of the Soviet Union and the other socialist countries. He said Du Bois welcomed "their rejection of racism" and their efforts for "the welfare of the vast majority of the people."[10]

* * *

As Robeson's sixty-seventh birthday approached in 1965, he authorized *Freedomways* to hold a "birthday salute" to raise money for the journal. It took place the evening of April 22 in the ballroom of the Americana Hotel in midtown Manhattan. Two thousand people attended, a mixture of whites

Robeson returning home, greeted by his family at the airport on December 22, 1963. Photographed by Allyn Baum, *New York Times*.

and blacks, filling all the seats, with many more standing along the walls of the huge room.[11]

Among the participants in the program were folksinger Pete Seeger, composer Earl Robinson, writer James Baldwin, musician Billy Taylor, and actors Roscoe Lee Browne, Morris Carnovsky, Howard Da Silva, and Ruby Dee. Ossie Davis served as master of ceremonies. Robeson embraced Pete Seeger, kissed tiny James Baldwin on the cheek, and shook hands with several others.

John Lewis, the young black chairman of the radical Student Nonviolent Coordinating Committee, delivered a keynote speech in which he declared, "We of S.N.C.C. are Paul Robeson's spiritual children." He quoted a Robeson statement in *Here I Stand* that "the goal of 'Equal Rights Now' can be achieved." He added, "Mr. Robeson, we hope to honor you best by performing that task."

A veteran Harlem leader, Hope R. Stevens, told the audience that after the "pygmies" who defamed Paul Robeson were long forgotten, "this moral giant of our time will live in the hearts of his people."

Around a table at the front of the ballroom, Robeson sat with Essie, Paul Jr. and Marilyn, their two children, and Paul's sister, Mrs. Marian Forsythe, a matronly woman with gold-rimmed glasses who beamed with sisterly pride. They linked arms and swayed back and forth when Seeger sang the civil rights anthem "We Shall Overcome."

Robeson, dressed as usual in a conservative double-breasted suit, now with a white carnation in the left lapel, rose to speak at 10 p.m. as the audience cheered and applauded. He smiled and applauded in return to acknowledge the warm reception. He looked rather thin and tired, seeming to lack the vitality that he had projected in the past. As the applause finally subsided, he put on a pair of horn-rimmed glasses to read from notes for his speech.

"Well, I am certainly proud and happy to be with you tonight," he began, in that familiar, deeply resonant voice. He hailed *Freedomways* as a magazine that had become part of "the thrust of the Negro Freedom Movement." And he called the crowd's attention to "my friend and colleague, Mr. Lawrence Brown, an authority on Negro and classical music, who has been my partner in concerts for forty years."

Then, making it clear that his views had not changed, he said art reflected common aspirations of people throughout the world, and he praised "socialist development" in the Soviet Union, the People's Republic of China, Cuba, and the other Communist countries. As for which system was better for humanity, he said, the different social systems should "compete with one another under conditions of peaceful co-existence."

Turning to civil rights, he said that during all his time away in Europe, he had "kept in touch with the remarkable progress of the freedom struggle here at home." He asserted, "The Negro people are claiming their rights and they are in every way determined to have those rights and nothing can turn us back." He added that achieving black rights would not reduce white rights and would in fact "enormously strengthen the base of democracy for all Americans."

Robeson concluded by reciting a stanza of the Warsaw Ghetto song and repeating the final words of the current rallying song: "We shall overcome, deep in my heart I do believe, we shall overcome some day."[12]

Despite this successful birthday event, Paul Robeson had been relegated to the sidelines, largely irrelevant and forgotten, as Dr. Martin Luther King Jr. and a new generation of black leaders led the fight for civil rights.

* * *

Under the forceful urging of President Lyndon B. Johnson, Congress passed the Civil Rights Act and Voting Rights Act of 1964 and 1965, legislation that advanced the political rights of black people. Robeson must have been pleasantly surprised by the leadership of this forceful Texan. Congress also passed his important Medicare bill, providing health insurance for elderly Americans.

Robeson, accompanied by his wife, flew from New York to Los Angeles in May 1965 on his first trip since returning home. They stayed at a friend's house in the city's black community and attended a celebration for them at the First Presbyterian Church. Paul spoke to the congregation, then sang "Jacob's Ladder" without accompaniment. Noting it was the first time he had sung for some while, he said with a smile, "I guess the voice is still around somewhere."

The *Los Angeles Times* published a friendly article on May 16 under the headline "Robeson Cherishes His U.S. Heritage." It quoted an "optimistic" Robeson as saying he believed that the Negro would become "a full American in every sense of the word."

The Robesons went on to San Francisco, where they stayed at the home of an old friend. They attended a fund-raising dinner for a Du Bois Club and a lunch at another friend's house. But both of them were fading with fatigue and failed to go to an elaborate "Salute to Paul Robeson" affair on June 4. Instead, they flew back to New York to rest.

* * *

Back home, Robeson felt lethargic and depressed. His wife found him holding a pair of scissors to his chest one morning, and later that day, his son found him holding a razor blade to his neck. They called Dr. Samuel Rosen, a good friend, who rushed to the house and took Paul to the Gracie Square Hospital.[13]

It is painful to think of one who achieved so much and touched so many lives wanting to take his own life. Depression can be a hard taskmaster. Paul believed that he had nothing more to contribute, nothing meaningful left to do.

He entered the psychiatric hospital under the assumed name of Frank Robertson on June 11 and remained there for three weeks under treatment with antidepressants. When he returned home, he seemed better. He went with his son to see Dr. Ari Kiev, a psychiatrist who found that Robeson suffered from a great sadness with an underlying cerebral arteriosclerosis. Given all the hostility that he had endured, Dr. Kiev said, it was surprising that he had not broken down sooner.[14]

* * *

In early August it was Essie who had to go to the hospital. Paul took her to Beth Israel Hospital, where she remained for a series of cobalt treatments for breast cancer. Surgeons operated on her on August 10.

Paul Robeson Jr. went to 16 Jumel Terrace every evening to cook dinner for his father while Essie was in the hospital. He also took him back to see the psychiatrist, who found Robeson depressed and concerned about his wife's hospitalization. The doctor readmitted him to the Gracie Square Hospital, where his condition deteriorated under high doses of medication.

Concerned about his father's condition, Paul Jr. summoned Dr. Rosen, who rushed to the hospital with Dr. Richard Nachtigall. They ordered several tests and placed Robeson on the critical list, acutely ill with pneumonia, high fever, dehydration, and kidney damage. They transferred him to University Hospital, where he improved slowly for three weeks.[15]

Both Paul and Essie came home from their hospitals in September. She was dying of cancer. He stayed in the house, deep in his own depression. Two old friends, Frankie Sims and Marie Bowden, came to help Paul Jr. and Marilyn take care of his parents.

* * *

On the evening of October 15, Robeson walked out the front door and disappeared. Paul Jr. called Lloyd Brown, who lived nearby, and they drove through the neighborhood in search of him. At midnight, they called the police, who issued a missing persons report. Early the next morning, a man walking his dog spotted Robeson and called the police. They found a semiconscious Robeson lying in some bushes near Highbridge Park, a few blocks from home.

The police took him to the Vanderbilt Clinic at Presbyterian Hospital for treatment of minor lacerations and bruises, then transferred him to University Hospital. Essie left her sickbed to go there with Paul Jr. and Lloyd Brown to see him. Paul told them that he had no memory of leaving the house. He kept asking them, "What happened to me?"

Eslanda Robeson issued a statement reporting that her husband had a circulatory illness and suffered from some dizzy spells. He remained in the hospital for several days; then Paul Jr. took him to Marian's house in Philadelphia.[16]

* * *

Essie returned to the hospital in November for a final time. This was an illness that even she could not overcome. On December 13, 1965, two days before her seventieth birthday, the indomitable Eslanda Goode Robeson died of cancer in Beth Israel Hospital.

Paul Robeson Jr. went to Philadelphia to inform his father. He said his father signed the death certificate, then turned away, saying not a word. Robeson stayed in Philadelphia. Paul Jr. and Marilyn, with their two children, attended the funeral for his mother in New York.[17]

For more than four decades, Essie had been the most important person in Paul's life. They had stayed together though good times and bad; their emotions had remained deeply entwined, even though Paul preferred to put some distance between them at times. Now, with her death, he seemed to withdraw into himself, essentially removing himself from daily life.

Eslanda Robeson was a modern woman a generation ahead of her time. She was well educated, accomplished, and assertive, a feminist and a writer, independent and indomitable. She suffered numerous illnesses over the years, endured them largely without complaint, and continued to fulfill her obligations. Despite her troubled relationship with her husband, she remained married to him for forty-four years and always relished her role as Mrs. Paul Robeson.

She had earned an undergraduate degree from Columbia University and later studied anthropology at London University and the Hartford Seminary. Her books included the first biography of her husband, a journal of her journey through Africa, and a discourse with the Nobel novelist Pearl S. Buck. Essie also participated in progressive politics. She played an extremely important part in her husband's early career, chronicled much of their life together, and remained with him to the end. She never faltered in working for his best interests.[18]

An obituary in the *New York Times* described Eslanda Robeson as an anthropologist and author who encouraged her husband's career and "worked actively for civil rights causes throughout her life." Even in death, Essie could trim a year from her age; the *Times* obituary said she was sixty-eight.

Her most significant contribution came in the mass of material—diaries, letters, and documents—that she preserved for the legacy of Paul Robeson.

Paul's relationship with Essie had been complex and troubled but loving and enduring to the end. Afflicted by loneliness, he sought solace in the arms of caring women. His romantic affairs constituted a character flaw, a failure of fidelity to his wife. Even on that score, however, it can be said that he was not a promiscuous man; he always treated women with respect and never exploited or abused them. His half dozen affairs, in a period of almost half a century, were long-lasting ones with women who invariably retained their affection for him.

With the passing of his wife, Robeson's final years would be reclusive ones in the care of his sister in Philadelphia.

* * *

"Swing Low, Sweet Chariot"

Swing low, sweet chariot,
Coming for to carry me home.
Swing low, sweet chariot
Coming for to carry me home.

I looked over Jordan and what did I see,
Coming for to carry me home,
A band of angels coming after me,
Coming for to carry me home.

Swing low, sweet chariot,
Coming for to carry me home,
Swing low, sweet chariot,
Coming for to carry me home.

If you get there before I do,
Coming for to carry me home,
Tell all of my friends I'm coming too,
Coming for to carry me home.

Swing low, sweet chariot,
Coming for to carry me home,
Swing low, sweet chariot,
Coming for to carry me home.

—arranged by Lawrence Brown

• 20 •

Our Tallest Tree Has Fallen

I'm going to tell God all of my troubles.

—spiritual

Paul Robeson lived in his sister Marian's comfortable twelve-room house in Philadelphia at the beginning of 1966.

In February, Paul Robeson Jr. took his father back to New York, where he moved his own family into the house at 16 Jumel Terrace, so they could stay together. This arrangement did not work well. Paul Jr. then decided to rent and refurbish a spacious apartment on West 86th Street for his family, with a separate suite for his father. This arrangement also failed to work, however, as the senior Robeson grew emotionally withdrawn.

It seemed clear that he could stay more comfortably in the care of his sister in Philadelphia, so he returned there permanently in October 1966. The house at 16 Jumel Terrace was sold for almost $18,000.

* * *

Marian Robeson Forsythe, a retired schoolteacher, was seventy-two years old at this time. Her husband, Dr. William Forsythe, had died several years before. Marian lived with their daughter, Paulina, in the spacious three-story house at 4951 Walnut Street in West Philadelphia. Paul had a large bedroom with a bay window on the second floor in the rear of the house.

Marian, always the devoted sister, said she hoped God would spare her long enough to take care of Paul in his final years.

On a Sunday afternoon, Marian invited Charlotte Turner Bell, a piano teacher who lived two blocks away, for a visit. Bell discussed music with Paul, whom she described as friendly and gracious. Then, Marian arranged for her to play the piano for Paul a few times a week. He would sit next to her at the

197

piano for an hour or so and sing some of his favorite songs, usually spirituals, while she accompanied him on the piano.

He sang softly, she said, but his voice retained its fine quality. Songs he sang most often included "Witness," "Break Bread Together," and "Climbing Jacob's Ladder," as well as "All Through the Night," "Water Boy," and "Ol' Man River."

Bell said she served as Paul's "private accompanist" during this period. He usually woke up around noon, took a shower, and walked downstairs conservatively dressed, complete with a tie and fresh white shirt, according to Bell. He tended to stay up late, watching sports or musical programs on television. On some days, he rested in bed, and a cook served his meals in his room.

Bell also recalled that Paul sometimes read aloud to her and his sister from the French and German newspapers that he received, translating the news into English for them.[1]

Robeson continued to have good days when he seemed a little more like his old self and bad days when he withdrew silently into himself. Unlike Bell, who emphasized the good periods and ignored the bad, Paul Jr. and Lloyd Brown realized that the bad days predominated and that he would never recover.

* * *

Robeson's seventieth birthday on April 9, 1968, came less than a week after Martin Luther King Jr. was assassinated. Major celebrations of the Robeson birthday took place in London, Berlin, and Moscow. The event in London included tributes to him by Peggy Ashcroft, Peter O'Toole, Michael Redgrave, and Mary Ure, as well as fond messages from Marie Burke, John Gielgud, Yehudi Menuhin, Flora Robson, Sybil Thorndike, and Elisabeth Welch.[2]

Paul's sister made a special dinner for him, complete with a birthday cake, at home in Philadelphia. She held a celebration of his birthday every year.

In discussions with his son, Robeson expressed his great respect and admiration for Martin Luther King Jr. and sadness at his assassination. About this time, doctors inserted a pacemaker to improve Robeson's blood circulation to his brain.[3]

Paul Robeson Jr. managed his father's affairs during the Philadelphia years. He limited his father's visitors to the family, Lloyd Brown and his wife, Sam and Helen Rosen, and very few others. Lloyd wanted Lawrence Brown to visit too, but Paul Jr. rejected the idea, contending it might disturb his father. Other disagreements arose between the two men, each devoted to Paul in his own way. Paul Jr. finally dismissed Lloyd as the official Robeson biographer, giving Martin Duberman access to the Robeson Archives for a biography.[4]

Robeson had been born into a world without automobiles or airplanes. Now, in July 1969, the United States launched a rocket into space that enabled two American astronauts to walk on the moon.

* * *

On May 17, 1971, a month after Robeson's seventy-third birthday, a public television station in New Jersey broadcast "A Tribute to Paul Robeson." The actor Ossie Davis said on the program that the American establishment had conducted a deliberate policy to eliminate Robeson from our history: "It just didn't accidentally happen, that this tremendous oak of a human being should be blotted out from memory."

Paul Robeson Jr. said on the program, "My father challenged the cultural, political and economic foundations of racism in America," and "he linked this struggle for black liberation in America with the struggle of the oppressed all over the world."

"He survived an unprecedented onslaught. . . . And there's a certain majestic triumph in the fact that he's retired a sort of undefeated champion. He never took a word back, and he retired unbowed and undefeated."[5]

On a visit to the Philadelphia house in the summer of 1972, Lloyd Brown brought a copy of *Ebony* magazine to Paul. It contained an article in which a panel of historians named Paul Robeson as one of the ten greatest black men in American history. When Brown showed the article to him, Paul responded, "Pop would have been pleased."[6]

Another honor came to Robeson in November 1972 when the National Theater Hall of Fame inducted him as a charter member.

* * *

When Clara Rockmore and her nephew, Robert Sherman, visited Paul about this time, they found him friendly but withdrawn. He made very brief replies to their questions; there were long moments of silence. He looked well, but he seemed depressed.

Ruby Dee and her husband, Ossie Davis, also visited Paul at his sister's house. She recalled that they had heard rumors of his ill health but were still surprised at his condition. They had fondly remembered Paul as "an incredible human being." But now, he did not focus on them; he just mumbled a bit.

"I was heartbroken," Dee said, at finding how much he had deteriorated. She added, "Ossie almost broke down and cried."[7]

* * *

On Christmas Day 1972, Lawrence Brown died. He was seventy-nine years old. He had not seen Paul in recent years.

Born in Jacksonville, Florida, he displayed an early talent for music, went to Boston to study and then to London, and remained in Europe for several years as the piano accompanist for the great black tenor Roland Hayes. He conducted research into black folk songs, arranged many traditional spirituals, and returned to America in late 1924.

The quiet, elegant, loyal Larry Brown served as the principal arranger and accompanist for Paul Robeson for the rest of his career. He maintained his home in a small apartment at 188 West 135th Street in Harlem, while he traveled through much of the world. He never married, and he died alone.[8]

* * *

Harry Belafonte visited Robeson in Philadelphia to discuss plans for a seventy-fifth birthday tribute to him in 1973. Harry observed that Paul was now "a stooped and frail figure." He said Paul was depressed about what had happened in the Soviet Union under Stalin but would say nothing that could "give ammunition to the anti-communist zealots who'd hounded him for so long."[9]

Paul Jr. helped present the major "Salute to Paul Robeson" at Carnegie Hall on April 15, 1973, with a star-filled program produced by Belafonte, who also sang, as did Odetta and Pete Seeger. The actors paying tribute to Robeson included Ossie Davis, Ruby Dee, and James Earl Jones.

Mrs. Martin Luther King Jr. said Robeson tapped into black militancy earlier than her husband. Sidney Poitier said no black actor before Robeson played any movie role except racist stereotypes. Dizzy Gillespie said Robeson was "my personal champion." And Mayor Richard G. Hatcher of Gary, Indiana, called him "our own black prince and prophet."

Paul Robeson Jr. told the audience that his father was "in command of all his faculties" but that he was still suffering from a circulatory ailment. The program presented a "theatrical biography" of Robeson with recordings, slides, and movies. The audience broke into loud applause for a film scene from *Show Boat* with Robeson singing "Ol' Man River."[10]

Remaining in Philadelphia, Paul Robeson sent a recorded message played to the audience in Carnegie Hall. These were his last public words:

Warmest thanks to all the many friends here and throughout the world who have sent me greetings on my seventy-fifth birthday. Though I have not been able to be active for several years, I want you to know that I am the same Paul dedicated as ever to the worldwide cause of humanity for freedom, peace and brotherhood.

Cover of Vanguard Records LP album, titled simply *Robeson* (c. 1959), with chorus and orchestra. The album contained a mixture of spirituals and other songs, including "Water Boy," "Deep River," and "Loch Lomond." Courtesy Vanguard.

Here at home, my heart is with the continuing struggle of my people to achieve complete liberation from racist domination, and to gain for all black Americans and the other minority groups not only equal rights but an equal share. In the same spirit, I salute the colonial liberation movements of Africa, Latin America and Asia. . . .

Together with the partisans of peace—the peoples of the socialist countries and the progressive elements of all other countries—I rejoice that the movement for peaceful co-existence has made important gains and that the advocates of "cold war" and "containment" have had to retreat.

Though ill health has compelled my retirement, you can be sure that in my heart I go on singing.

And then he recited the lines

> But I keeps laughing instead of crying,
> I must keep fighting until I'm dying,
> And Ol' Man River, he just keeps rolling along.

* * *

On Robeson's seventy-sixth birthday, April 9, 1974, Lloyd Brown and his wife, Lily, attended a festive dinner that Marian served at home. As they sat around the table, Marian nodded to Paul, who then said grace. The meal included roast chicken and baked ham, followed by a sweet potato pie with whipped cream, all accompanied by pitchers of iced tea.[11]

The *Philadelphia Evening Bulletin* observed, "Perhaps Paul Robeson was born thirty years too soon." Writer Hans Knight said the same Robeson who was vilified as a Communist in the past would be welcomed on talk shows now as a goodwill ambassador. He said times had changed "and not least because of the courage of Paul Robeson, singer, actor, activist."

Paul made a sad comment to his son at Thanksgiving in 1975, saying if not for his family and the public, he would have "checked myself out long ago."[12]

So many famous men have been arrogant, self-centered, and inconsiderate; not Our Paul. This good and gentle man was invariably modest, unassuming, and generous. He had given so much to the things he believed in—his art, his politics, his friends. His accomplishments were long behind him. With nothing more to give, he waited quietly for the end of his life.

On December 28, 1975, Robeson entered Presbyterian Hospital of the University of Pennsylvania Medical Center in Philadelphia. He was diagnosed as suffering from a slight stroke. But then he had a second stroke. Paul Jr. and Marilyn visited him in the hospital on January 22.

It was the next day—January 23, 1976—that Paul Robeson died in the hospital in Philadelphia. A hospital spokesman attributed the death to complications from "severe cerebral vascular disorder."

* * *

Virtually all newspapers published substantial obituaries of Paul Robeson. The *Philadelphia Inquirer* ran one that began on the front page and filled a full inside page with text and pictures. Overseas, the lead of the obituary in the *London Times* said, "Mr. Paul Robeson, the Negro singer with the magnificent voice and the actor with the majestic presence, died yesterday at the age of 77."

Under a two-column headline on its front page, the *New York Times* carried a factual, neutrally worded obituary, written by Alden Whitman, which continued for half an inside page. It summarized his career, then said, "One of the most influential performers and political figures to emerge from black America, Mr. Robeson was under a cloud in his native land during the Cold War as a political dissenter and an outspoken admirer of the Soviet Union."

On January 31, its first issue after his death, the weekly *Amsterdam News* in Harlem devoted much of its front page to Robeson under a big, bold headline that exclaimed, "Goodbye, Paul!" It contained a full page of articles inside the paper, another page on the funeral, and the editorial page, all focused on him.

The paper's editorial characterized Robeson as "a charismatic leader of Black people all over the world."

* * *

For two days before Robeson's funeral, hundreds of mourners came to view his body in an open mahogany coffin at Benta's Funeral Home in Harlem. He was dressed, as so often in life, in a conservative double-breasted suit with a snowy white shirt and silk tie. A purple orchid rested on his folded hands.

His recordings of "Amazing Grace," "Go Tell It on the Mountain," and "Ol' Man River" sounded softly in the chapel as the mourners, many of them elderly, walked slowly past his body. His impressive frame appeared terribly diminished in death, a shock to those who remembered him from years past.

* * *

Robeson's funeral on Tuesday, January 24, 1976, filled the large sanctuary of the Mother AME Zion Church in Harlem, with an overflow of mourners standing in the cold rain on the sidewalks outside the front door. Inside, at the front of the sanctuary, rested the sealed mahogany coffin, covered by a blanket of red carnations.[13]

The church's pastor, Dr. George McMurray, began the funeral service, saying, "We have come this evening to memorialize an ambassador of justice and equality . . . who stood as a giant in a society rocked by social prejudice."

Bishop J. Clinton Hoggard, a family friend and prelate of the AME Zion Church, spoke at length, noting that Paul's brother had served as pastor of this congregation from 1936 to 1963. He said Paul had evoked great hostility and harassment in the McCarthy era but made "no compromise with any man on the matter of conscience, human rights, civil rights or personal dignity."

Dr. Samuel Rosen spoke in moving, personal tones about Paul's strong friendship with the Rosen family. He said, "His warmth and love and humor and wisdom spread across our lives. His music filled our house and our hearts, his companionship our souls."

Lloyd Brown eulogized Robeson with a simple eloquence that began, "The tallest tree in our forest has fallen." He added, "I think that Nature herself must feel that with the passing of Paul Robeson something uniquely wonderful has departed from the earth."

Describing him as a modern African American with "the manifold talents of a Renaissance man," Brown said, "He became an impassioned advocate of social justice, with a special concern for black liberation at home and for colonial liberation abroad." He quoted Robeson's last statement that "everybody should know that I am the same Paul Robeson."

Paul Robeson Jr. rose to conclude the eulogies by speaking of "the family's personal grief and overwhelming sense of loss." Looking to the front row, where Marian sat somberly with the family, he lauded the loving care that Paul's sister had provided in his final years. He said, "My father's immense power and great gentleness, his intense spiritual force and great intellect, his unbending courage and his deep compassion have left each one of us with special memories that will always sustain us, for each was touched by him in a special way."

He referred to his father as "a great and gentle warrior" whose last years contained disappointment because illness had forced him to retire from public life. But he stressed there was also triumph "because he retired undefeated and unrepentant."

With the eulogies finished, the recorded voice of Paul Robeson singing "Deep River" filled the church. Pallbearers carried the flower-strewn coffin down the aisle and out the front door to the hearse. Hundreds of mourners, many weeping, stood in a chill rain to bear final witness to his passing.

* * *

More than five thousand people attended the funeral of Paul Robeson, the *New York Times* reported. Attending were most of the living men and women who had played important parts in Robeson's life—a testament to the hold he retained on the affection of virtually all who knew him. They included Geraldine Neale Bledsoe, Freda Diamond, Uta Hagen, Leontyne Price, and Clara Rockmore, as well as Helen Rosen and her family, with her son John as a pallbearer.[14]

Burial of Robeson's remains, after cremation in a private ceremony, took place at the Ferncliff Cemetery in Hartsdale, New York. The grave site, beside that of his wife, is marked by a simple bronze plaque with his name, the dates of his birth and death, and the words, "The artist must elect to fight for freedom or slavery. I have made my choice. I had no alternative."[15]

Four days after Robeson's funeral, Democratic congressman John Conyers of Michigan led a tribute to him in the House of Representatives. Conyers said, "Paul Robeson stands as a monument to the capacity of the human spirit to achieve excellence in the face of adversity. His talent and courage fused to manifest personal greatness. . . . He sang, struggled, suffered, and died for the cause of human dignity."

Even Roy Wilkins of the NAACP, who had been one of Robeson's severest critics, lauded him in a *New York Post* column on February 14. Wilkins wrote, "There is one among the citizens of this country who eminently deserved the title of 'great'—Paul Robeson."

Robeson's will was filed in Surrogates Court in New York, disclosing that he left $150,000 in U.S. Treasury Notes and a personal checking account. His will allocated three-quarters of this estate to his son and one-quarter to his sister.

* * *

On April 11, two days after what would have been his seventy-eighth birthday, television newscaster Gil Noble presented a laudatory documentary on Robeson. It included recollections of him by Harry Belafonte, Dizzy Gillespie, Charlie Parker, and Paul Robeson Jr.[16]

The Friends of the Paul Robeson Archives presented a tribute to him at Carnegie Hall on October 18, 1976. The board of directors included Belafonte, with Paul Jr. as its president. Others were Freda Diamond, Jane Fonda, Sidney Lumet, Gil Noble, and Helen and Sam Rosen.[17]

Artists participating in the evening's program included Sidney Poitier, Pete Seeger, and Mary Travers. Proceeds of the program went to the Paul Robeson Archives, formed to assemble, preserve, and catalogue the papers, records, films, and photographs documenting his life.

Belafonte later extolled Robeson for his honesty and compassion, calling him "the most powerful voice for freedom and democracy." Sidney Poitier wrote that Robeson projected a new black image, a forerunner of the civil rights movement, adding, "He was my hero and my friend." Pete Seeger said simply, "Paul Robeson was one of the greatest human beings of all time."[18]

On February 17, 1977, little more than a year after Robeson's death, his devoted sister, Marian, died in Philadelphia at the age of eighty-two. She had fulfilled her wish to live long enough to take care of Paul in his last years.

The years following Robeson's death saw his son conduct a concerted effort to protect and promote his father's legacy.

* * *

"I'm Going to Tell God All of My Troubles"

I'm going to tell God all of my troubles,
Tell Him all of my troubles,
When I get home,
When I get home.

I'm going to tell God all of my troubles,
Tell Him all of my troubles,
I'm going to tell God all of my troubles,
When I get home.

I'm going to tell Him I had hard trials,
When I get home.
I'm going to tell Him I had hard trials,
When I get home.

I'm going to tell Him I had hard trials,
Tell Him I had hard trials,
I'm going to tell God all of my troubles,
When I get home.

—arranged by Lawrence Brown

Postscript

Centennial

$\mathscr{P}$aul Robeson Jr. continued to protect and promote his father's legacy in the latter years of the twentieth century. His efforts culminated in 1998 with celebrations of the hundredth anniversary of Paul Robeson's birth.

Robeson's extraordinary life contained a wide range of groundbreaking accomplishments for so many years; then it was crushed by the overwhelming weight of racism and anticommunism that virtually erased his name from the nation's history. The centennial of his birth finally restored his reputation to some extent, but he remained unknown to most young people.

The Paul Robeson Archives and a supporting foundation were established under the leadership of Paul Jr. and his wife, Marilyn, to preserve his legacy. They subsequently sent the bulk of his documents to the Moorland-Spingarn Research Center at Howard University in Washington, DC.

* * *

As a prelude to the centennial celebration in 1998, tributes to Paul Robeson took place to mark three birthday anniversaries in 1978, 1983, and 1988 with Harry Belafonte, Sidney Poitier, and numerous others participating.

An original play titled *Paul Robeson*, based on his life with James Earl Jones portraying Robeson, appeared off Broadway in 1977. This production did not please Paul Robeson Jr., who sparked a campaign against it, contending that it presented Robeson as naive rather than revolutionary. The play was revived in 1988 with Avery Brooks as the star, drawing little interest or controversy.[1]

A long list of artists produced essays, poems, and sculptures in honor of Paul Robeson over the years, including Nobel poet Pablo Neruda.

Paul Robeson Jr. gave the first access to the Robeson papers to Professor Martin Duberman for a biography. When published in 1988, however, it failed to please Paul Jr. So he went on to write his own two-volume biography.

In 1989, East Germans tore down the Berlin Wall, bringing unity back to Germany amid joyful cheering. And in 1991, the Soviet Union disintegrated as communism collapsed in Europe. History had rendered its verdict.

The U.S. Postal Service issued a thirty-seven-cent commemorative stamp bearing the picture of Paul Robeson in 2004, part of the Black Heritage Series. And the College Football Hall of Fame belatedly inducted him in 1995, rectifying the absurdity of ten-man all-American teams in 1917 and 1918 that had removed his name.

* * *

On April 9, 1998, former mayor David N. Dinkins appeared with Paul Robeson Jr. and his family at the main centennial celebration at the New York Historical Society in Manhattan. It included an extensive exhibition of Robeson memorabilia, recordings, and photographs, as well as an award-winning documentary on his life narrated by Sidney Poitier.

A docent wandered through the audience, offering assistance and asking people if they had a special memory of Robeson. He said he was amazed at the number of people who told him of a memorable encounter, some personal way that Robeson had touched their lives.

Mayor Dinkins, who always had a large Robeson photograph in a place of honor above the fireplace in his office at city hall, was asked why he held this man in such high esteem. He replied crisply, "It was his integrity."[2]

Pete Seeger was one of so many who encountered Robeson's generosity. In a book of tributes for the centennial, he recalled visiting Paul's dressing room to seek help for his young quartet of folksingers. "He took time to help us, to advise us," Seeger said. This unknown quartet then sang at many Robeson rallies before becoming the famous group known as the Weavers.

* * *

Paul Robeson dedicated his life to advancing equal rights for his people, freedom for colonial people, and human dignity for all people. He also believed in socialism, friendship with the Soviet Union, and world peace.

On civil rights, colonialism, and peace, Robeson stood in the forefront of the struggle, a generation ahead of his time. With regard to communism and the Soviet Union, however, he was on the wrong side of history.

Even his admirers understood that his most serious fault was a steadfast refusal to criticize the Soviet Union when its actions clearly called for censure.

But he felt that any negative comments by him would be used to attack the country that he still believed stood for racial equality. And he was stubborn; once he made up his mind, no amount of pressure could make him change it.

His belief in socialism developed at a time when capitalism appeared to be in shambles. Many idealistic people, mainly in Europe, looked to the Soviet Union as a worthy experiment to build a better society. But this hope foundered on the rocks of reality—people worked best for their own self-interest, not for the common good in a regimented society. And Soviet leaders created a brutal totalitarian state.

* * *

Most people have recognized that history has reached its decision; communism has been discredited, and the Soviet Union has disintegrated. British historian Max Hastings wrote that it took decades to realize that the Soviet Union's vast devastation and concentration on military necessities in World War II had "sown the seeds of the Communist system's eventual collapse."[3]

Long before the Soviet Union collapsed, some Western intellectuals who had believed in communism renounced it, notably writers in *The God that Failed*, published in 1950. One of them, Andre Gide, had written in 1932 that the Soviet Union seemed to "point to salvation" for a world being ruined by capitalism. Ignazio Silone called it "a bitter disillusionment" when the promise of a better world turned into a repressive dictatorship.[4]

Many more Soviet sympathizers were finally disillusioned by two major events in 1956: Khrushchev's denunciation of Stalin as a brutal despot, three years after Stalin's death, and the invasion of Soviet tanks to suppress a new government in Hungary.

* * *

If Robeson ever felt disillusioned with Soviet communism, he never expressed it, and there is no evidence that he felt it. Some critics contended that he had been duped by his royal treatment in Russia, seeing only what the Russians wanted him to see. But he was no dupe. He was an intelligent observer who spoke Russian fluently, traveled widely in the Soviet Union, and spoke with many people, both famous and ordinary. He knew the faults of the Soviet system, but he concluded that its benefits, most particularly official opposition to racism, outweighed its faults.[5]

One could certainly come to a different conclusion, but his was founded on his own experience and his own convictions. The tragedy for our country was not that one of its noblest sons believed in communism but that our democracy could not tolerate political dissent. We allowed the hysteria of McCarthyism to trample on freedom of speech.

At the conclusion of his classic documentary on Senator Joseph McCarthy, Edward R. Murrow warned, "We must not confuse dissent with disloyalty." He ended with this portentous line from Shakespeare: "The fault, dear Brutus, is not in our stars but in ourselves."[6]

There have been significant periods when our admirable country acted less than admirably. Among its most notorious failings have been the brutal treatment of Native Americans, slavery and segregation, the waging of unnecessary wars, and restrictions on freedom of speech.

* * *

A history book by Harold Evans declared that the treatment of Paul Robeson was "one of the most shameful episodes in our history."[7] Historians might do well to ponder the fact that W. E. B. Du Bois—the other great black American activist of the first half of the twentieth century—also turned to communism. Unlike Paul Robeson, he became a member of the Communist Party and lived the last years of his life in exile in Ghana.

It should also be noted that most of the democratic countries of Western Europe have adopted aspects of socialism to soften the harsher elements of capitalism, which may provide a rational road to the future.

* * *

In an interview with me in 1993, Paul Robeson Jr. said, "My father combined immense power with great gentleness—that was the human quality about him that I remember most." He said his father "never joined the Communist Party—or any other party for that matter—because he was an independent artist and would never submit to any kind of organizational discipline."

As for himself, Paul Jr. did belong to the Communist Party from 1948 to 1962 and served on its national committee, because he believed it was "a radical instrument that could help advance the interests of African Americans." He left the party in 1962 after "it became bureaucratic and corrupt."

He had no difficulty being the son of such a famous man, he said, because his father had told him to be himself. "So I never remember having any need to compete with him. He gave me a sense of being my own man."[8]

Paul Robeson Jr. worked as a translator of Russian technical journals and as a freelance journalist who wrote four books. He and his wife had two children, a son, David, and a daughter, Susan.[9]

* * *

Speaking for myself now, I saw Paul Robeson perform more than twenty times; on most of those occasions, I observed him closely backstage and spoke with him briefly several times. He treated everyone with consideration. His modest demeanor and generous spirit never faltered.

My observations confirmed the views expressed by others who found him to be a man of enormous decency without a trace of arrogance or artifice. This great and good man remained forever "Our Paul," a black giant who touched the lives of so many of us with the unsurpassed beauty of his voice, the grandeur of his character, and the generosity of his spirit.

It is my belief that no one else possessed his combination of qualities. It is a tragedy for our country that so many of our citizens have never heard of this remarkable American.

Robeson wore his dignity like a suit of armor to protect that special place reserved for his deepest emotions, while the epidemic of racism and political hysteria drove him into depression and eradicated his name from our history. He was a real man, larger than life, possessing a grandeur and gravitas rooted in the soil of his native land. It was no accident that astute observers likened him to a great tree—a mighty oak, a soaring redwood, the tallest tree in our forest.

For me, Robeson's essence was his conviction that all men are brothers, with similar aspirations for human dignity regardless of race or nationality, and that this principle lives in their music, the songs that he sang. He traveled through much of the world but remained forever a man of America, with deep roots in his native land. We are left with the recordings of his wonderful voice singing songs of America—the many spirituals, the labor anthem "Joe Hill," the historic "Ballad for Americans," and his signature "Ol' Man River."

His life should be remembered by our people, restored to its rightful place in our history, secured in the soul of our nation—it is a ballad of America.

Notes

Chapter 1

1. Birth date of July 27, 1845, for William at Lloyd L. Brown, *The Young Paul Robeson* (Boulder, CO: Westview Press, 1997), 9. Brown's meticulous research said William escaped in 1862 at age seventeen. But 1843 for birth and fifteen for age of escape cited at Paul Robeson Jr., *The Undiscovered Paul Robeson*, vol. 1, *An Artist's Journey, 1898–1939* (New York: John Wiley & Sons, 2001), 4. He relied on his father's faulty memory for dates. Material from Paul Robeson Jr., *The Undiscovered Paul Robeson*, appears under fair use and also some specifically used under © 2001 Paul Robeson Jr.; reprinted with permission of John Wiley & Sons. My thanks to Sheik Safdar, permissions coordinator.

2. Early catalogue of Lincoln University in Lower Oxford, Pennsylvania. Catalogues with names of students obtained from Lincoln's special collections library, with help of librarian Susan Pevar. In 1867, William entered Lincoln's program to prepare students for college. He graduated with an AB in 1873 as an honor student and received AM and sacred theology degrees in 1876.

3. Maria Louisa Bustill was born in Philadelphia on November 8, 1853. Her great-grandfather, Cyrus Bustill, earned freedom from slavery working for Quakers; baked bread for Washington's soldiers in Revolutionary War. Officer's letter thanking Cyrus at Paul Robeson, *Here I Stand* (New York: Othello Associates, 1958; Boston: Beacon Press, 1971 and 1988), 16; pages cited from original.

4. Paul's birth certificate (for unnamed male child) on April 9, 1898, from New Jersey State Archives; gave father's age as fifty-two, mother's age as forty-five, but she turned forty-five later in the year. Also birth certificates for Paul's siblings. Weather for April 9, 1898, from state climatologist at Rutgers.

5. In decade of Reconstruction after Civil War, Northern troops enforced voting rights for freed slaves in defeated South; some freedmen won elective offices. But troops withdrew in 1877, and South soon disenfranchised Negroes. Segregation went into full force with *Plessy v. Ferguson*.

6. Edison invented incandescent light bulb in 1879; street lights in lower Manhattan in 1882; invented recording machine and motion-picture camera. Bell patented telephone in 1876, with service developing slowly. War of 1898 saw United States invade Cuba and force out Spain; United States also acquired Puerto Rico and Philippines from Spain.

7. *Princeton Press* articles on microfilm at library of Princeton University. It reported on December 3, 1898, that "the colored people of Princeton" held meeting at Witherspoon church to protest racial violence in South. Rev. W. D. Robeson spoke on need to prevent "such disgraceful outrages." Article on November 10, 1900, said church meeting discussed pastor; large majority voted to retain him but decision was left to white presbytery. Brief notice in paper on November 17, 1900, said he resigned, effective February 1. Less charitable view of reverend at Sheila Tully Boyle and Andrew Bunie, *Paul Robeson: The Years of Promise and Achievement* (Amherst: University of Massachusetts Press, 2001), 18–21; they suggest vague misconduct by him.

8. Backyard ashes at Robeson, *Here I Stand*, 20. His first-person account of childhood, in first chapter, primary source on his early years. All quotations from this book are credited to Robeson, *Here I Stand*, © 1958, 1988 Paul Robeson; reprinted with permission of Beacon Press, Boston.

9. Limited memory of mother at Robeson, *Here I Stand*, 15: remembered her lying in coffin but said, "It must be that the pain and shock of her death blotted out all other personal recollections." Motherless child comment on pp. 22–23; songs of his people on p. 23; community seeing something special in him on p. 24.

10. Bill recalled noting young Paul's voice in 1952 *Freedom* magazine article: "An Intimate Portrait, My Brother, Paul," by Rev. Benjamin C. Robeson.

11. Reeve reacted to racial insults, arrested for brawling; father finally ordered him to leave because he set bad example for young Paul. He went to Detroit, lost touch with family.

12. Comments on father at Robeson, *Here I Stand*, 14 and 17.

13. Report card at Eslanda Goode Robeson, *Paul Robeson, Negro* (New York: Harper and Brothers, 1930), 19–22.

14. *The Valkyrie* monthly publication with student editors and English teacher Anna Miller as consultant. Photocopies of old issues obtained with assistance of Mrs. June Ambs at library of Somerville High School.

15. Father teaching him public speaking, with recitations from Virgil and Homer, at Robeson, *Here I Stand*, 26–27.

16. Harsher view of Paul's childhood at Boyle and Bunie, *Paul Robeson*, 42: they write that a "gnawing sense of inferiority" troubled him for much of his life. But his own positive recollection is more credible. Classmate Margaret Potter Gibbons is quoted about Paul sleeping late at Boyle and Bunie, *Paul Robeson*, 36. Arriving late, rare fault, contributed to displeasure of principal, Dr. William A. Ackerman, whom Paul detested.

17. Scholarship to Rutgers as "decisive point" at Robeson, *Here I Stand*, 33.

Chapter 2

1. James D. Carr, a Phi Beta Kappa student, first black to graduate from Rutgers in 1892; only one earlier black student attended in obscure past. Rutgers chartered in 1766 as Queens College, eighth oldest college in United States. Named Rutgers in 1825; State University of New Jersey after World War II.

2. Interview by Robert Van Gelder in *New York Times* on January 16, 1944. Robeson said recalling this incident helped him portray rage in *Othello*.

3. Conversation with Cameron at Brown, *The Young Paul Robeson*, 77. Permission to use this from Sarah Sheppard, subsidiary rights administrator.

4. Description of olive-skinned "Gerry" at Paul Robeson Jr., *The Undiscovered Paul Robeson*, 1:25.

5. Student newspaper, *The Targum*, reported all Rutgers football games in next issue. *Targum* articles obtained at Alexander Library of Rutgers University in New Brunswick, New Jersey.

6. *Targum* reported Walter Camp's account of "eleven Robesons." *Tribune* and *World* articles reprinted at Eslanda Robeson, *Paul Robeson, Negro*, 172–78.

7. First black all-American was William Henry Lewis in 1892 and 1893; played for Harvard while in law school. Pollard first as running back in 1916.

8. Sad comment on father's death in his scrapbook of clippings in Paul and Eslanda Robeson papers in Moorland-Spingarn Research Center at Howard University in Washington, DC. What "Pop" would have said at Brown, *The Young Paul Robeson*, 7 and 141; also family gathering for funeral in 1918 on pp. 85–87.

9. Senior thesis in Robeson Archive of Alexander Library at Rutgers. Analysis of official academic records, noted in numerals rather than letters, such as 90 instead of A, indicated thirty As, thirty-six Bs, eleven Cs, and one D (64 in economics). These records from research of Stephen Dalina, university records management coordinator, from Rutgers Archives.

10. At Robeson's funeral in 1976, Gerry told his son, "Even that far back I understood that he was a man of destiny." She went to Howard University; moved to Detroit; worked for state agencies, campaigned for women's rights; was inducted into Michigan Women's Hall of Fame in 1983.

11. His words about Gerry at Brown, *The Young Paul Robeson*, 67.

12. Stendhal's treatise *On Love* (Liveright Publishing, 1947).

13. Perhaps only comparable scholar-athlete was Byron "Whizzer" White, University of Colorado, with seven varsity letters in football, baseball, and basketball; all-American in 1937; three years in National Football League; Rhodes Scholar, Yale Law School, U.S. Supreme Court. Later scholar-athlete Bill Bradley lacked some versatility of White and Robeson.

14. *The Targum* and yearbook both cited eleven varsity letters for Robeson; some books erroneously said he received twelve to fifteen varsity letters. Careful search by Rutgers archivist, Thomas Frusciano, confirmed eleven; four for football, three for basketball, two each for baseball and track; Robeson apparently did not win a varsity letter in baseball until junior year.

15. Valedictory text in Robeson Archive of Alexander Library at Rutgers. His favorite poem in college was "If" by Rudyard Kipling.

Chapter 3

1. Essie sometimes said she met Paul first in 1919, citing brief encounter on street; she sometimes said they met in 1920.

2. Play at YWCA, with visit of Macgowan and Jones, at Brown, *The Young Paul Robeson*, 119.

3. Several books said Robeson played for Akron in 1920. But according to John M. Carroll, *Fritz Pollard: Pioneer in Racial Advancement* (Champaign: University of Illinois Press, 1992), Robeson coached Lincoln in 1920, joined Akron in 1921. Nora Hill of *Akron Beacon Journal* searched 1920 files for me; found no mention of Robeson. Professional Football Hall of Fame had no record of him in 1920. American Professional Football Association began in 1920, name changed to National Football League after 1922 season, at George S. Halas with Gwen Morgan and Arthur Veysey, *Halas: An Autobiography* (New York: McGraw-Hill Book Company, 1979; Chicago: Bonus Books, 1986), 60 and 91.

4. Eslanda Cardozo Goode born on December 15, 1895. Birth certificate obtained from Department of Health records of District of Columbia. For much of her life she trimmed one year from her age. Her grandfather, Francis Lewis Cardozo, was state treasurer of South Carolina; apparently not related to Benjamin Cardozo of U.S. Supreme Court.

5. Campaign to win Paul in Eslanda Robeson's book of conversations with Pearl S. Buck, *American Argument* (New York: John Day Company, 1949), 23 and 25. Her family on pp. 8–9; school and chemistry on pp. 14–15. Buck's estate granted permission to use her material.

6. Family disapproval (p. 50) and abortion (p. 51) in Paul Robeson Jr., *The Undiscovered Paul Robeson*, vol. 1. Son's account of courtship and marriage of parents on pp. 46–52, based on memoir, diaries, and his conversations with them.

7. Essie's determination comment at Eslanda Robeson with Pearl S. Buck, *American Argument*, 11.

8. Marriage proposal in Essie's diary that day. Marriage certificate, issued August 17, 1921, by Town of Rye, in Paul Robeson Collection in Moorland-Spingarn Research Center at Howard University in Washington, DC. Marriage certificate identified them as "colored."

9. Patterson, who became a Communist, said Robeson often visited his law office; see William L. Patterson, *The Man Who Cried Genocide* (New York: International Publishers, 1971), 65–66.

10. Paul "out of sync" with Essie at Paul Robeson Jr., *The Undiscovered Paul Robeson*, 53. © 2001 Paul Robeson Jr.; reprinted with permission of John Wiley & Sons. Essie on their differences at Eslanda Robeson, *Paul Robeson, Negro*, 73. His personal habits at Eslanda Robeson with Pearl S. Buck, *American Argument*, 58.

11. Woollcott's first meeting with Robeson at Alexander Woollcott, *While Rome Burns* (New York: Grosset & Dunlap, 1934), 128.

12. Browning and *Shuffle Along* in Martin Duberman's thoroughly researched biography, *Paul Robeson* (New York: Alfred A. Knopf, 1988), 44.

13. Letters in Paul Robeson Collection in Moorland-Spingarn Research Center at Howard University in Washington, DC.

14. Brown at London apartment at Brown, *The Young Paul Robeson*, 120–22. Also on Marie Seton, *Paul Robeson* (London: Dennis Dobson, 1958), 10.

15. Her illness at Paul Robeson Jr., *The Undiscovered Paul Robeson*, 67–68.

16. Davis on Gerald Horne's article "Comrades and Friends," in *Paul Robeson: Artist and Citizen*, ed. Jeffrey C. Stewart (New Brunswick, NJ: Rutgers University Press and the Paul Robeson Cultural Center, 1998), 198.

17. Stotesbury firm at Duberman, *Paul Robeson*, 54–55.

Chapter 4

1. Benjamin's article "My Brother Paul," in *Freedom* magazine of February 1952.

2. Exchange of letters, role in *All God's Chillun Got Wings*, at Paul Robeson Jr., *The Undiscovered Paul Robeson*, 1:73.

3. Controversy over *All God's Chillun Got Wings* widely reported in New York newspapers.

4. Opening of *The Emperor Jones* in Essie's diary dated May 6, 1924. Her diaries in extensive collection, the Paul and Eslanda Robeson papers, in Moorland-Spingarn Research Center at Howard University in Washington, DC.

5. Threats of violence resulted in police outside and personal security by friends inside theater for opening of *All God's Chillun Got Wings*.

6. Stallings review in *World*, reprinted at Eslanda Robeson, *Paul Robeson, Negro*, 84–86. Nathan in *American Mercury*, 81–84.

7. Provincetown Players at Eslanda Robeson, *Paul Robeson, Negro*, 77–78.

8. Stewart on Murray's nude photographs at Stewart, *Paul Robeson: Artist and Citizen*, 153. In artistic Greenwich Village, where beautiful nudity seemed acceptable, Robeson's large, powerful figure attracted interest for his full-formed statue and for Murray's photographs of him as works of art.

9. Renaissance optimism at David Levering Lewis, *When Harlem Was in Vogue* (New York: Alfred A. Knopf, 1981; paperback, Oxford: Oxford University Press, 1989), 103. His literary agent gave permission as fair use of quotation.

10. White on experience with Robesons in his essay "The Paradox of Color" in notable anthology *The New Negro: Voices of the Harlem Renaissance*, edited by Alain Locke (New York: Albert and Charles Boni, 1925; New York: Macmillan, 1992), 361–62; pages cited here from 1992 reprinted edition.

11. Changing career in profile by Elizabeth Shepley Sergeant in *The New Republic*, March 3, 1926.

12. *Body and Soul* in Essie's diary on October 17, 1924. Paul's style of naturalism in this first silent film "differs very little" from his later sound films, according to Scott Allen Nollen, *Paul Robeson: Film Pioneer* (Jefferson, NC: McFarland & Company, 2010), 18.

13. Van Vechten parties with Gershwin and Dreiser at Howard Pollack, *George Gershwin: His Life and Work* (Berkeley: University of California, 2005), 105. Dreiser published his novel *An American Tragedy* in 1925.

14. Contract for *The Emperor Jones* in London was marked improvement over his acting for minimal pay in New York.

15. Brown meeting Robeson in Harlem at Seton, *Paul Robeson*, 34–36. Brown gave similar account in Robeson documentary on Gil Noble's television program *Like It Is* on ABC in 1976.

16. Robeson introduced Brown to Van Vechten at party on March 29, 1925; Essie's diary noted that guests included Mr. and Mrs. Alfred Knopf.

Chapter 5

1. Preparations for Robeson's first concert in 1925 at Eslanda Robeson, *Paul Robeson, Negro*, 99–100.

2. Lawrence Brown on preparations at Seton, *Paul Robeson*, 36.

3. Spirituals, with original spellings, from program in Lawrence Brown papers at Schomburg Center for Research in Black Culture, in Harlem.

4. Applause and reaction at Eslanda Robeson, *Paul Robeson, Negro*, 102. Later profile of Robeson by Elizabeth Shepley Sergeant in *The New Republic*, March 3, 1926, said, "I have never seen on the stage a more civilized artistic gesture than his nod to his accompanist, the signal to begin the song."

5. Essie's diaries in Paul and Eslanda Robeson papers in Moorland-Spingarn Research Center at Howard University in Washington, DC.

6. James Weldon Johnson, ed., introduction to *The Book of American Negro Spirituals* (New York: Viking Press, 1925). Slaves accepted Christianity despite "vast gulf" between what whites preached and practiced; spirituals "true folk songs."

7. Visit to Kahn and his $5,000, with Essie's comments, recorded in her diary.

8. Freda Diamond at Paul Robeson Jr., *The Undiscovered Paul Robeson*, 93. Father said he was deeply offended by Essie saying she would "no more let some other woman sleep with Paul than I would let her use my toothbrush." Freda Diamond material cited here under © 2001 Paul Robeson Jr.; reprinted with permission of John Wiley & Sons.

9. London and lack of racism at Eslanda Robeson, *Paul Robeson, Negro*, 105–11. And Emma Goldman in Essie's diary on August 22 and September 23 and 25, 1925. Copies of Essie's many letters to Van Vechtens obtained from Beinecke Rare Book and Manuscript Library at Yale University.

10. London opening of *The Emperor Jones* in Essie's diary on September 10, 1925. Essie's September 28 letter to Van Vechtens, replying to their complaint that Larry avoided them, noted his distrust of whites: "his black and white complex—which is very strong."

11. Beach's party in Essie's diary on November 8; McKay on November 21 and December 1. Villefranche at Eslanda Robeson, *Paul Robeson Negro*, 112.

12. Reviews in Brown's scrapbooks in Schomburg Center for Research in Black Culture, in Harlem. Essie on Chicago and Boston concerts at Eslanda Robeson, *Paul Robeson, Negro*, 123–27.

13. With no formal musical training, Robeson contacted teachers to correct his breathing and protect his voice from strain.

14. Woollcott's account of Kern seeking Robeson for "Ol' Man River" at Woollcott, *While Rome Burns*, 124–25.

15. Fredi affair and "tacit solution" at Paul Robeson Jr., *The Undiscovered Paul Robeson*, 100–101. Son's personal knowledge of parents made him most authoritative source on their complex relationship.

16. Essie pregnant at Paul Robeson Jr., *The Undiscovered Paul Robeson*, 142. Paul believed she "unilaterally" decided to have baby to tie him to their marriage. Her account of having child at Eslanda Robeson, *Paul Robeson, Negro*, 135–37. Essie's book contains valuable information but also some fanciful material.

17. Letter to Essie from ship in Robeson papers in Moorland-Spingarn Research Center.

Chapter 6

1. Letters and diaries in extensive collection of Paul and Eslanda Robeson papers in Moorland-Spingarn Research Center at Howard University in Washington, DC.

2. Letter to Essie about future and finances on December 12, 1927.

3. As young actor-singer in need of money, Robeson made mistake of signing to do popular revue and also to sing Porgy role.

4. Essie took active role in managing Paul's career as singer and actor. She told him that Larry was essential to his concert career.

5. Marie Burke, who played Julie in show, described scene and quoted Kern in interview in excellent Robeson documentary on Gil Noble's ABC television program *Like It Is* in 1976.

6. Essie wrote in diary about finding "a charming flat in St. John's Wood, facing Regents Park." She added, "Great news!!—that we are to remain in London for a year or two."

7. Joe Andrews described at Boyle and Bunie, *Paul Robeson*, 191–98. Everyone liked Joe except Essie, who believed he helped Paul arrange romantic assignations.

8. Robesons invited to lavish British parties but ignored by U.S. embassy, at Seton, *Paul Robeson*, 44. H. G. Wells, prominent socialist writer, on p. 45.

9. Comments on socialism at Seton, *Paul Robeson*, 46–47; Seton, an English journalist, became Robeson's friend.

10. Renting house and sending for Pauli at Paul Robeson Jr., *The Undiscovered Paul Robeson*, 1:154. Salary for *Show Boat* on p. 155; also Kahn's loan and dispute with producer, Caroline Dudley Reagan, who sued Robeson. During dispute, *The New Yorker* profile "King of Harlem" by Mildred Gilman said, "Here at least he will be freely forgiven if he doesn't come back. For, in Harlem, Paul Robeson can do no wrong."

11. *Die Stunde* review at Seton, *Paul Robeson*, 48; Robeson comment on Jews in Europe, affinity between Negro and Hungarian music, on pp. 48–49.

12. Carnegie Hall concerts and Lawrence Tibbett in pocket-sized notebook Robeson used in November 1929; this notebook diary in Robeson papers in Moorland-Spingarn Research Center at Howard University. Personal musings in notebook provided his intriguing view of God. Paul Robeson Jr. told me that his father would kneel beside him to say prayers at bedtime when he was young child, but they stopped because his mother objected; his mother was agnostic, her mother, atheist.

13. Encounter with Welsh miners at Paul Robeson Jr., *The Undiscovered Paul Robeson*, 156. Robeson bonded with miners and began to focus on working class in Britain. He told story of marching with miners to his son. Used here under © 2001 Paul Robeson Jr.; reprinted with permission of John Wiley & Sons.

14. Queens at Bucharest concert in Essie's diary dated January 18, 1930. Comments about *Borderline* film also in diary.

15. Yolande from well-connected family; her father a judge. Essie found love letter but put her anger aside as they prepared for *Othello*.

Chapter 7

1. Rupert Hart-Davis, Peggy's husband, described director at rehearsals in his memoir, *The Power of Change* (London: Sinclair-Stevenson, 1991), 44. Paul "lost" in Essie's diary on April 16, 1930. Her diaries and letters in Robeson papers in Moorland-Spingarn Research Center at Howard University in Washington, DC.

2. Rehearsals at Gary O'Connor, *The Secret Woman: A Life of Peggy Ashcroft* (London: Orion Books, 1998), 19. Ashcroft had long, distinguished acting career. Peggy called Paul "a folk-hero, a legendary figure to us all" at Michael Billington, *Peggy Ashcroft* (London: John Murray, 1988), 37.

3. Essie's letter to Van Vechtens added, "The Desdemona is beautiful beyond words, so simple and appealing, and such a fine actress too." Her letters to them in Beinecke Rare Book and Manuscript Library at Yale.

4. Thorndike's recollection of Robeson at Elizabeth Sprigge, *Sybil Thorndike Casson* (London: Victor Gollancz Ltd., 1971), 193.

5. Titterton interviews in Robeson Archive at Akademie der Künste in Berlin.

6. Need to improve his mind at Paul Robeson Jr., *The Undiscovered Paul Robeson*, 1:185.

7. Affair with Ashcroft and her comment at Duberman, *Paul Robeson*, 140. For her quote about falling in love, see Billington, *Peggy Ashcroft*, 41. Essie's discovery of Ashcroft letter in diary dated September 1, 1930. Ashcroft's husband said in his memoir, "Both [of us] became very fond of him. He was gentle, modest, affectionate and full of fun" (Hart-Davis, *The Power of Change*, 46).

8. Troubled letter to wife in Robeson papers in Moorland-Spingarn Research Center.

9. Yolande described at Paul Robeson Jr., *The Undiscovered Paul Robeson*, 163–64.

10. Reviews of concerts in Lawrence Brown's scrapbooks on microfilm at Schomburg Center for Research in Black Culture, in Harlem.

11. Abortion hinted at as "job" in diary. Abortion at Paul Robeson Jr., *The Undiscovered Paul Robeson*, 184, with Paul's suspicion of Noel Coward. Diary noted Noel "often" came to apartment; Coward, widely known as homosexual, was apparently bisexual.

12. Essie on Paul "degenerating" in her diary for November 10, 1931. Also, entries on November 29 about "red letter day" and on Christmas about divorce.

13. *New York Times* on January 18, 1932, reported that Robeson "returned in triumph." Also, in January he spoke of God to *Daily Gleaner* of Jamaica, cited at Nollen, *Paul Robeson: Film Pioneer*, 31.

14. Ferber on audience reaction to Robeson in *Show Boat* on May 19, 1932, at Woollcott, *While Rome Burns*, 125–26.

15. Key diary entry on September 27: visits Paul, learns he will not marry "Yo."

16. Letter to Rockmore at Paul Robeson Jr., *The Undiscovered Paul Robeson*, 195–96. © 2001 Paul Robeson Jr.; reprinted with permission of John Wiley & Sons. Yolande soon had short-lived marriage to Russian aristocrat in Paris but pursued Paul again to no avail; little more known about her.

17. Diary in October and December reported reconciliation and her birthday. Tacit agreement to stay together at Paul Robeson Jr., *The Undiscovered Paul Robeson*, 199–200.

Chapter 8

1. West's letter in chapter titled "Colossal Bronze" at Woollcott, *While Rome Burns*, 131.

2. Funds for refugees, comment on Jews, at Seton, *Paul Robeson*, 67–69; Seton claimed credit for Robeson's political awareness in 1933.

3. Pollard complained he had difficulty working with Robeson on this film; see Boyle and Bunie, *Paul Robeson*, 277–78 for a rare complaint about working with him. See also Nollen, *Paul Robeson: Film Pioneer*, 43. Nollen quoted Donald Bogle saying his "greatest contribution to film history . . . was his proud defiant portrait of the black man" (p. 32).

4. Essie's letter on April 5, 1933, about studying at London University. Copies of her many letters to Carl Van Vechten obtained from Beinecke Rare Book and Manuscript Library at Yale.

5. His articles on Africa in Robeson Archive at Akademie der Künste in Berlin.

6. Stuckey, history professor at University of California, Riverside, wrote "The Cultural Philosophy of Paul Robeson" in *Paul Robeson: The Great Forerunner*, ed. Editors of *Freedomways* (New York: Dodd, Mead, 1978; New York: International Publishers, 1998). Northrop at F. S. C. Northrop, *The Meeting of East and West: An Inquiry Concerning World Understanding* (London: Macmillan Publishing, 1946; Woodbridge, CT: Ox Bow Press, 1979), 160.

7. Brown calling Robeson "genius" at Seton, *Paul Robeson*, 59.

8. Son's recollection at Paul Robeson Jr., *The Undiscovered Paul Robeson*, 211–12. © 2001 Paul Robeson Jr.; reprinted with permission of John Wiley & Sons.

9. Eisenstein's invitation at Seton, *Paul Robeson*, 80. Robesons asked Seton to accompany them because she had been there and knew Eisenstein. Eisenstein, son of Jewish father and Russian mother; director of classic 1925 silent film *Battleship Potemkin* and others; fell out of favor with Stalin. Seton had close, apparently Platonic, relationship with him.

10. Berlin in Essie's diary on December 21, 1934; treatment of Jews made her see how blacks felt in Mississippi. Soviet visit in daily diary in Moorland-Spingarn Research Center at Howard University in Washington, DC.

11. Robeson and Eisenstein, talking and playing records, at Marie Seton, *Sergei M. Eisenstein*, 327.

12. Christmas Eve with Litvinovs in Essie's diary. Ivy was English-born wife of Maxim Litvinov, who was Jewish. Parties at Dom Kino, buying coat, visits by Essie's brothers, New Year's Eve—all noted in her diary.

13. Factory visit and "full dignity" quote at Seton, *Paul Robeson*, 94–95. Quote ignored his stature in Britain, but he often said his personal success was negated by discrimination against other blacks.

14. Vern Smith of *Daily Worker* conducted interview at House of Kino. Interview and "breathe freely" quote in Robeson papers in Moorland-Spingarn Research Center at Howard University in Washington, DC.

15. Woollcott's defining description at Woollcott, *While Rome Burns*, 123. Permission to use this as fair use given by Sam Moore of permissions department of Penguin Group.

Chapter 9

1. Robeson contended editing of *Sanders of the River* changed it, but change more in him than in film; his anticolonialism had intensified. *New York Times* on April 3, 1935, reported "brilliant premiere" of *Sanders of the River* in London. "Robeson made an impressive figure of Bosambo." *London Times* praised film, Robeson, and Leslie Banks.

2. British version of American western at Boyle and Bunie, *Paul Robeson*, 328. This book's publisher, University of Massachusetts Press, granted permission to me under fair use.

3. *New York Times* on May 7 reported *Stevedore* stirred audience "in spite of its obvious propaganda." Lawrence Brown made "successful stage debut." *Telegraph* called Robeson's "nobility of bearing" his greatest stage asset.

4. His 1935 notebook in Robeson papers in Moorland-Spingarn Research Center.

5. *Show Boat* contract and Greta Garbo at Boyle and Bunie, *Paul Robeson*, 332. Film added song "I Still Suits Me" for Robeson to sing.

6. Concert on October 31, 1935, at Fred Jerome and Rodger Taylor, *Einstein on Race and Racism* (New Brunswick, NJ: Rutgers University Press, 2005), 54–56. Einstein lived in Princeton, saw Robeson whenever he performed there.

7. Visit to Pauli, comment about rich black kid, father's promise, at Paul Robeson Jr., *The Undiscovered Paul Robeson*, 1:232–33. © 2001 Paul Robeson Jr.; reprinted with permission of John Wiley & Sons.

8. Essie on "grand flat" and orchestra applauding in letter to Van Vechtens on November 21. When *Show Boat* opened at Radio City Music Hall in May, *New York Times* called it "one of the finest musical films we have seen."

9. Concert reviews in Lawrence Brown's scrapbooks, preserved on microfilm at Schomburg Center for Research in Black Culture, in Harlem.

10. Welch "adored" Robeson at Stephen Bourne, *Elisabeth Welch: Soft Lights and Sweet Music* (Lanham, MD: Scarecrow Press, 2005), 44. Welch talking with him on p. 47.

11. Interview with Davis at Philip S. Foner, ed., *Paul Robeson Speaks* (New York: Brunner/Mazel, 1978), 105–8. All material from this book used with kind permission of Laura and Elizabeth Foner.

12. Will Rogers cited at *Dictionary of Quotations* (Edinburgh: Chambers, 1997), 820. Current example of Jon Stewart compared to pundits on cable news.

13. Her diary of trip turned into Eslanda Robeson, *African Journey* (New York: John Day Company, 1945).

14. Essie on set of *Big Fella* at Bourne, *Elisabeth Welch*, 48.

15. Paul Robeson Jr. said, "I didn't speak a word of Russian" when parents entered him in Moscow school. Father's "endless questions" at Paul Robeson Jr., *The Undiscovered Paul Robeson*, 280.

16. Socialism in original edition of Robeson, *Here I Stand*, 47.

17. Quotation at Michael Kazin, *American Dreamers: How the Left Changed a Nation* (New York: Alfred A. Knopf, 2011), 156. Union leader Eugene Debs and Presbyterian minister Norman Thomas both idealistic socialists and pacifists, not Communists. Socialism could never take hold in United States.

Chapter 10

1. Pyramid at Henry Wilcoxon with Katherine Orrison, *Lionheart in Hollywood: The Autobiography of Henry Wilcoxon* (Metuchen, NJ: Scarecrow Press, 1991), 90–93. Wilcoxon called Paul's singing at pyramid "the most extraordinary experience of my life." Pyramid anecdote cited here with copyright permission of Patricia Zline, permissions manager, Rowman & Littlefield Publishing Group. Mozart aria a Robeson favorite.

2. Essie's remarks to Van Vechtens in letter to them obtained from Beinecke Rare Book and Manuscript Library at Yale.

3. Council on African Affairs at David Henry Anthony III, *Max Yergan: Race Man, Internationalist, Cold Warrior* (New York: New York University Press, 2006), 170.

4. Political ally of left at Paul Robeson Jr., *The Undiscovered Paul Robeson*, 1:285–86.

5. Text of speech on June 24, 1937, in collection of Robeson papers in Moorland-Spingarn Research Center at Howard University in Washington, DC. Guernica referred to slaughter in Spanish Civil War, immortalized in famous Picasso painting.

6. Pauli's reluctance to leave Moscow in Essie's letter to Van Vechtens on April 4, 1938, from Beinecke Rare Book and Manuscript Library at Yale.

7. *New York Times* reported on December 19, 1937, that nine thousand members of Labour Party filled the Royal Albert Hall to demand aid for Spain. It said Robeson changed "Ol' Man River" lyrics to "I must keep on struggling until I'm dying." Oscar Hammerstein's comment in footnote at Brown, *The Young Paul Robeson*, 143.

8. Essie quoted Paul about going to Spain, fighting fascism, in her diary. Spain visit recorded daily in her diary, January 22–31, 1938, all in Moorland-Spingarn Research Center.

9. Spain visit as turning point in his life at Robeson, *Here I Stand*, 61 (original 1958 edition); © 1958, 1988 Paul Robeson; reprinted with permission of Beacon Press, Boston.

10. Decision to move again and subsequent visitors at Paul Robeson Jr., *The Undiscovered Paul Robeson*, 307–8. Son attended Soviet school in London.

11. Interview in London *Daily Worker* about Unity Theatre at Foner, *Paul Robeson Speaks*, 119–20.

12. Interview with *Worthington Herald* on September 23, 1938, in Paul Robeson Archive at Akademie der Künste in Berlin. Interviewer said he never before had "such an impression of a powerful mind combined with a simply lovable nature."

13. Mrs. Roosevelt resigned from the Daughters of the American Revolution to protest their barring Anderson; used her influence as president's wife to arrange concert at Lincoln Memorial on Easter Sunday 1939.

14. "N-word" expunged from revival at Robeson's insistence; revival drew packed houses and excellent reviews.

15. Complaint about elusive behavior in letter from Essie dated May 31, 1939.

16. *Jericho* and *The Proud Valley* his best movies; he had some editorial control over them; latter film virtually song of praise for Welsh miners.

17. Quotation about "sheer cynicism" at William L. Shirer, *The Rise and Fall of the Third Reich: A History of Nazi Germany* (New York: Simon & Schuster, 1960), 528.

Chapter 11

1. *Afro-American* had photograph of Robesons "as they left first class quarters on the SS *Washington*" on arrival Thursday, October 12, 1939. *Amsterdam News* on October 21 reported Robeson's return and quoted him as saying he saw no reason for United States to enter war. Stalin-Hitler pact put Robeson in dilemma; he strongly opposed Nazi Germany but supported Moscow's position, contending Stalin needed time to prepare for war; dilemma ended when Germany attacked Russia.

2. Essie's diary in November 1939 described "our glorious 5-room flat." Her diaries in Robeson papers in Moorland-Spingarn Research Center at Howard University in Washington, DC.

3. Brown and Robinson working with Robeson at Seton, *Paul Robeson*, 127. Robbins Music Corp. published "Ballad for Americans." Sony/ATV Music Publishing now provided lyric reprint license to me.

4. Robinson's account of autobiography at Earl Robinson with Eric A. Gordon, *Ballad of an American: The Autobiography of Earl Robinson* (Lanham, MD: Scarecrow Press, 1998), 93–95. Permission to use material provided by Patricia Zline, permissions manager, Rowman & Littlefield Publishing Group.

5. Audience at "Ballad for Americans" in *Time* magazine, November 20, 1939. Original album of two ten-inch 78-rpm discs, recorded on both sides. First time I ever heard Robeson.

6. Atkinson's letter in Robeson papers in Moorland-Spingarn Research Center.

7. Hamilton ceremony in *New York Times* on January 22, 1940. Letter at Edwin P. Hoyt, *Paul Robeson: The American Othello* (Cleveland, OH: World Publishing Company, 1967), 103–4.

8. Unpopular actions of Soviet Union put Robeson in difficult position, but he continued to support Moscow.

9. *Show Boat* included John Boles, Norma Terris, Guy Kibbee, and Helen Morgan. *Chicago Defender* articles obtained from Hayden Library of Arizona State University in Tempe.

10. Reports on concerts, including Lewisohn Stadium, in Lawrence Brown's scrapbook in Schomburg Center for Research in Black Culture, in Harlem.

11. Theremin instrument invented by Russian scientist, Leon Theremin. Clara recalled tours with Paul, racism they encountered, and speaking Russian with him in public, on website of Nadia-Clara Foundation. Hundreds of programs, reviews, and articles obtained from Clara Rockmore Collection at library of University of Maryland, with aid of Vincent J. Novara of Special Collection in Performing Arts.

12. Horne's view of Robeson at *In Person, Lena Horne; As Told to Helen Arstein and Carlton Moss* (Greenberg, 1950), 184–90.

13. Connecticut house at Hoyt, *Paul Robeson: The American Othello*, 109–10. *Look* magazine on March 10, 1942, ran glowing picture article on the Robesons in Enfield house.

14. "King Joe" on ten-inch 78-rpm disc; lyrics by Richard Wright.

15. After concert years later, I asked why he sometimes held hand over his ear when he sang; he said it helped him hear his own voice more clearly.

16. FBI reports on Robeson began in 1941; eventually there were thousands of them; obtained under Freedom of Information Act, on microfilm at Schomburg Center for Research in Black Culture, in Harlem.

17. Based on 1938 hearing by Senator Robert LaFollette of Wisconsin.

Chapter 12

1. Concern about Robeson's acting at Margaret Webster, *Don't Put Your Daughter on the Stage* (New York: Alfred A. Knopf, 1972), 110–11.

2. Cousin's story at Dorothy Butler Gilliam, *Paul Robeson, All-American* (Washington, DC: New Republic Book Company, 1976), 108.

3. "Songs of Free Men" recorded for Columbia Records. Taubman's highly favorable review appeared in *New York Times* on February 28, 1942. CD "Songs of Free Men" issued years later; it diluted power of original album by adding spirituals, all beautiful but distracting from political tone of 1942 album of 78-rpm records.

4. Labor rally in Yankee Stadium on May 2 at Charles H. Wright, *Robeson: Labor's Forgotten Champion* (Detroit, MI: Balamp, 1975), 37.

5. Morehouse ceremony in *New York Times* on June 2, 1943.

6. Father-son talks at Paul Robeson Jr., *The Undiscovered Paul Robeson*, vol. 2, *Quest for Freedom, 1939–1976* (New York: John Wiley & Sons, 2010), 55–56. Used here under © Paul Robeson Jr. 2010; reprinted with permission of John Wiley & Sons.

7. Webster's "big bear of a man" at Webster, *Don't Put Your Daughter on the Stage*, 116.

8. Audience's ovation on opening night and Webster's speech in brief article next to review in *New York Times* on October 20, 1943.

9. Reaction to *Othello* reviews at Seton, *Paul Robeson*, 154. Earlier Robeson comments on acting in *Othello* also on p. 154.

10. Reviews of *Othello* in Lawrence Brown's scrapbook at Schomburg Center for Research in Black Culture, in Harlem. Atkinson, who saw later performance, described Robeson as "a slow and ponderous Othello." Webster said Atkinson saw one of Robeson's weaker performances.

11. Uta's view of Paul's acting at Duberman, *Paul Robeson*, 278. Cast very fond of Paul, who played on cast's softball team in Central Park.

12. Text at forum in Paul Robeson Collection at Schomburg Center for Research in Black Culture, in Harlem. Honorary union member at Wright, *Robeson: Labor's Forgotten Champion*, 44.

13. Baseball at Foner, *Paul Robeson Speaks*, 151–52.

14. Radio broadcast reported in *Pittsburgh Courier* on January 8, 1944. *Courier* articles on microfilm obtained from library of University of Arizona, Tucson.

15. Baltimore *Afro-American* on April 22, 1944, reported his forty-sixth birthday. Article from ProQuest Historical Newspapers digital database at library of Princeton University. Bethune, who had spoken at birthday celebration, wrote to Robeson a few days later, saying, "Keep on being our brave and courageous Paul."

16. *American Magazine* article of May 1944 in Robeson Archive at Rutgers. *Chicago Defender* on December 30 from library of Arizona State University in Tempe.

17. Affair with Hagen at Duberman, *Paul Robeson,* 286–91, based on his interviews with her. Used with Duberman's generous permission. Uta Hagen born in Germany; family moved to United States when she was seven. Jose Ferrer born in Puerto Rico and went to Princeton University. Hagen became teacher of acting; divorced Ferrer in 1948; later married Herbert Berghof. Ferrer married Phyllis Hill, then Rosemary Clooney.

18. Segregation stand at Lindsey R. Swindall, *The Politics of Paul Robeson's Othello* (Jackson: University Press of Mississippi, 2011), 104.

Chapter 13

1. Report of Spingarn ceremony in *Pittsburgh Courier* on October 17, 1945. *Courier* on microfilm in library of University of Arizona in Tucson.

2. Nehru discussing Soviets at Northrop, *The Meeting of East and West*, 433, quoting from Nehru's book *Toward Freedom* (New York: John Day Company, 1941).

3. Concert programs and reviews in Lawrence Brown's scrapbooks on microfilm at Schomburg Center for Research in Black Culture, in Harlem.

4. America needed an enemy, and Soviet communism clearly filled this role according to historian H. W. Brands, *The Devil We Knew: Americans and the Cold War* (Oxford: Oxford University Press, 1993), 218.

5. Text of speech at South African rally on September 11, 1947, in Robeson papers at Schomburg Center for Research in Black Culture, in Harlem.

6. Einstein for antilynching crusade at Jerome and Taylor, *Einstein on Race and Racism*, 92.

7. Most authoritative account of Robeson's meeting with Truman in *Chicago Defender* on September 28, because its editor participated in this meeting. Baltimore *Afro-American* on October 5 quoted Robeson's reply to reporter after meeting. Articles

obtained from library of Arizona State University in Tempe. Tammy Kelly, archivist of Harry S. Truman Presidential Library, informed me that Truman did not have stenographers or other note takers in his office with him during meetings, and the library did not find any additional information about his meeting with Robeson.

8. Radio speech in Robeson Archive at Akademie der Künste in Berlin.

9. Tenney transcript on October 7, 1946, in Robeson Archive at Akademie der Künste.

10. Hagen on Christmas Eve incident at Duberman, *Paul Robeson*, 311–13, based on his interviews with her; she died in 2004. Apparently, Paul called his friend Harlem gangster "Bumpy" Johnson, who provided armed escort to protect him from any harm.

11. Copy of Essie's letter to Paul about finances on December 1, 1946, in Moorland-Spingarn Research Center at Howard University in Washington, DC. She trimmed one year from her age here.

12. Robeson as role model at Harry Belafonte with Michael Shnayerson, *My Song: A Memoir* (New York: Alfred A. Knopf, 2011), 64. And turning to folksinging on p. 94.

13. Brown on Robeson's mood at Seton, *Paul Robeson*, 168–69.

14. Paul Robeson Jr. suggested FBI behind attempt to kill his father. He learned FBI had Robeson and driver under twenty-four-hour surveillance at that time, but no evidence of wrongdoing.

15. Concert at University of Utah at Seton, *Paul Robeson*, 177.

16. Truman Doctrine (p. 105) and Marshall Plan (p. 119) in Harry S. Truman, *Memoirs of Harry S. Truman: 1946–1952, Years of Trial and Hope* (Garden City, NY: Doubleday & Company, 1956). Historians might differ as to whether he could have averted, or limited, the Cold War by following conciliatory policy advocated by Henry Wallace. Marshall Plan proved great success as humanitarian and political policy.

17. Clara's nephew, Robert Sherman, recalled Robeson's relationship with Rockmores and listening to baseball games with Paul in telephone interview with me on January 13, 2011.

18. Wallace speech, noting Communist support, on September 11 at Richard J. Walton, *Henry Wallace, Harry Truman, and the Cold War* (New York: Viking Press 1976), 164–65.

19. On arms race, see Robert Dallek, *The Lost Peace: Leadership in a Time of Horror and Hope, 1945–1953* (New York: HarperCollins Publishers, 2010).

Chapter 14

1. Wallace committee in *New York Times* on January 29, 1948. His supporters included Aaron Copeland, Albert Einstein, Edna Ferber, Jose Ferrer, Uta Hagen, Dashiell Hammett, Lillian Hellman, Gene Kelly, Norman Mailer, Thomas Mann, Arthur Miller, and Eugene O'Neill.

2. Wallace described in John C. Culver and John Hyde, *American Dreamer: The Life and Times of Henry A. Wallace* (New York: W. W. Norton & Company, 2000).

3. Wallace on Communists in campaign at Zachary Karabell, *The Last Campaign: How Harry Truman Won the 1948 Election* (New York: Alfred A. Knopf, 2000), 66. Karabell said TV transformed later campaigns for president.

4. Campaign expectations at Walton, *Henry Wallace, Harry Truman, and the Cold War*, 195. According to Michael Kazin, "Wallace hoped to win enough votes to pressure the winner to restore the wartime alliance with the USSR, establish a more generous welfare state, and enact a sweeping civil rights law" (Kazin, *American Dreamers*, 202).

5. Hawaiian tour at Robinson, *Ballad of an American*, 220–22. Permission to use quote kindly given by Patricia Zline, permissions manager, Rowman & Littlefield Publishing Group.

6. Press conference reported in *Honolulu Star-Bulletin* on March 22, 1948.

7. Yergan turned against Robeson at Anthony, *Max Yergan*, 233 and 242.

8. Chanting for vice president at Seton, *Paul Robeson*, 184.

9. Transcript of testimony obtained with help of Shirley Whitehouse and Kathleen Jones in Government Documents Section of Hayden Library at Arizona State University. From then on, Robeson refused to answer if he was a Communist. Mundt-Nixon Bill passed two years later as McCarran Internal Security Act.

10. Gene Dennis described childhood event in television documentary film *Children of the Left* by Eric Stange, producer-director in Arlington, Massachusetts. Documentary viewed at New York Public Library. Gene became longshoreman, broke with Communists. Father imprisoned.

11. Kazin wrote that, with possible exception of Joe Louis, Robeson was the "most celebrated black person" in the United States and best-known American in world (Kazin, *American Dreamers*, 200).

12. Truman's diary at Robert H. Ferrell, ed., *Off the Record: The Private Papers of Harry S. Truman* (Columbia: University of Missouri Press, 1980), 143.

13. Brown's reluctance to go to Florida at Seton, *Paul Robeson*, 190.

14. Official 1948 election results from Federal Election Commission.

15. Quotation of English philosopher Dr. Samuel Johnson at *Bartlett's Familiar Quotations*, 17th ed. (New York: Little, Brown and Co., 2002), 327.

Chapter 15

1. Peace Congress report from Paris in *New York Times* on April 21, 1949. *Times* did not mention "unthinkable" remark reported by Associated Press.

2. His imprecise words, without preparation, did not intend to speak for all Negroes. He had previously used "unthinkable" to express opinions, so Associated Press story seemed credible. Lloyd Brown spoke on DVD of 1998 documentary *Speak of Me as I Am*, narrated by Pam Grier, produced and directed by Rachel Harmer; coproduction of BBC Wales, NJN Public Television, NVC Arts.

3. Prague conversation at Seton, *Paul Robeson*, 201–2.

4. Account of meeting Feffer in notes Paul Robeson Jr. wrote for CD of Moscow concert; Soviet official sent concert tape to him. Similar account at Paul Robeson Jr., *The Undiscovered Paul Robeson*, 2:153–55. Sergei Eisenstein died in 1947.

5. On disk, one hears all songs, introductions in Russian, sustained applause; ends with Robeson singing Warsaw Ghetto song.

6. Paul Robeson Jr. said his father's words at concert's end deleted from tape sent to him; missing words could not be corroborated. Feffer's execution delayed three years.

7. Paul Robeson Jr. and Marilyn told me about their time at Cornell.

8. *Amsterdam News* of June 25, 1949, published details of wedding. *Time* magazine quoted Robeson's angry words to photographers.

9. Text of Rockland Palace speech in Robeson papers at Schomburg Center for Research in Black Culture, in Harlem.

10. Jackie Robinson's testimony at David Falkner, *Great Time Coming: The Life of Jackie Robinson—from Baseball to Birmingham* (New York: Simon & Schuster, 1995), 200–201. *New York Times* put it on front page. Robinson "light in his touch" when he criticized Robeson at Arnold Rampersad, *Jackie Robinson* (New York: Alfred A. Knopf, 1997), 214.

11. Jackie Robinson regretted words against Robeson in his autobiography, told to Alfred Duckett, *I Never Had It Made* (New York: Putnam, 1972; New York: Ecco, HarperCollins, 1995).

12. Most of speech denounced colonialism but included "contempt for the Western press." *New York Times* on July 21 put fifty pickets in fourth paragraph. Conversation witnessed by me, standing behind reporter; I was a teenager with no idea at that time of becoming a reporter. Student at subsequent "Make Marc Mayor" rallies also was me.

13. Helen's account at Duberman, *Paul Robeson*, 364–65, used here with his kind permission. Helen's son, Dr. John Rosen, confirmed quote attributed to him but rejected my request to discuss Robeson beyond that. In long telephone interview with me on August 13, 2009, Pete Seeger said he arrived at blocked entrance; policeman told him, "There's not going to be any concert." No one could get in, so he turned his car around and left.

14. Howard Fast described August 27 events inside concert grounds in his brief book *Peekskill USA: Inside the Infamous 1949 Riots* (New York: Civil Rights Congress, 1951; Mineola, NY: Dover Publications, 2006).

15. Peekskill concerts sponsored by People's Artists, agency founded by Seeger. Straus, unions, and security at Howard Fast, *Freedom Road*, with a forward by W. E. B. Du Bois and an introduction by Eric Foner (Armonk, NY: M. E. Sharpe, 1995), 75–76 and 81–83. Also described by Paul Robeson Jr. in radio interview "Episode 6: Reds." Seeger said he felt "honored to be asked to sing a few songs" at Peekskill; see Editors of *Freedomways, Paul Robeson: The Great Forerunner*, 313.

16. September 4 concert, songs, and collection from audience reported next day in *New York Times*; story focused on police efforts to quell violence.

17. In his telephone interview with me, Seeger described violence in detail. Seeger, Lee Hays, Freddie Hellerman, and Ronnie Gilbert formed quartet, later called the Weavers, which had number one hit "Goodnight Irene." Essie wrote open letter to her sorority that summer: "Now for the record, I am not a Communist. I have never been a Communist."

18. Jury convicted all eleven defendants. Medina sentenced them to full five years in prison, except for one who got "only" three years because of his heroic military service. Judge also sent defense lawyers to prison for contempt of court. Not a great time for dissent and democracy.

Chapter 16

1. FBI files on Robeson on microfilm at Schomburg Center for Research in Black Culture, in Harlem.

2. Rejected suggestion and Wilkerson comment at Duberman, *Paul Robeson,* 382–83.

3. NBC controversy in *New York Times* on March 14, 1950.

4. For Stendhal, who wrote classic French novel *The Red and the Black* more than a century earlier, red seemed to stand for the army and black for the clergy, main careers open to his hero at that time.

5. At Carnegie Hall on April 15, 1950: term paper was about Paul Robeson; student was me. His immediate willingness to help this young student made strong impression on me. Coretta Scott, music student on program with Robeson at Antioch College, said he impressed her and encouraged her; see Coretta Scott King, *My Life with Martin Luther King Jr.* (New York: Henry Holt, 1969; rev. ed., London: Puffin, 1993), 43.

6. Text of speech on June 10, 1950, in Robeson papers at Schomburg Center for Research in Black Culture, in Harlem.

7. *Amsterdam News* editor James Hicks witnessed incident in Red Rooster. He gave this account on Gil Noble's *Like It Is* television program, which broadcast special Robeson documentary on April 11, 1976.

8. On June 10, 1951, friend of my sister went with me to Robeson concert; she had never heard him before; deeply impressed with his "Water Boy-oy-oy."

9. Poitier described him as "hero and mentor." His recollection at Aram Goudsouzian, *Sidney Poitier: Man, Actor, Icon* (Chapel Hill: University of North Carolina Press, 2004), 88–90.

10. Du Bois indictment, marriage to Shirley Graham at David Levering Lewis, *W. E. B. Du Bois: The Fight for Equality and the American Century* (New York: Henry Holt, 2000), 2:548–52.

11. Genocide petition at Patterson, *The Man Who Cried Genocide,* 169–84.

12. Blocked at border, singing by telephone in notes by Ian Shaw for Folk Era disk made from tape of subsequent concert; songs and speech from disk.

13. His 1952 quote on father on Omega CD titled *The Odyssey of Paul Robeson.*

14. Visit to Einstein, recalled by Brown, at Jerome and Taylor, *Einstein on Race and Racism,* 123–24. Recounted here by permission of Rutgers University Press

15. Stalin Peace Prize at Hoyt, *Paul Robeson: The American Othello,* 208–9.

16. Camus statement, which echoed Robeson's speech fifteen years earlier, came from his essay "The Artist and His Time" in Albert Camus, *The Myth of Sisyphus and Other Essays,* translated from French (New York: Vintage Books, Alfred A. Knopf, and Random House, 1959), 147.

17. Transcript of her Senate testimony obtained by Shirley Whitehouse and Kathleen Jones in Government Documents Section of Hayden Library at Arizona State University. United Press story in *Washington Post* on July 8, 1953, described Essie as "smiling and calm during her testimony." Roy M. Cohn later became good news source for me at *New York Times.*

Chapter 17

1. Description in notes by Ian Shaw for Folk Era disk of concert on August 16, 1953. Program and speech from disk of live concert. Those in range of his voice alluded to FBI agents monitoring him. Alan Booth, young black pianist, became principal accompanist when Lawrence Brown wanted to reduce his schedule.

2. Rosen family at Duberman, *Paul Robeson*, 407–8, based on his interviews with Helen. Rosen material used here with Duberman's generous permission.

3. Du Bois bought Brooklyn Heights town house from Arthur Miller; for entertaining of visitors there, see Murali Balaji, *The Professor and the Pupil: The Politics of W. E. B. Du Bois and Paul Robeson* (New York: Nation Books, 2007), 354–55. Du Bois the professor, Robeson the pupil, wives "the undisputed first ladies of the struggle."

4. Du Bois 1953 Christmas party at Shirley Graham Du Bois, *His Day Is Marching On: A Memoir of W. E. B. Du Bois* (New York: J. B. Lippincott, 1971), 213–14. His speech about Robeson at Balaji, *The Professor and the Pupil*, 374.

5. Description of McCarthyism in *Freedom* at Foner, *Paul Robeson Speaks*, 375–77.

6. "Salute to Paul Robeson" on May 26, 1954, at Robin G. Kelley, *Thelonious Monk: The Life and Times of an American Original* (New York: Free Press, 2009), 168–69.

7. "My Brother, Paul" profile in *Freedom* magazine of April 1952; copy in Paul Robeson Archive at Akademie der Künste in Berlin.

8. Wheel coming off Robeson's car at Duberman, *Paul Robeson*, 431. Wheel also at Paul Robeson Jr., *The Undiscovered Paul Robeson*, 2:239–40.

9. *New York Times* reported passport fight and judge's rejection of Robeson's request.

10. Manchester on March 11, 1956. Reported in *Manchester Guardian* next day. Also Wright, *Robeson: Labor's Forgotten Champion*, 24.

11. Depression at Paul Robeson Jr., *The Undiscovered Paul Robeson*, 2:248–49, and Duberman, *Paul Robeson*, 437–39.

12. House Un-American Activities Committee transcript on June 12, 1956, obtained for me by Shirley Whitehouse and Kathleen Jones in Government Documents Section of Arizona State University. Michael Kazin said U.S. Communist Party never had over one hundred thousand members; in 1956, it had only about five thousand members, "perhaps a third of whom were secret agents of the FBI."

13. Twain's comment cited at *Bartlett's Familiar Quotations,* 17th ed. (New York: Little, Brown and Co., 2002), 562.

14. Lloyd Brown on working with Robeson at Brown, *The Young Paul Robeson*, 132. Brown said they shared political viewpoint and Negro culture.

15. Telephone concert in 1957 at Wright, *Robeson: Labor's Forgotten Champion*, 19.

16. Book expanded on his oft-stated views, including socialism at Robeson, *Here I Stand*, 47 (original edition); © 1958, 1988 Paul Robeson; reprinted with permission of Beacon Press, Boston. Added words here from interview on Pacifica Radio in San Francisco on March 15, 1958. Book "widely praised in the African-American press" at Manning Marable, *Malcolm X: A Life of Reinvention* (New York: Viking Press, 2011), 157.

17. Praise by Du Bois reprinted at W. E. B. Du Bois, *The Autobiography of W. E. B. Du Bois* (New York: International Publishers, 1968), 396–97. Also in *National Guardian* of April 7, 1958.

18. Printed programs of concerts May 9 and 23, both of which I attended.

Chapter 18

1. Bevan left-wing leader in Labour Party; wife, Jennie Lee, in Parliament.

2. Essie wrote about Soviet trip in articles for *Afro-American* on October 11 and 18, 1958. She reported tremendous welcome; also Khrushchev and volleyball in Yalta. Film clip of laughing Khrushchev and Robeson, made by Soviet film crew for national television, later in documentary *Speak of Me as I Am*, produced and directed by Rachel Harmer for BBC in 1998.

3. *London Times* articles obtained from its online archive.

4. Du Bois–Robeson encounter at Kremlin party at Shirley Graham Du Bois, *His Day Is Marching On*, 269–70.

5. Stratford family at Duberman, *Paul Robeson*, 476. Description from family of son-in-law Andrew Faulds. He told press Robeson inspired him to enter politics.

6. Richardson's assessment at Tony Richardson, *The Long-Distance Runner: An Autobiography* (New York: William Morrow and Co., 1993), 129–30.

7. Robinson as Robeson's accompanist in Prague at Robinson, *Ballad of an American*, 223. On p. 224, he said lonely Paul wanted to go home to United States.

8. *Express* interview in Robeson Archive at Akademie der Künste in Berlin, which contains thousands of articles about Robeson, most of them in English and some in German.

9. Humboldt University reports in archive at Akademie der Künste.

10. Reports from Australia and New Zealand also at Akademie der Künste.

11. Helen's visit, Paul's departure at Duberman, *Paul Robeson*, 496.

12. Singing at factory, later confronting Khrushchev at Robert Robinson with Jonathan Slevin, *Black on Red: My 44 Years inside the Soviet Union* (Washington, DC: Acropolis Books, 1988), 317–19. Mournful song probably "Hassidic Chant."

13. Some of Robinson's details questionable, but factory visit and Khrushchev rumor sounded credible. He said he heard about Robeson-Khrushchev incident from three party members; this report of Khrushchev harshly criticizing Robeson might explain suicide attempt.

14. Paul Robeson Jr. was primary source on suicide attempt at Duberman, *Paul Robeson*, 498–500, and Paul Robeson Jr., *The Undiscovered Paul Robeson*, 2:311–20. Also see his article in *The Nation* on December 20, 1999. This note and note 19 used under © 2010 Paul Robeson Jr.; reprinted with permission of John Wiley & Sons.

15. In sanatorium together, Robeson told his son about visitors who pleaded for help, but he provided no more information. Paul Jr. wrote in *The Nation* that he suspected CIA drugged father with LSD to induce suicide; raised questions but no hard evidence. A. E. Hotchner, in *New York Times* on fiftieth anniversary of Hemingway's suicide, said his friend suffered from depression and paranoia. Also, FBI files later revealed Hemingway had been under surveillance for many years because of suspicions over his activities in Cuba.

16. Received fifty-four electric-shock treatments at Priory, which son called "outrageous" amount. Paul and Essie attended concert by Ella Fitzgerald, who dedicated a song to him.

17. Essie's letter written to "Harry" from London on October 6, 1961.

18. *Telegraph* ran "exclusive" stories of intrigue involving Robeson trip. *New York Times* reported Robeson called *Telegraph* stories "completely absurd."

19. Buch Clinic treatment at Paul Robeson Jr., *The Undiscovered Paul Robeson*, 2:333–36, and Duberman, *Paul Robeson*, 516–20.

Chapter 19

1. Arrival at airport on front page of *New York Times* on December 23, 1963, in article by Peter Kihss, the most accurate, thorough, reliable reporter I ever knew. Separate feature with misleading headline "Disillusioned Native Son."

2. Brief notes Robeson wrote on flight home at Paul Robeson Jr., *The Undiscovered Paul Robeson*, 2:238.

3. United States had nuclear-armed missiles in bases close to Soviet Union but refused to tolerate similar Soviet base in range of United States. This 1962 Cuban Missile Crisis closest world came to nuclear war. For the *New York Times*, I reported Adlai Stevenson's dramatic speech at United Nations.

4. Copy of letter on Paul's progress in Paul Robeson Archive at Akademie der Künste.

5. His unpublished notes at Balaji, *The Professor and the Pupil*, 411.

6. Speech at Davis funeral at Foner, *Paul Robeson Speaks*, 470–71; all material from this book used with kind permission of Laura and Elizabeth Foner.

7. Black press statement in Robeson papers at Akademie der Künste.

8. *New York Times* reported that at Hansberry funeral Robeson spoke from pulpit in voice "still compelling in its richness and resonance." Paul Robeson Jr. revealed discussion with Malcolm X at Paul Robeson Jr., *The Undiscovered Paul Robeson*, 2:344–45.

9. C. Vann Woodward, *The Strange Career of Jim Crow*, commem. ed. (Oxford: Oxford University Press, 2002), 202. In a series of lectures in 1955 comprising this book, Woodward described history of segregation known as Jim Crow. Term "Jim Crow" apparently originated in song-and-dance written by entertainer Thomas D. Rice in 1832; became character in minstrel shows; used to characterize segregation by 1900.

10. Article on Du Bois at Foner, *Paul Robeson Speaks*, 474.

11. Description of Robeson and program at Americana on April 22, 1965, from notes I took as observer. At end of event, though obviously tired, he signed autographs for dozens of people who clamored around him. It was last time I saw him; older, thinner, but still "Our Paul."

12. Text of speeches by Lewis, Stevens, and Robeson from 1965 summer issue of *Freedomways*, called "quarterly review of Negro Freedom Movement." In late 1960s, Stokely Carmichael led more militant Black Power movement to fight white brutality.

13. Robeson with scissors and razor, then going to Gracie Square Hospital on June 11, 1965, at Paul Robeson Jr., *The Undiscovered Paul Robeson*, 2:354–55. Used here under © 2010 Paul Robeson Jr.; reprinted with permission of John Wiley & Sons.

14. Doctor's evaluation at Duberman, *Paul Robeson*, 534.

15. Return to hospital and acute illness at Paul Robeson Jr., *The Undiscovered Paul Robeson*, 2:357–58. Paul Jr. credited Dr. Nachtigall with saving father's life. Paul Jr. suspected CIA involved in drugging father in Moscow and in treatment at Priory in London and hospital in New York with excess medications, but no convincing proof.

16. *New York Times* reported on October 19: Robeson found semiconscious in vacant lot a few blocks north of home; wallet with $15 intact; no evidence of foul play.

17. Silently signed wife's death certificate at Paul Robeson Jr., *The Undiscovered Paul Robeson*, 2:361. He seemed weary of life.

18. Some said Essie received PhD from Hartford Seminary, but its registrar informed me that "there is no record of Eslanda Robeson having been granted a degree from here."

Chapter 20

1. Life at sister's house in first thirteen pages of slim book Charlotte Turner Bell, *Paul Robeson's Last Days in Philadelphia* (Bryn Mawr, PA: Dorrance & Company, 1986). Her firsthand account gives interesting details but glosses over his illness. Lloyd Brown gave tour of Marian's house in television documentary *Speak of Me as I Am*, produced by BBC and NJN in 1998.

2. Seventieth birthday and WBAI-Pacifica "Tribute to Paul Robeson" on DVD in Criterion Collection of Robeson movies issued in 2006.

3. Discussions with son, pacemaker at Paul Robeson Jr., *The Undiscovered Paul Robeson*, 2:364–65.

4. Paul Robeson Jr. managing father's affairs, limiting visitors at Brown, *The Young Paul Robeson*, 141.

5. Comments by Ossie Davis and Paul Robeson Jr. in three-part Robeson tribute on *New Jersey Speaks* on WNET, Channel 13, in May 1971.

6. Brown showed him August 1972 *Ebony* at Brown, *The Young Paul Robeson*, 141.

7. My telephone interview on January 13, 2011, with Sherman. Ruby Dee's comments in telephone interview with me on July 6, 2011. She and husband Ossie Davis also said of Paul that their "greatest joy was to just be in his presence" in *With Ossie and Ruby: In This Life Together* (New York: William Morrow and Co., 1998; New York: Perennial, 2000), 178.

8. Lawrence Brown papers, including his scrapbooks, at Schomburg Center for Research in Black Culture, a few blocks from his apartment in Harlem.

9. Belafonte's visit at Belafonte, *My Song*, 363.

10. Birthday salute to Robeson reported in *New York Times* on April 16, 1973. Text of speech appeared later in *Amsterdam News* and other publications.

11. Birthday dinner at Brown, *The Young Paul Robeson*, 141.

12. Sad words on Thanksgiving at Paul Robeson Jr., *The Undiscovered Paul Robeson*, 2:369. Robeson contemplated suicide more than once, feeling he had no more to contribute. No evidence he ever took drugs or drank to excess. Despite terrible toll of depression and hostility he endured, it is still painful to know this most remarkable man wished to end his own life.

13. Description of funeral from notes I took when attending it. Excerpts from eulogies in *Amsterdam News* and later booklet of tributes.

14. Names of mourners at funeral from *New York Times* and *Amsterdam News*.

15. Burial description from Lloyd Brown's book and documentary. Copy of Robeson's will obtained by me in Surrogates Court in Manhattan.

16. Gil Noble's *Like It Is* television program carried ninety-minute documentary titled "Paul Robeson: The Tallest Tree in Our Forest" on WABC on April 11, 1976. Noble kindly provided me with text of his excellent program.

17. Fund-raising tribute for Robeson Archive from printed program.

18. Belafonte extolled Robeson in television documentary *Scandalize My Name* presented on DVD in 1999 by Starz Encore Entertainment. Poitier spoke at Sidney Poitier, *Life beyond Measure: Letters to My Great-Granddaughter* (New York: HarperOne, 2008), 161, and Seeger wrote note for Criterion Collection of Robeson movies on DVD in 2006.

Postscript

1. Play *Paul Robeson* written by Phillip Hayes Dean. James Earl Jones recalled seeing Robeson in concert for first time: "I felt an energy sweep over me and rock my soul"; in "Our Paul" recollections by actors for Criterion Collection box set of Robeson movies in 2006.

2. Docent told me of many people with memorable moments. And my question elicited mayor's comment on Robeson's integrity. Pete Seeger at Editors of *Freedomways*, *Paul Robeson: The Great Forerunner*, 311. On p. 284 of this book, Shirley Graham Du Bois extolls, "That big smile embracing everybody in sight and beyond; the big Voice speaking or singing. All American, unexcelled . . . OUR PAUL!"

3. Hastings, *Winston's War: Churchill, 1940–1945*, 475. According to historian H. W. Brands, communism was its own "worst enemy," destined to collapse without U.S. opposition in Cold War (Brands, *The Devil We Knew*, 227–28).

4. Arthur Koestler, Richard Wright, and others renounced Communist beliefs relatively early; see Richard H. Crossman, ed., *The God that Failed* (London: Hamilton, 1950). Gide (p. 173) and Silone (p. 102) at Crossman, *The God that Failed* (New York: Columbia University Press, 2001). Khrushchev's denunciation of Stalin in his speech to Twentieth Congress of Soviet Communist Party in February 1956. Soviet

invasion of Hungary in October destroyed myth that Eastern European countries were voluntary, independent allies of Soviet Union.

5. According to Eric Foner, *Who Owns History? Rethinking the Past in a Changing World* (New York: Hill and Wang, 2002), Communist Party was "only predominantly white organization to make fighting racism central to its political program" in United States in 1930s. Michael Kazin wrote that Robeson believed United States "succeeded the British and French as the chief sponsors of colonial rule" (Kazin, *American Dreamers*, 201). And "only the USSR stood in its way." Kazin believed leftist "dreamers" changed U.S. attitudes, particularly on race.

6. Murrow's television broadcast on Senator McCarthy on March 9, 1954. Quotation of Cassius speaking in Shakespeare's *Julius Caesar*.

7. Profile of Robeson noting his fight for civil rights "two decades before the civil rights movement" at Harold Evans, *The American Century* (New York: Alfred A. Knopf, 1998), 457.

8. My article in *New York Times* on October 21, 1993, based on extensive interviews with him after his first book, *Paul Robeson, Jr. Speaks to America* (New Brunswick, NJ: Rutgers University Press, 1993). It took time for me to overcome his intense suspicion of press, but we became friends. BBC Radio 2 documentary titled *The Robeson Files,* produced by Hilary Robinson, broadcast in Britain summer of 2011, focused on FBI and MI5 surveillance of Robeson. His godson, Eric Goode, said, "Paul was a very courageous and principled man and also very obstinate." Broadcast disk kindly provided by Rosemary Foxcroft of BBC.

9. Susan became television writer-producer; also did pictorial biography of Paul Robeson titled *The Whole World in His Hands* (Secaucus, NJ: Citadel Press, 1981). David worked as entertainer; committed suicide at age forty-six in 1998. As of this writing, Paul Robeson Jr. is living with his wife, Marilyn, in Hoboken, New Jersey.

Selected Bibliography

BY THE ROBESON FAMILY

Robeson, Eslanda Goode. *African Journey.* New York: John Day Company, 1945.

———. *Paul Robeson, Negro.* New York: Harper and Brothers, 1930.

———, with Pearl S. Buck. *American Argument.* New York: John Day Company, 1949.

Robeson, Paul. *Here I Stand.* New York: Othello Associates, 1958. Reissued with preface by Lloyd L. Brown, Boston: Beacon Press, 1971; reissued again with introduction by Sterling Stuckey, Boston: Beacon Press, 1988.

Robeson, Paul, Jr. *A Black Way of Seeing Things.* New York: Seven Stories Press, 2006.

———. *Paul Robeson, Jr. Speaks to America.* New Brunswick, NJ: Rutgers University Press, 1993.

———. *The Undiscovered Paul Robeson.* Vol. 1, *An Artist's Journey, 1898–1939.* New York: John Wiley & Sons, 2001.

———. *The Undiscovered Paul Robeson.* Vol. 2, *Quest for Freedom, 1939–1976.* New York: John Wiley & Sons, 2010.

Robeson, Susan. *The Whole World in His Hands: A Pictorial Biography of Paul Robeson.* Secaucus, NJ: Citadel Press, 1981.

BIOGRAPHIES OF ROBESON

Bell, Charlotte Turner. *Paul Robeson's Last Days in Philadelphia.* Bryn Mawr, PA: Dorrance & Company, 1986.

Boyle, Sheila Tully, and Andrew Bunie. *Paul Robeson: The Years of Promise and Achievement.* Amherst: University of Massachusetts Press, 2001.

Brown, Lloyd L. *The Young Paul Robeson.* Boulder, CO: Westview Press, 1997.

Duberman, Martin Bauml. *Paul Robeson.* New York: Alfred A. Knopf, 1988.

Gilliam, Dorothy Butler. *Paul Robeson, All-American*. Washington, DC: New Republic Book Company, 1976.

Graham, Shirley. *Paul Robeson: Citizen of the World*. New York: Julian Messner, 1948.

Hamilton, Virginia. *Paul Robeson: The Life and Times of a Free Black Man*. New York: Harper & Row, 1974.

Hoyt, Edwin P. *Paul Robeson: The American Othello*. Cleveland, OH: World Publishing Company, 1967.

Nollen, Scott Allen. *Paul Robeson: Film Pioneer*. Jefferson, NC: McFarland & Company, 2010.

Seton, Marie. *Paul Robeson*. London: Dennis Dobson, 1958.

Wright, Charles H. *Robeson: Labor's Forgotten Champion*. Detroit, MI: Balamp, 1975.

ESSAYS, LETTERS, AND SPEECHES

Davis, Lenwood G. *A Paul Robeson Handbook: Everything You Want to Know about Paul Robeson*. Rockland, ME: Angelis Press, 1998.

———. *A Paul Robeson Research Guide and Selected Annotated Bibliography*. Westport, CT: Greenwood Press, 1982.

Dorinson, Joseph, and William Pencak, eds. *Paul Robeson: Essays on His Life and Legacy*. Jefferson, NC: McFarland & Company, 2002.

Editors of *Freedomways*, ed. *Paul Robeson: The Great Forerunner*. New York: Dodd, Mead, 1978. Reissued, New York: International Publishers, 1998.

Foner, Eric. *Who Owns History? Rethinking the Past in a Changing World*. New York: Hill and Wang, 2002.

Foner, Philip S., ed. *Paul Robeson Speaks*. New York: Brunner/Mazel, 1978.

———. *The Voice of Black America: Major Speeches by Negroes in the United States, 1797–1971*. New York: Simon & Schuster, 1972.

Gates, Henry Louis, Jr., and Evelyn Brooks Higgenbotham, eds. *African American Lives*. Oxford: Oxford University Press, 2004.

Locke, Alain, ed. *The New Negro: Voices of the Harlem Renaissance*. New York: Albert and Charles Boni, 1925. Reissued with introduction by Arnold Rampersad, New York: Macmillan, 1992.

Russell, Dick. *Black Genius*. New York: Carroll & Graf Publishers, 1998.

Stewart, Jeffrey C., ed. *Paul Robeson: Artist and Citizen*. New Brunswick, NJ: Rutgers University Press and the Paul Robeson Cultural Center, 1998.

BLACK HISTORY

Balaji, Murali. *The Professor and the Pupil: The Politics of W. E. B. Du Bois and Paul Robeson*. New York: Nation Books, 2007.

Belafonte, Harry, with Michael Shnayerson. *My Song: A Memoir*. New York: Alfred A. Knopf, 2011.

Bynum, Cornelius L. *A. Philip Randolph and the Struggle for Civil Rights*. Champaign: University of Illinois Press, 2010.

Cruse, Harold. *The Essential Harold Cruse*. New York: Palgrave, 2002.

Davis, Ossie, and Ruby Dee. *With Ossie and Ruby: In This Life Together*. New York: Perennial, 2000. Hardcover published by New York: William Morrow and Co., 1998.

Dierenfield, Bryce J. *The Civil Rights Movement*. Rev. ed. London: Pearson Education Limited, 2008. First published in Great Britain in 2004.

Du Bois, Shirley Graham. *His Day Is Marching On: A Memoir of W. E. B. Du Bois*. New York: J. B. Lippincott, 1971.

Du Bois, W. E. B. *The Autobiography of W. E. B. Du Bois*. New York: International Publishers, 1968.

——. *The Souls of Black Folks*. New York: Pocket Books, 2005.

Embree, Edwin R. *Thirteen against the Odds*. New York: Viking Press, 1944.

Franklin, John Hope, and Alfred A. Moss Jr. *From Slavery to Freedom: A History of Negro Americans*. 6th ed. New York: Alfred A. Knopf, 1988.

Hemenway, Robert E. *Zora Neale Hurston: A Literary Biography*. Champaign: University of Illinois Press, 1977.

Johnson, James Weldon, ed. *The Book of American Negro Spirituals*. New York: Viking Press, 1925.

Lewis, David Levering. *W. E. B. Du Bois, 1868–1919: Biography of a Race*. New York: Henry Holt, 1993.

——. *W. E. B. Du Bois: The Fight for Equality and the American Century*. New York: Henry Holt, 2000.

——. *When Harlem Was in Vogue*. New York: Alfred A. Knopf, 1981. Reissued, Oxford: Oxford University Press, 1989.

Marable, Manning. *Malcolm X: A Life of Reinvention*. New York: Viking Press, 2011.

Norrell, Robert J. *Up from History: The Life of Booker T. Washington*. Cambridge, MA: Harvard University Press, 2009.

Parks, Gordon. *A Hungry Heart*. New York: Atria Books, 2005.

Patterson, William L. *The Man Who Cried Genocide*. New York: International Publishers, 1971.

Rampersad, Arnold. *The Life of Langston Hughes*. Oxford: Oxford University Press, 2002.

Robinson, Robert, with Jonathan Slevin. *Black on Red: My 44 Years inside the Soviet Union*. Washington, DC: Acropolis Books, 1988.

Rustin, Bayard. *Down the Line: The Collected Writings of Bayard Rustin*, with an introduction by C. Vann Woodward. Chicago: Quadrangle Books, 1971.

Stuckey, Sterling. *Slave Culture: Nationalist Theory and the Foundations of Black America*. Oxford: Oxford University Press, 1987.

Washington, Booker T. *Up from Slavery*. Secaucus, NJ: Carol Publishing Group, 1997.

White, Walter. *A Man Called White: Autobiography*. New York: Viking Press, 1948.

Woodward, C. Vann. *The Strange Career of Jim Crow*. Commemorative edition with a new afterword by William S. McFeely. Oxford: Oxford University Press, 2002.

MISCELLANEOUS HISTORY

Allen, Frederick Lewis. *Only Yesterday*. New York: Perennial Classics, 2000.

Conn, Peter. *Pearl S. Buck: A Cultural Biography*. Cambridge: Cambridge University Press, 1996.

Evans, Harold. *The American Century*. New York: Alfred A. Knopf, 1998.

Fast, Howard. *Freedom Road*, with a forward by W. E. B. Du Bois and an introduction by Eric Foner. Armonk, NY: M. E. Sharpe, 1995. First published in 1944.

Goebel, Julius, Jr., and staff under his direction. *A History of the School of Law, Columbia University*. New York: Columbia University Press, 1955.

Hoffman, David E. *The Dead Hand: The Untold Story of the Cold War Arms Race and Its Dangerous Legacy*. New York: Doubleday, 2009.

Isaacson, Walter. *Einstein: His Life and Universe*. New York: Simon & Schuster, 2007.

Kazin, Michael. *American Dreamers: How the Left Changed a Nation*. New York: Alfred A. Knopf, 2011.

Leinwand, Gerald. *1927: High Tide of the Twenties*. New York: 4 Walls 8 Windows, 2001.

Northrop, F. S. C. *The Meeting of East and West: An Inquiry Concerning World Understanding*. London: Macmillan Publishers, 1946. Reprint, Woodbridge, CT: Ox Bow Press, 1979.

Seton, Marie. *Sergei M. Eisenstein* [a biography]. New York: Grove, 1960.

Shirer, William L. *The Rise and Fall of the Third Reich: A History of Nazi Germany*. New York: Simon & Schuster, 1960.

Thomas, Evan. *The War Lovers*. New York: Little, Brown and Co., 2010.

Traxel, David. *1898*. New York: Alfred A. Knopf, 1998.

POLITICS: COLD WAR, HENRY WALLACE, AND MCCARTHYISM

Bentley, Eric, ed. *Thirty Years of Treason: Excerpts from Hearings before the House Committee on Un-American Activities, 1938–1968*. New York: Thunder's Mouth Press, 2002. Originally published by New York: Viking Press, 1971.

Brands, H. W. *The Devil We Knew: Americans and the Cold War*. Oxford: Oxford University Press, 1993.

Crossman, Richard H., ed. *The God that Failed*. New York: Columbia University Press, 2001; edition by arrangement with HarperCollins. Originally published by London: Hamilton, 1950.

Culver, John C., and John Hyde. *American Dreamer: The Life and Times of Henry A. Wallace*. New York: W. W. Norton & Company, 2000.

Dallek, Robert. *The Lost Peace: Leadership in a Time of Horror and Hope, 1945–1953*. New York: HarperCollins Publishers, 2010.

Donaldson, Gary A. *Truman Defeats Dewey*. Lexington: University Press of Kentucky, 1999.

Fariello, Griffin. *Red Scare: Memories of the American Inquisition*. New York: W. W. Norton & Company, 1995.

Fast, Howard. *Peekskill USA: Inside the Infamous 1949 Riots*. Mineola, NY: Dover Publications, 2006. Originally published by New York: Civil Rights Congress, 1951.

Haldane, Charlotte. *Truth Will Out*. London: Right Book Club; Peal, Ashdown & Hart Ltd., 1949.

Jerome, Fred. *The Einstein File*. New York: St. Martin's Press, 2002.

Jerome, Fred, and Rodger Taylor. *Einstein on Race and Racism*. New Brunswick, NJ: Rutgers University Press, 2005.

Johnson, Haynes. *The Age of Anxiety: McCarthyism to Terrorism*. Boston: Harcourt, 2005.

Karabell, Zachary. *The Last Campaign: How Harry Truman Won the 1948 Election*. New York: Alfred A. Knopf, 2000.

LaFeber, Walter. *America, Russia, and the Cold War, 1945–2002*. New York: McGraw-Hill, 2002.

Patterson, William L. *The Man Who Cried Genocide*. New York: International Publishers, 1971.

Robinson, Earl, with Eric A. Gordon. *Ballad of an American: The Autobiography of Earl Robinson*. Lanham, MD: Scarecrow Press, 1998.

Robinson, Robert, with Jonathan Slevin. *Black on Red: My 44 Years inside the Soviet Union*. Washington, DC: Acropolis Books, 1988.

Truman, Harry S. *Memoirs of Harry S. Truman: 1946–1952, Years of Trial and Hope*. Garden City, NY: Doubleday & Company, 1956.

———. *Off the Record: The Private Papers of Harry S. Truman*, edited by Robert H. Ferrell. Columbia: University of Missouri Press, 1980. Originally published by New York: Harper & Row

Walton, Richard J. *Henry Wallace, Harry Truman, and the Cold War*. New York: Viking Press, 1976.

SPORTS

Carroll, John M. *Fritz Pollard: Pioneer in Racial Advancement*. Champaign: University of Illinois Press, 1992.

Falkner, David. *Great Time Coming: The Life of Jackie Robinson—from Baseball to Birmingham*. New York: Simon & Schuster, 1995.

Halas, George S., with Gwen Morgan and Arthur Veysey. *Halas: An Autobiography*. Chicago: Bonus Books, 1986. Originally published by New York: McGraw-Hill Book Company, 1979.

Peterson, Robert W. *Pigskin: The Early Years of Pro Football*. Oxford: Oxford University Press, 1997.

Piascik, Andy. *Gridiron Gauntlet: The Story of the Men Who Integrated Pro Football in Their Own Words*. Lanham, MD: Taylor Trade Publishing, 2009.

Robinson, Jackie, with Alfred Duckett. *I Never Had It Made*. New York: Ecco, HarperCollins, 1995. Originally published by New York: Putnam, 1972.

THEATER AND MUSIC

Barranger, Milly S. *Margaret Webster: A Life in the Theater*. Ann Arbor: University of Michigan Press, 2004.

Belafonte, Harry, with Michael Shnayerson. *My Song: A Memoir*. New York: Alfred A. Knopf, 2011.

Billington, Michael. *Peggy Ashcroft*. London: John Murray, 1988.

Bourne, Stephen. *Elisabeth Welch: Soft Lights and Sweet Music*. Lanham, MD: Scarecrow Press, 2005.

Davis, Ossie, and Ruby Dee. *With Ossie and Ruby: In This Life Together*. New York: Perennial, 2000. Hardcover published by New York: William Morrow and Co., 1998.

Gelb, Arthur, and Barbara Gelb. *O'Neill: Life with Monte Cristo*. New York: Applause, 2000.

Goudsouzian, Aram. *Sidney Poitier: Man, Actor, Icon*. Chapel Hill: University of North Carolina Press, 2004.

Hagen, Uta, with Haskel Frankel. *Respect for Acting*. Hoboken, NJ: John Wiley & Sons, 1973.

———. *Sources: A Memoir*. New York: Performing Arts Journal Publications, 1983.

Hart-Davis, Rupert. *The Power of Change* [memoir]. London: Sinclair-Stevenson, 1991.

Horne, Lena. *In Person, Lena Horne; As Told to Helen Arstein and Carlton Moss*. Greenberg, 1950.

———, and Richard Schickel. *Lena*. New York: New American Library, 1965.

O'Connor, Gary. *The Secret Woman: A Life of Peggy Ashcroft*. London: Orion Books, 1998.

Swindall, Lindsey R. *The Politics of Paul Robeson's Othello*. Jackson: University Press of Mississippi, 2011.

Webster, Margaret. *Don't Put Your Daughter on the Stage*. New York: Alfred A. Knopf, 1972.

Wilcoxon, Henry, with Katherine Orrison. *Lionheart in Hollywood: The Autobiography of Henry Wilcoxon*. Metuchen, NJ: Scarecrow Press, 1991.

Woollcott, Alexander. *While Rome Burns*. New York: Grosset & Dunlap, 1934.

BROADCAST INTERVIEWS AND DOCUMENTARIES

BBC Radio, 1958 [TV interview and documentary].

Here I Stand. American Masters, Thirteen WNET. Narrated by Ossie Davis.

Paul Robeson: The Rise and Fall of an American Legend. BBC Wales/NJN Public Television/NVBC Arts coproduction. Narrated by Pam Grier.

Paul Robeson: Tribute to an Artist. Janus Films. Directed by Saul J. Turell. Narrated by Sidney Poitier. Part of Criterion Collection box set in 2006.

Pete Seeger: The Power of a Song. PBS. February 27, 2008.

The Robeson Files. BBC Radio 2. Produced by Hillary Robinson, summer 2011.

Scandalize My Name. Starz Encore Entertainment. Hosted by Morgan Freeman.

Song of Freedom. Screen Edge, 2008.

Speak of Me as I Am. BBC Wales/NJN Public Television. Narrated by Pam Grier.

Index

About the Author

Arnold H. Lubasch went to the College of William and Mary, where he edited the student newspaper, and he served in the Second Armored Division in Germany, where he edited the division newspaper and wrote articles for the *Stars and Stripes*. After his army service, he joined the *New York Times* in 1956 and remained there for thirty-eight years, working as a reporter, rewrite man, and United Nations correspondent; he also covered major trials in the federal court in New York for many years. He now lives in Scottsdale, Arizona.